The Gifts of the Child Christ

The George MacDonald family, ca. *1872* (permission for publication kindly granted by the Bettmann Archive).

The Gifts of the Child Christ

Fairytales and Stories for the Childlike

by
George MacDonald

edited by
GLENN EDWARD SADLER

VOLUME II

WILLIAM B. EERDMANS PUBLISHING COMPANY
Grand Rapids, Michigan

Library of Congress Cataloging in Publication Data

Macdonald, George, 1824-1905
The gifts of the child Christ.
I. Title.
PZ3.M144Gi6 [PR4967]   823'.8   72-96406
ISBN 0-8028-3428-0
ISBN 0-8028-1518-9 (pbk.)

First printing, November 1973
Fifth printing, June 1979

Contents

"The Girl That Lost Things" by George MacDonald   6

I.   THE LIGHT PRINCESS   9

II.   THE GIANT'S HEART   51

III.   THE CARASOYN   73

IV.   THE GRAY WOLF   113

V.   THE CRUEL PAINTER   121

VI.   THE BROKEN SWORDS   153

VII.   THE WOW O' RIVVEN [THE BELL]   175

VIII.   UNCLE CORNELIUS, HIS STORY   191

IX.   THE BUTCHER'S BILLS   215

X.   BIRTH, DREAMING, DEATH [THE SCHOOLMASTER'S STORY]   249

"That Holy Thing" by George MacDonald   261

"The Girl That Lost Things"

There was a girl that lost things—
  Nor only from her hand;
She lost, indeed—why, most things,
  As if they had been sand!

She said, "But I must use them,
  And can't look after all!
Indeed I did not lose them,
  I only let them fall!"

That's how she lost her thimble,
  It fell upon the floor:
Her eyes were very nimble
  But she never saw it more.

And then she lost her dolly,
  Her very doll of all!
That loss was far from jolly,
  But worse things did befall.

She lost a ring of pearls
  With a ruby in them set;
But the dearest girl of girls
  Cried only, did not fret.

And then she lost her robin;
  Ah, that was sorrow dire!
He hopped along, and—bob in—
  Hopped bob into the fire!

And once she lost a kiss
  As she came down the stair;

But that she did not miss,
   For sure it was somewhere!

Just then she lost her heart too,
   But did so well without it
She took that in good part too,
   And said—not much about it.

But when she lost her health
   She did feel rather poor,
Till in came loads of wealth
   By quite another door!

And soon she lost a dimple
   That was upon her cheek,
But that was very simple—
   She was so thin and weak!

And then she lost her mother,
   And thought that she was dead;
Sure there was not another
   On whom to lay her head!

And then she lost her self—
   But that she threw away;
And God upon his shelf
   It carefully did lay.

And then she lost her sight,
   And lost all hope to find it;
But a fountain-well of light
   Came flashing up behind it.

At last she lost the world:
   In a black and stormy wind
Away from her it whirled—
   But the loss how could she mind?

For with it she lost her losses,
   Her aching and her weeping,

Her pains and griefs and crosses,
  And all things not worth keeping;

It left her with the lost things
  Her heart had still been craving;
'Mong them she found—why, most things,
  And all things worth the saving.

She found her precious mother,
  Who not the least had died;
And then she found that other
  Whose heart had hers inside.

And next she found the kiss
  She lost upon the stair;
'Twas sweeter far, I guess,
  For ripening in that air.

She found her self, all mended,
  New-drest, and strong, and white;
She found her health, new-blended
  With a radiant delight.

She found her little robin:
  He made his wings go flap,
Came fluttering, and went bob in,
  Went bob into her lap.

So, girls that cannot keep things,
  Be patient till to-morrow;
And mind you don't beweep things
  That are not worth such sorrow;

For the Father great of fathers,
  Of mothers, girls, and boys,
In his arms his children gathers,
  And sees to all their toys.
                              —*George MacDonald*

I

The Light Princess

The Christening (woodcut by Arthur Hughes; reprinted from *Dealings with the Fairies* [1867]).

I

What! No Children?

Once upon a time, so long ago that I have quite forgotten the date, there lived a king and queen who had no children.

And the king said to himself, "All the queens of my acquaintance have children, some three, some seven, and some as many as twelve; and my queen has not one. I feel ill-used." So he made up his mind to be cross with his wife about it. But she bore it all like a good patient queen as she was. Then the king grew very cross indeed. But the queen pretended to take it all as a joke, and a very good one too.

"Why don't you have any daughters, at least?" said he. "I don't say *sons;* that might be too much to expect."

"I am sure, dear king, I am very sorry," said the queen.

"So you ought to be," retorted the king; "you are not going to make a virtue of *that,* surely."

But he was not an ill-tempered king, and in any matter of less moment would have let the queen have her own way with all his heart. This, however, was an affair of state.

The queen smiled.

"You must have patience with a lady, you know, dear king," said she.

She was, indeed, a very nice queen, and heartily sorry that she could not oblige the king immediately.

The king tried to have patience, but he succeeded very badly. It was more than he deserved, therefore, when, at last, the queen gave him a daughter—as lovely a little princess as ever cried.

Reprinted from *Adela Cathcart* (1864).

II

Won't I, Just?

The day grew near when the infant must be christened. The king wrote all the invitations with his own hand. Of course somebody was forgotten.

Now it does not generally matter if somebody *is* forgotten, only you must mind who. Unfortunately, the king forgot without intending to forget; and so the chance fell upon the Princess Makemnoit, which was awkward. For the princess was the king's own sister; and he ought not to have forgotten her. But she had made herself so disagreeable to the old king, their father, that he had forgotten her in making his will; and so it was no wonder that her brother forgot her in writing his invitations. But poor relations don't do anything to keep you in mind of them. Why don't they? The king could not see into the garret she lived in, could he?

She was a sour, spiteful creature. The wrinkles of contempt crossed the wrinkles of peevishness, and made her face as full of wrinkles as a pat of butter. If ever a king could be justified in forgetting anybody, this king was justified in forgetting his sister, even at a christening. She looked very odd, too. Her forehead was as large as all the rest of her face, and projected over it like a precipice. When she was angry, her little eyes flashed blue. When she hated anybody, they shone yellow and green. What they looked like when she loved anybody, I do not know; for I never heard of her loving anybody but herself, and I do not think she could have managed that if she had not somehow got used to herself. But what made it highly imprudent in the king to forget her was—that she was awfully clever. In fact, she was a witch; and when she bewitched anybody, he very soon had enough of it; for she beat all the wicked fairies in wickedness, and all the clever ones in cleverness. She despised all the modes we read of in history, in which offended fairies and witches have taken their revenges; and therefore, after waiting and waiting in vain for an invitation, she made up her mind at last to go without one, and make the whole family miserable, like a princess as she was.

So she put on her best gown, went to the palace, was kindly

received by the happy monarch, who forgot that he had forgotten her, and took her place in the procession to the royal chapel. When they were all gathered about the font, she contrived to get next to it, and throw something into the water; after which she maintained a very respectful demeanour till the water was applied to the child's face. But at that moment she turned round in her place three times, and muttered the following words, loud enough for those beside her to hear:—

> "Light of spirit, by my charms,
>   Light of body every part,
> Never weary human arms—
>   Only crush thy parents' heart!"

They all thought she had lost her wits, and was repeating some foolish nursery rhyme; but a shudder went through the whole of them notwithstanding. The baby, on the contrary, began to laugh and crow; while the nurse gave a start and a smothered cry, for she thought she was struck with paralysis: she could not feel the baby in her arms. But she clasped it tight and said nothing.

The mischief was done.

III

She Can't Be Ours

Her atrocious aunt had deprived the child of all her gravity. If you ask me how this was effected, I answer, "In the easiest way in the world. She had only to destroy gravitation." For the princess was a philosopher, and knew all the *ins* and *outs* of the laws of gravitation as well as the *ins* and *outs* of her boot-lace. And being a witch as well, she could abrogate those laws in a moment; or at least so clog their wheels and rust their bearings, that they would not work at all. But we have more to do with what followed than with how it was done.

The first awkwardness that resulted from this unhappy privation was, that the moment the nurse began to float the baby up and down, she flew from her arms towards the ceiling. Happily, the resistance of the air brought her ascending career to a close within a foot of it. There she remained, horizontal as when she left her nurse's arms, kicking and laughing amazingly. The nurse in terror flew to the bell, and begged the footman, who answered it, to bring up the house-steps directly. Trembling in every limb, she climbed upon the steps, and had to stand upon the very top, and reach up, before she could catch the floating tail of the baby's long clothes.

When the strange fact came to be known, there was a terrible commotion in the palace. The occasion of its discovery by the king was naturally a repetition of the nurse's experience. Astonished that he felt no weight when the child was laid in his arms, he began to wave her up and—not down; for she slowly ascended to the ceiling as before, and there remained floating in perfect comfort and satisfaction, as was testified by her peals of tiny laughter. The king stood staring up in speechless amazement, and trembled so that his beard shook like grass in the wind. At last, turning to the queen, who was just as horror-struck as himself, he said, gasping, staring, and stammering,—

"She *can't* be ours, queen!"

Now the queen was much cleverer than the king, and had begun already to suspect that "this effect defective came by cause."

"I am sure she is ours," answered she. "But we ought to have taken better care of her at the christening. People who were never invited ought not to have been present."

"Oh, ho!" said the king, tapping his forehead with his forefinger, "I have it all. I've found her out. Don't you see it, queen? Princess Makemnoit has bewitched her."

"That's just what I say," answered the queen.

"I beg your pardon, my love; I did not hear you.—John! bring the steps I get on my throne with."

For he was a little king with a great throne, like many other kings.

The throne-steps were brought, and set upon the dining-table, and John got upon the top of them. But he could not reach the little princess, who lay like a baby-laughter-cloud in the air, exploding continuously.

"Take the tongs, John," said his Majesty; and getting up on the table, he handed them to him.

John could reach the baby now, and the little princess was handed down by the tongs.

IV

Where Is She?

One fine summer day, a month after these her first adventures, during which time she had very carefully watched, the princess was lying on the bed in the queen's own chamber, fast asleep. One of the windows was open, for it was noon, and the day was so sultry that the little girl was wrapped in nothing less ethereal than slumber itself. The queen came into the room, and not observing that the baby was on the bed, opened another window. A frolicsome fairy wind, which had been watching for a chance of mischief, rushed in at the one window, and taking its way over the bed where the child was lying, caught her up, and rolling and floating her along like a piece of flue, or a dandelion seed, carried her with it through the opposite window, and away. The queen went down-stairs, quite ignorant of the loss she had herself occasioned.

When the nurse returned, she supposed that her Majesty had carried her off, and, dreading a scolding, delayed making inquiry about her. But hearing nothing, she grew uneasy, and went at length to the queen's boudoir, where she found her Majesty.

"Please, your Majesty, shall I take the baby?" said she.

"Where is she?" asked the queen.

"Please forgive me. I know it was wrong."

"What do you mean?" said the queen, looking grave.

"Oh! don't frighten me, your Majesty!" exclaimed the nurse, clasping her hands.

The queen saw that something was amiss, and fell down in a faint. The nurse rushed about the palace, screaming, "My baby! my baby!"

Every one ran to the queen's room. But the queen could give no orders. They soon found out, however, that the princess was missing, and in a moment the palace was like a beehive in a garden; and in one minute more the queen was brought to herself by a great shout and a clapping of hands. They had found the princess fast asleep under a rose-bush, to which the elvish little wind-puff had carried her, finishing its mischief by shaking a shower of red rose-leaves all over the little white sleeper. Startled by the noise the servants made, she woke, and, furious with glee, scattered the rose-leaves in all directions, like a shower of spray in the sunset.

She was watched more carefully after this, no doubt; yet it would be endless to relate all the odd incidents resulting from this peculiarity of the young princess. But there never was a baby in a house, not to say a palace, that kept the household in such constant good humour, at least below-stairs. If it was not easy for her nurses to hold her, at least she made neither their arms nor their hearts ache. And she was so nice to play at ball with! There was positively no danger of letting her fall. They might throw her down, or knock her down, or push her down, but couldn't *let* her down. It is true, they might let her fly into the fire or the coal-hole, or through the window; but none of these accidents had happened as yet. If you heard peals of laughter resounding from some unknown region, you might be sure enough of the cause. Going down into the kitchen, or *the room,* you would find Jane and Thomas, and Robert and Susan, all and sum, playing at ball with the little princess. She was the ball herself, and did not enjoy it the less for that. Away she went, flying from one to another, screeching with laughter. And the servants loved the ball itself better even than the game. But they had to take some care how they threw her, for if she received an upward direction, she would never come down again without being fetched.

V

What Is to Be Done?

But above-stairs it was different. One day, for instance, after breakfast, the king went into his counting-house, and counted out his money.

The operation gave him no pleasure.

"To think," said he to himself, "that every one of these gold sovereigns weighs a quarter of an ounce, and my real, live, flesh-and-blood princess weighs nothing at all!"

And he hated his gold sovereigns, as they lay with a broad smile of self-satisfaction all over their yellow faces.

The queen was in the parlour, eating bread and honey. But at the second mouthful she burst out crying, and could not swallow it. The king heard her sobbing. Glad of anybody, but especially of his queen, to quarrel with, he clashed his gold sovereigns into his money-box, clapped his crown on his head, and rushed into the parlour.

"What is all this about?" exclaimed he. "What are you crying for, queen?"

"I can't eat it," said the queen, looking ruefully at the honey-pot.

"No wonder!" retorted the king. "You've just eaten your breakfast—two turkey eggs, and three anchovies."

"Oh, that's not it!" sobbed her Majesty. "It's my child, my child!"

"Well, what's the matter with your child? She's neither up the chimney nor down the draw-well. Just hear her laughing."

Yet the king could not help a sigh, which he tried to turn into a cough, saying,—

"It is a good thing to be light-hearted, I am sure, whether she be ours or not."

"It is a bad thing to be light-headed," answered the queen, looking with prophetic soul far into the future.

"'Tis a good thing to be light-handed," said the king.

"'Tis a bad thing to be light-fingered," answered the queen.

"'Tis a good thing to be light-footed," said the king.

"'Tis a bad thing—" began the queen; but the king interrupted her.

"In fact," said he, with the tone of one who concludes an argument in which he has had only imaginary opponents, and in which, therefore, he has come off triumphant—"in fact, it is a good thing altogether to be light-bodied."

"But it is a bad thing altogether to be light-minded," retorted the queen, who was beginning to lose her temper.

This last answer quite discomfited his Majesty, who turned on his heel, and betook himself to his counting-house again. But he was not half-way towards it, when the voice of his queen overtook him.

"And it's a bad thing to be light-haired," screamed she, determined to have more last words, now that her spirit was roused.

The queen's hair was black as night; and the king's had been, and his daughter's was, golden as morning. But it was not this reflection on his hair that arrested him; it was the double use of the word *light.* For the king hated all witticisms, and punning especially. And besides, he could not tell whether the queen meant light-*haired* or light-*heired;* for why might she not aspirate her vowels when she was ex-asperated herself?

He turned upon his other heel, and rejoined her. She looked angry still, because she knew that she was guilty, or, what was much the same, knew that he thought so.

"My dear queen," said he, "duplicity of any sort is exceedingly objectionable between married people of any rank, not to say kings and queens; and the most objectionable form duplicity can assume is that of punning."

"There!" said the queen, "I never made a jest, but I broke it in the making. I am the most unfortunate woman in the world!"

She looked so rueful, that the king took her in his arms; and they sat down to consult.

"Can you bear this?" said the king.

"No, I can't," said the queen.

"Well, what's to be done?" said the king.

"I'm sure I don't know," said the queen. "But might you not try an apology?"

"To my older sister, I suppose you mean?" said the king.

"Yes," said the queen.

"Well, I don't mind," said the king.

So he went the next morning to the house of the princess, and, making a very humble apology, begged her to undo the spell. But the princess declared, with a grave face, that she knew nothing at all about it. Her eyes, however, shone pink, which was a sign that she was happy. She advised the king and queen to have patience, and to mend their ways. The king returned disconsolate. The queen tried to comfort him.

"We will wait till she is older. She may then be able to suggest something herself. She will know at least how she feels, and explain things to us."

"But what if she should marry?" exclaimed the king, in sudden consternation at the idea.

"Well, what of that?" rejoined the queen.

"Just think! If she were to have children! In the course of a hundred years the air might be as full of floating children as of gossamers in autumn."

"That is no business of ours," replied the queen. "Besides, by that time they will have learned to take care of themselves."

A sigh was the king's only answer.

He would have consulted the court physicians; but he was afraid they would try experiments upon her.

VI

She Laughs Too Much

Meantime, notwithstanding awkward occurrences, and griefs that she brought upon her parents, the little princess laughed and grew—not fat, but plump and tall. She reached the age of seventeen, without having fallen into any worse scrape than a chimney; by rescuing her from which, a little bird-nesting urchin got fame and a black face. Nor, thoughtless as she was, had she committed anything worse than laughter at everybody and everything that came in her way. When she was told, for the sake of experiment, that General Clanrunfort was cut to pieces with all his troops, she laughed; when she heard that the enemy was on his way to besiege her papa's capital, she laughed hugely; but when she was told that the city would certainly be abandoned to the mercy of the enemy's soldiery—why, then she laughed immoderately. She never could be brought to see the serious side of anything. When her mother cried, she said,—

"What queer faces mamma makes! And she squeezes water out of her cheeks! Funny mamma!"

And when her papa stormed at her, she laughed, and danced round and round him, clapping her hands, and crying—

"Do it again, papa. Do it again! It's such fun! Dear, funny papa!"

And if he tried to catch her, she glided from him in an instant, not in the least afraid of him, but thinking it part of the game not to be caught. With one push of her foot, she would be floating in the air above his head; or she would go dancing backwards and forwards and sideways, like a great butterfly. It happened several times, when her father and mother were holding a consultation about her in private, that they were interrupted by vainly repressed outbursts of laughter over their heads; and looking up with indignation, saw her floating at full length in the air above them, whence she regarded them with the most comical appreciation of the position.

One day an awkward accident happened. The princess had come out upon the lawn with one of her attendants, who held her by the hand. Spying her father at the other side of the lawn, she snatched her hand from the maid's, and sped across to him. Now when she wanted to run alone, her custom was to catch up a stone in each hand, so that she might come down again after a bound. Whatever she wore as part of her attire had no effect in this way: even gold, when it thus became as it were a part of herself, lost all its weight for the time. But whatever she only held in her hands retained its downward tendency. On this occasion she could see nothing to catch up but a huge toad, that was walking across the lawn as if he had a hundred years to do it in. Not knowing what disgust meant, for this was one of her peculiarities, she snatched up the toad and bounded away. She had almost reached her father, and he was holding out his arms to receive her, and take from her lips the kiss which hovered on them like a butterfly on a rosebud, when a puff of wind blew her aside into the arms of a young page, who had just been receiving a message from his Majesty. Now it was no great peculiarity in the princess that, once she was set agoing, it always cost her time and trouble to check herself. On this occasion there was no time. She *must* kiss—and she kissed the page. She did not mind it much; for she had no shyness in her composition; and she knew, besides, that she could not help it. So she only laughed, like a musical box. The poor page fared the worst. For the princess, trying to correct the unfortunate tendency of the kiss, put out her hands to keep her off the page; so that, along with the kiss, he received, on the other cheek, a slap with the hugh black toad, which she poked right into his eye. He tried to laugh, too, but the attempt resulted in such an odd contortion of countenance, as showed that there was no danger of his pluming himself on the kiss. As for the king, his dignity was greatly hurt, and he did not speak to the page for a whole month.

I may here remark that it was very amusing to see her run, if her mode of progression would properly be called running. For first she would make a bound; then, having alighted, she would run a few steps, and make another bound. Sometimes she would fancy she had reached the ground before she actually had, and her feet would go backwards and forwards, running upon nothing at all, like those of a chicken on its back. Then she would laugh like the very spirit of fun; only in her laugh there was something missing. What it was, I find myself unable to describe. I think it was a certain tone, depending upon the possibility of sorrow—*morbidezza,* perhaps. She never smiled.

VII

Try Metaphysics

After a long avoidance of the painful subject, the king and queen resolved to hold a council of three upon it; and so they sent for the princess. In she came, sliding and flitting and gliding from one piece of furniture to another, and put herself at last in an arm-chair, in a sitting posture. Whether she could be said *to sit,* seeing she received no support from the seat of the chair, I do not pretend to determine.

"My dear child," said the king, "you must be aware by this time that you are not exactly like other people."

"Oh, you dear funny papa! I have got a nose, and two eyes, and all the rest. So have you. So has mamma."

"Now be serious, my dear, for once," said the queen.

"No, thank you, mamma; I had rather not."

"Would you not like to be able to walk like other people?" said the king.

"No indeed, I should think not. You only crawl. You are such slow coaches!"

"How do you feel, my child?" he resumed, after a pause of discomfiture.

"Quite well, thank you."

"I mean, what do you feel like?"

"Like nothing at all, that I know of."

"You must feel like something."

"I feel like a princess with such a funny papa, and such a dear pet of a queen-mamma!"

"Now really!" began the queen; but the princess interrupted her.

"Oh yes," she added, "I remember. I have a curious feeling sometimes, as if I were the only person that had any sense in the whole world."

She had been trying to behave herself with dignity; but now she burst into a violent fit of laughter, threw herself backwards over the chair, and went rolling about the floor in an ecstasy of enjoyment. The king picked her up easier than one does a down quilt, and replaced her in her former relation to the chair. The exact preposition expressing this relation I do not happen to know.

"Is there nothing you wish for?" resumed the king, who had learned by this time that it was useless to be angry with her.

"Oh, you dear papa!—yes," answered she.

"What is it, my darling?"

"I have been longing for it—oh, such a time!—ever since last night."

"Tell me what it is."

"Will you promise to let me have it?"

The king was on the point of saying *Yes,* but the wiser queen checked him with a single motion of her head.

"Tell me what it is first," said he.

"No no. Promise first."

"I dare not. What is it?"

"Mind, I hold you to your promise.—It is—to be tied to the end of a string—a very long string indeed, and be flown like a kite. Oh such fun! I would rain rose-water, and hail sugar-plums, and snow whipped-cream, and—and—and—"

A fit of laughing checked her; and she would have been off again over the floor, had not the king started up and caught her just in time. Seeing that nothing but talk could be got out of her, he rang the bell, and sent her away with two of her ladies-in-waiting.

"Now, queen," he said, turning to her Majesty, "what *is* to be done?"

"There is but one thing left," answered she. "Let us consult the college of Metaphysicians."

"Bravo!" cried the king; "we will."

Now at the head of this college were two very wise Chinese philosophers—by name Hum-Drum, and Kopy-Keck. For them the king sent; and straightway they came. In a long speech he communicated to them what they knew very well already—as who did not?—namely, the peculiar condition of his daughter in relation to the globe on which she dwelt; and requested them to consult together as to what might be the cause and probable cure of her *infirmity*. The king laid stress upon the word, but failed to discover his own pun. The queen laughed; but Hum-Drum and Kopy-Keck heard with humility and retired in silence.

Their consultation consisted chiefly in propounding and supporting, for the thousandth time, each his favourite theories. For the condition of the princess afforded delightful scope for the discussion of every question arising from the division of thought—in fact, of all the Meta-physics of the Chinese Empire. But it is only justice to say that they did not altogether neglect the discussion of the practical question, *what was to be done.*

Hum-Drum was a Materialist, and Kopy-Keck was a Spiritualist. The former was slow and sententious; the latter was quick and flighty: the latter had generally the first word; the former the last.

"I reassert my former assertion," began Kopy-Keck, with a plunge. "There is not a fault in the princess, body or soul; only they are wrong put together. Listen to me now, Hum-Drum, and I will tell you in brief what I think. Don't speak. Don't answer me. I *won't* hear you till I have done.—At that decisive moment, when souls seek their appointed habi-tations, two eager souls met, struck, rebounded, lost their way, and arrived each at the wrong place. The soul of the princess was one of those, and she went far astray. She does not belong by rights to this world at all, but to some other planet, probably Mercury. Her proclivity to her true sphere destroys all the natural influence which this orb would otherwise possess over her corporeal frame. She cares for nothing here. There is no relation between her and this world.

"She must therefore be taught, by the sternest compulsion, to take an interest in the earth as the earth. She must study every department of its history—its animal history; its vegetable history; its mineral history; its social history; its moral history; its political history; its scientific history; its literary history; its musical history; its artistical history; above all, its metaphysical history. She must begin with the Chinese dynasty and end with Japan. But first of all she must study geology, and especially the history of the extinct races of animals—their natures, their habits, their loves, their hates, their revenges. She must—"

"Hold, h-o-o-old!" roared Hum-Drum. "It is certainly my turn now. My rooted and insubvertible conviction is, that the causes of the anomalies evident in the princess's condition are strictly and solely physical. But that is only tantamount to acknowledging that they exist. Hear my opinion.—From some cause or other, of no importance to our inquiry, the motion of her heart has been reversed. That remarkable combination of the suction and the force-pump works the wrong way—I mean in the case of the unfortunate princess: it draws in where it should force out, and forces out where it should draw in. The offices of the auricles and the ventricles are subverted. The blood is sent forth by the veins, and returns by the arteries. Consequently it is running the wrong way through all her corporeal organism—lungs and all. Is it then at all mysterious, seeing that such is the case, that on the other particular of gravitation as well, she should differ from normal humanity? My proposal for the cure is this:—

"Phlebotomize until she is reduced to the last point of safety. Let it be effected, if necessary, in a warm bath. When she is reduced to a state of perfect asphyxy, apply a ligature to the left ankle, drawing it as tight as the bone will bear. Apply, at the same moment, another of equal tension around the right wrist. By means of plates constructed for the purpose, place the other foot and hand under the receivers of two air-pumps. Exhaust the receivers. Exhibit a pint of French brandy, and await the result.

"Which would presently arrive in the form of grim Death," said Kopy-Keck.

"If it should, she would yet die in doing our duty," retorted Hum-Drum.

But their Majesties had too much tenderness for their volatile offspring to subject her to either of the schemes of the equally unscrupulous philosophers. Indeed, the most complete knowledge of the laws of nature would have been unserviceable in her case; for it was impossible to classify her. She was a fifth imponderable body, sharing all the other properties of the ponderable.

VIII

Try a Drop of Water

Perhaps the best thing for the princess would have been to fall in love. But how a princess who had no gravity could fall into anything is a difficulty—perhaps *the* difficulty. As for her own feelings on the subject, she did not even know that there was such a beehive of honey and stings to be fallen into. But now I come to mention another curious fact about her.

The palace was built on the shores of the loveliest lake in the world; and the princess loved this lake more than father or mother. The root of this preference no doubt, although the princess did not recognise it as such, was, that the moment she got into it, she recovered the natural right of which she had been so wickedly deprived—namely, gravity. Whether this was owing to the fact that water had been employed as the means of conveying the injury, I do not know. But it is certain that she could swim and dive like the duck that her old nurse said she was. The manner in which this alleviation of her misfortune was discovered was as follows.

One summer evening, during the carnival of the country, she had been taken upon the lake by the king and queen, in the royal barge. They were accompanied by many of the courtiers in a fleet of little boats. In the middle of the lake she wanted to get into the lord chancellor's barge, for his daughter, who was a great favourite with her, was in it with her father. Now though the old king rarely condescended to make light of his misfortune, yet, happening on this occasion to be in a particularly good humour, as the barges approached each other, he caught up the princess to throw her into the chancellor's barge. He lost his balance, however, and dropping into the bottom of the barge, lost his hold of his daughter; not, however, before imparting to her the downward tendency of his own person, though in a somewhat different direction; for, as the king fell into the boat, she fell into the water. With a burst of delighted laughter she disappeared in the lake. A cry of horror ascended from the boats. They had never seen the Princess go down before. Half the men were under water in a moment; but they had all, one after another, come up to the surface again for breath, when—tinkle, tinkle, babble, and gush! came the princess's laugh over the water from far away. There she was, swimming like a swan. Nor would she come out for king or queen, chancellor or daughter. She was perfectly obstinate.

But at the same time she seemed more sedate than usual. Perhaps that was because a great pleasure spoils laughing. At all events, after this, the passion of her life was to get into the water, and she was always the better behaved and the more beautiful the more she had of it. Summer and winter it was quite the same; only she could not stay so long in the water when they had to break the ice to let her in. Any day, from morning till evening in summer, she might be descried—a streak of white in the blue water—lying as still as the shadow of a cloud, or shooting along like a dolphin; disappearing, and coming up again far off, just where one did not expect her. She would have been in the lake of a night too, if she could have had her way; for the balcony of her window overhung a deep pool in it; and through a shallow reedy passage she could have swum out into the wide wet water, and no one would have been any the wiser. Indeed, when she happened to wake in the moonlight, she could hardly resist the temptation. But there was the sad difficulty of getting into it. She had as great a dread of the air as some children have of the water. For the slightest gust of wind would blow her away; and a gust might arise in the stillest moment. And if she gave herself a push towards the water and just failed of reaching it, her situation would be dreadfully awkward, irrespective of the wind; for at best there she would have to remain, suspended in her night-gown, till she was seen and angled for by somebody from the window.

"Oh! if I had my gravity," thought she, contemplating the water, "I would flash off this balcony like a long white sea-bird, headlong into the darling wetness. Heigh-ho!"

This was the only consideration that made her wish to be like other people.

Another reason for her being fond of the water was that in it alone she enjoyed any freedom. For she could not walk out without a cortége, consisting in part of a troop of light-horse, for fear of the liberties which the wind might take with her. And the king grew more apprehensive with increasing years, till at last he would not allow her to walk abroad at all without some twenty silken cords fastened to as many parts of her dress, and held by twenty noblemen. Of course horseback was out of the question. But she bade good-by to all this ceremony when she got into the water.

And so remarkable were its effects upon her, especially in restoring her for the time to the ordinary human gravity, that Hum-Drum and Kopy-Keck agreed in recommending the king to bury her alive for three years; in the hope that, as the water did her so much good, the earth would do her yet more. But the king had some vulgar prejudices against the experiment, and would not give his consent. Foiled in this, they yet agreed in another recommendation; which, seeing that one imported his opinions from China and the other from Thibet, was very remarkable indeed. They argued that, if water of external origin and application could be so efficacious, water from a deeper source might work a perfect cure; in short, that if the poor afflicted princess could by any means be made to cry, she might recover her lost gravity.

But how was this to be brought about? Therein lay all the difficulty—to meet which the philosophers were not wise enough. To make the princess cry was as impossible as to make her weigh. They sent for a professional beggar; commanded him to prepare his most touching oracle of woe; helped him out of the court charade-box, to whatever he wanted for dressing up, and promised great rewards in the event of his success. But it was all in vain. She listened to the mendicant artist's story, and gazed at his marvellous make-up, till she could contain herself no longer, and went into the most undignified contortions for relief, shrieking, positively screeching with laughter.

When she had a little recovered herself, she ordered her attendants to drive him away, and not give him a single copper; whereupon his look of mortified discomfiture wrought her punishment and his revenge, for it sent her into violent hysterics, from which she was with difficulty recovered.

But so anxious was the king that the suggestion should have a fair trial, that he put himself in a rage one day, and, rushing up to her room, gave her an awful whipping. Yet not a tear would flow. She looked grave, and her laughing sounded uncommonly like screaming—that was all. The good old tyrant, though he put on his best gold spectacles to look, could not discover the smallest cloud in the serene blue of her eyes.

IX

Put Me in Again

It must have been about this time that the son of a king, who lived a thousand miles from Lagobel, set out to look for the daughter of a queen. He travelled far and wide, but as sure as he found a princess, he found some fault in her. Of course he could not marry a mere woman, however beautiful; and there was no princess to be found worthy of him. Whether the prince was so near perfection that he had a right to demand perfection itself, I cannot pretend to say. All I know is, that he was a fine, handsome, brave, generous, well-bred, and well-behaved youth, as all princes are.

In his wanderings he had come across some reports about our princess; but as everybody said she was bewitched, he never dreamed that she could bewitch him. For what indeed could a prince do with a princess that had lost her gravity? Who could tell what she might not lose next? She might lose her visibility, or her tangibility; or, in short, the power of making impressions upon the radical sensorium; so that he should never be able to tell whether she was dead or alive. Of course he made no further inquiries about her.

One day he lost sight of his retinue in a great forest. These forests are very useful in delivering princes from their courtiers, like a sieve that keeps back the bran. Then the princes get away to follow their fortunes. In this they have the advantage of the princesses, who are forced to marry before they have had a bit of fun. I wish our princesses got lost in a forest sometimes.

One lovely evening, after wandering about for many days, he found that he was approaching the outskirts of this forest; for the trees had got so thin that he could see the sunset through them; and he soon came upon a kind of heath. Next he came upon signs of human neighbourhood; but by this time it was getting late, and there was nobody in the fields to direct him.

After travelling for another hour, his horse, quite worn out with long labour and lack of food, fell, and was unable to rise again. So he continued his journey on foot. At length he entered another wood—not a wild forest, but a civilized wood, through which a footpath led him to the side of a lake. Along this path the prince pursued his way through the gathering darkness. Suddenly he paused, and listened. Strange sounds came across the water. It was, in fact, the princess laughing. Now there was something odd in her laugh, as I have already hinted; for the hatching of a real hearty laugh requires the incubation of gravity; and perhaps this was how the prince mistook the laughter for screaming. Looking over the lake, he saw something white in the water; and, in an instant, he had torn off his tunic, kicked off his sandals, and plunged in. He soon reached the white object, and found that it was a woman. There was not light enough to show that she was a princess, but quite enough to show that she was a lady, for it does not want much light to see that.

Now I cannot tell how it came about,—whether she pretended to be drowning, or whether he frightened her, or caught her so as to embarrass her,—but certainly he brought her to shore in a fashion ignominious to a swimmer, and more nearly drowned than she had ever expected to be; for the water had got into her throat as often as she had tried to speak.

At the place to which he bore her, the bank was only a foot or two above the water; so he gave her a strong lift out of the water, to lay her on the bank. But, her gravitation ceasing the moment she left the water, away she went up into the air, scolding and screaming.

"You naughty, *naughty*, NAUGHTY, *NAUGHTY* man!" she cried.

No one had ever succeeded in putting her into a passion before.— When the prince saw her ascend, he thought he must have been bewitched, and have mistaken a great swan for a lady. But the princess caught hold of the topmost cone upon a lofty fir. This came off; but she caught at another; and, in fact, stopped herself by gathering cones, dropping them as the stalks gave way. The prince, meantime, stood in the water, staring, and forgetting to get out. But the princess disappearing, he scrambled on shore, and went in the direction of the tree. There he found her climbing down one of the branches towards the stem. But in the darkness of the wood, the prince continued in some bewilderment as to what the phenomenon could be; until, reaching the ground, and seeing him standing there, she caught hold of him, and said,—

"I'll tell papa."

"Oh no, you won't!" returned the prince.

"Yes, I will," she persisted. "What business had you to pull me down out of the water, and throw me to the bottom of the air? I never did you any harm."

"Pardon me. I did not mean to hurt you."

"I don't believe you have any brains; and that is a worse loss than your wretched gravity. I pity you."

The prince now saw that he had come upon the bewitched princess, and had already offended her. But before he could think what to say next, she burst out angrily, giving a stamp with her foot that would have sent her aloft again but for the hold she had of his arm,—

"Put me up directly."

"Put you up where, you beauty?" asked the prince.

He had fallen in love with her almost, already; for her anger made her more charming than any one else had ever beheld her; and, as far as he could see, which certainly was not far, she had not a single fault about her, except, of course, that she had not any gravity. No prince, however, would judge of a princess by weight. The loveliness of her foot he would hardly estimate by the depth of the impression it could make in mud.

"Put you up where, you beauty?" asked the prince.

"In the water, you stupid!" answered the princess.

"Come, then," said the prince.

The condition of her dress, increasing her usual difficulty in walking, compelled her to cling to him; and he could hardly persuade himself that he was not in a delightful dream, notwithstanding the torrent of musical abuse with which she overwhelmed him. The prince being therefore in no hurry, they came upon the lake at quite another part, where the bank was twenty-five feet high at least; and when they had reached the edge, he turned towards the princess, and said,—

"How am I to put you in?"

"That is your business," she answered, quite snappishly. "You took me out—put me in again."

"Very well," said the prince; and, catching her up in his arms, he sprang with her from the rock. The princess had just time to give one delighted shriek of laughter before the water closed over them. When they came to the surface, she found that, for a moment or two, she could not even laugh, for she had gone down with such a rush, that it was with difficulty she recovered her breath. The instant they reached the surface—

"How do you like falling in?" said the prince.

After some effort the princess panted out,—

"Is that what you call *falling in?*"

"Yes," answered the prince, "I should think it a very tolerable specimen."

"It seemed to me like going up," rejoined she.

"My feeling was certainly one of elevation too," the prince conceded.

The princess did not appear to understand him, for she retorted his question:—

"How do *you* like falling in?" said the princess.

"Beyond everything," answered he; "for I have fallen in with the only perfect creature I ever saw."

"No more of that: I am tired of it," said the princess.

Perhaps she shared her father's aversion to punning.

"Don't you like falling in, then?" said the prince.

"It is the most delightful fun I ever had in my life," answered she. "I never fell before. I wish I could learn. To think I am the only person in my father's kingdom that can't fall!"

Here the poor princess looked almost sad.

"I shall be most happy to fall in with you any time you like," said the prince, devotedly.

"Thank you. I don't know. Perhaps it would not be proper. But I don't care. At all events, as we have fallen in, let us have a swim together."

"With all my heart," responded the prince.

And away they went, swimming, and diving, and floating, until at last they heard cries along the shore, and saw lights glancing in all directions. It was now quite late, and there was no moon.

"I must go home," said the princess. "I am very sorry, for this is delightful."

"So am I," returned the prince. "But I am glad I haven't a home to go to—at least, I don't exactly know where it is."

"I wish I hadn't one either," rejoined the princess; "it is so stupid! I have a great mind," she continued, "to play them all a trick. Why couldn't they leave me alone? They won't trust me in the lake for a single night!—You see where that green light is burning? That is the window of my room. Now if you would just swim there with me very quietly, and when we are all but under the balcony, give me such a push—up you call it—as you did a little while ago, I should be able to catch hold of the balcony, and get in at the window; and then they may look for me till tomorrow morning!"

"With more obedience than pleasure," said the prince, gallantly; and away they swam, very gently.

"Will you be in the lake to-morrow night?" the prince ventured to ask.

"To be sure I will. I don't think so. Perhaps," was the princess's somewhat strange answer.

But the prince was intelligent enough not to press her further; and merely whispered, as he gave her the parting lift, "Don't tell." The only answer the princess returned was a roguish look. She was already a yard above his head. The look seemed to say, "Never fear. It is too good fun to spoil that way."

So perfectly like other people had she been in the water, that even yet the prince could scarcely believe his eyes when he saw her ascend slowly, grasp the balcony, and disappear through the window. He turned, almost expecting to see her still by his side. But he was alone in the water. So he swam away quietly, and watched the lights roving about the shore for hours after the princess was safe in her chamber. As soon as they disappeared, he landed in search of his tunic and sword, and, after some trouble, found them again. Then he made the best of his way round the lake to the other side. There the wood was wilder, and the shore steeper—rising more immediately towards the mountains which surrounded the lake on all sides, and kept sending it messages of silvery streams from morning to night, and all night long. He soon found a spot whence he could see the green light in the princess's room, and where, even in the broad daylight, he would be in no danger of being discovered from the opposite shore. It was a sort of cave in the rock, where he provided himself a bed of withered leaves, and lay down too tired for hunger to keep him awake. All night long he dreamed that he was swimming with the princess.

X

Look at the Moon

Early the next morning the prince set out to look for something to eat, which he soon found at a forester's hut, where for many following days he was supplied with all that a brave prince could consider necessary. And having plenty to keep him alive for the present, he would not think of wants not yet in existence. Whenever Care intruded, this prince always bowed him out in the most princely manner.

When he returned from his breakfast to his watch-cave, he saw the princess already floating about in the lake, attended by the king and queen—whom he knew by their crowns—and a great company in lovely little boats, with canopies of all the colours of the rainbow, and flags and streamers of a great many more. It was a very bright day, and soon the prince, burned up with the heat, began to long for the cold water and the cool princess. But he had to endure till twilight; for the boats had provisions on board, and it was not till the sun went down that the gay party began to vanish. Boat after boat drew away to the shore, following that of the king and queen, till only one, apparently the princess's own boat, remained. But she did not want to go home even yet, and the prince thought he saw her order the boat to the shore without her. At all events, it rowed away; and now, of all the radiant company, only one white speck remained. Then the prince began to sing.

And this is what he sang:—

> "Lady fair,
> Swan-white,
> Lift thine eyes,
> Banish night
> By the might
> Of thine eyes.
>
> "Snowy arms,
> Oars of snow,
> Oar her hither,
> Plashing low.
> Soft and slow,
> Oar her hither.
>
> "Stream behind her
> O'er the lake,
> Radiant whiteness!
> In her wake
> Following, following for her sake,
> Radiant whiteness!
>
> "Cling about her,
> Waters blue;
> Part not from her,

But renew
Cold and true
Kisses round her.

"Lap me round,
Waters sad
That have left her;
Make me glad,
For ye had
Kissed her ere ye left her."

Before he had finished his song, the princess was just under the place where he sat, and looking up to find him. Her ears had led her truly.

"Would you like a fall, princess?" said the prince, looking down.

"Ah! there you are! Yes, if you please, prince," said the princess, looking up.

"How do you know I am a prince, princess?" said the prince.

"Because you are a very nice young man, prince," said the princess.

"Come up then, princess."

"Fetch me, prince."

The prince took off his scarf, then his sword-belt, then his tunic, and tied them all together, and let them down. But the line was far too short. He unwound his turban, and added it to the rest, when it was all but long enough; and his purse completed it. The princess just managed to lay hold of the knot of money, and was beside him in a moment. This rock was much higher than the other, and the splash and the dive were tremendous. The princess was in ecstasies of delight, and their swim was delicious.

Night after night they met, and swam about in the dark clear lake; where such was the prince's gladness, that (whether the princess's way of looking at things infected him, or he was actually getting light-headed) he often fancied that he was swimming in the sky instead of the lake. But when he talked about being in heaven, the princess laughed at him dreadfully.

When the moon came, she brought them fresh pleasure. Everything looked strange and new in her light, with an old, withered, yet unfading newness. When the moon was nearly full, one of their great delights was to dive deep in the water, and then, turning round, look up through it at the great blot of light close above them, shimmering and trembling and wavering, spreading and contracting, seeming to melt away, and again grow solid. Then they would shoot up through the blot; and lo! there was the moon, far off, clear and steady and cold, and very lovely, at the bottom of a deeper and bluer lake than theirs, as the princess said.

The prince soon found out that while in the water the princess was very like other people. And besides this, she was not so forward in her questions or pert in her replies at sea as on shore. Neither did she laugh so much; and when she did laugh, it was more gently. She seemed altogether more modest and maidenly in the water than out of it. But when the prince, who had really fallen in love when he fell in the lake, began to talk to her about love, she always turned her head towards him and laughed. After a while she began to look puzzled, as if she were trying to understand what he meant, but could not—revealing a notion that he meant something. But as soon as ever she left the lake, she was so altered, that the prince said to himself, "If I marry her, I see no help for it: we must turn merman and mermaid, and go out to sea at once."

XI

Hiss!

The princess's pleasure in the lake had grown to a passion, and she could scarcely bear to be out of it for an hour. Imagine then her consternation, when, diving with the prince one night, a sudden suspicion seized her that the lake was not so deep as it used to be. The prince could not imagine what had happened. She shot to the surface, and, without a word, swam at full speed towards the higher side of the lake. He followed, begging to know if she was ill, or what was the matter. She never turned her head, or took the smallest notice of his question. Arrived at the shore, she coasted the rocks with minute inspection. But she was not able to come to a conclusion, for the moon was very small, and so she could not see well. She turned therefore and swam home, without saying a word to explain her conduct to the prince, of whose presence she seemed no longer conscious. He withdrew to his cave, in great perplexity and distress.

Next day she made many observations, which, alas! strengthened her fears. She saw that the banks were too dry; and that the grass on the shore, and the trailing plants on the rocks, were withering away. She caused marks to be made along the borders, and examined them, day after day, in all directions of the wind; till at last the horrible idea became a certain fact—that the surface of the lake was slowly sinking.

The poor princess nearly went out of the little mind she had. It was awful to her to see the lake, which she loved more than any living thing, lie dying before her eyes. It sank away, slowly vanishing. The tops of rocks that had never been seen till now, began to appear far down in the clear water. Before long they were dry in the sun. It was fearful to think of the mud that would soon lie there baking and festering, full of lovely creatures dying, and ugly creatures coming to life, like the unmaking of a world. And how hot the sun would be without any lake! She could not bear to swim in it any more, and began to pine away. Her life seemed bound up with it; and ever as the lake sank, she pined. People said she would not live an hour after the lake was gone.

But she never cried.

Proclamation was made to all the kingdom, that whosoever should discover the cause of the lake's decrease, would be rewarded after a princely fashion. Hum-Drum and Kopy-Keck applied themselves to their physics and metaphysics; but in vain. Not even they could suggest a cause.

Now the fact was that the old princess was at the root of the mischief. When she heard that her niece found more pleasure in the water than any one else had out of it, she went into a rage, and cursed herself for her want of foresight.

"But," said she, "I will soon set all right. The king and the people shall die of thirst; their brains shall boil and frizzle in their skulls before I will lose my revenge."

And she laughed a ferocious laugh, that made the hairs on the back of her black cat stand erect with terror.

Then she went to an old chest in the room, and opening it, took out what looked like a piece of dried seaweed. This she threw into a tub of water. Then she threw some powder into the water, and stirred it with her bare arm, muttering over it words of hideous sound, and yet more hideous import. Then she set the tub aside, and took from the chest a

huge bunch of a hundred rusty keys, that clattered in her shaking
hands. Then she saw down and proceeded to oil them all. Before she
had finished, out from the tub, the water of which had kept on a slow
motion ever since she had ceased stirring it, came the head and half the
body of a huge gray snake. But the witch did not look round. It grew
out of the tub, waving itself backwards and forwards with a slow
horizontal motion, till it reached the princess, when it laid its head
upon her shoulder, and gave a low hiss in her hear. She started—but
with joy; and seeing the head resting on her shoulder, drew it towards
her and kissed it. Then she drew it all out of the tub, and wound it
round her body. It was one of those dreadful creatures which few have
ever beheld—the White Snakes of Darkness.

Then she took the keys and went down to her cellar; and as she
unlocked the door she said to herself,—

"This *is* worth living for!"

Locking the door behind her, she descended a few steps into the
cellar, and crossing it, unlocked another door into a dark, narrow
passage. She locked this also behind her, and descended a few more
steps. If any one had followed the witch-princess, he would have heard
her unlock exactly one hundred doors, and descend a few steps after
unlocking each. When she had unlocked the last, she entered a vast
cave, the roof of which was supported by huge natural pillars of rock.
Now this room was the under side of the bottom of the lake.

She then untwined the snake from her body, and held it by the tail
high above her. The hideous creature stretched up its head towards the
roof of the cavern, which it was just able to reach. It then began to
move its head backwards and forwards, with a slow oscillating motion,
as if looking for something. At the same moment the witch began to
walk round and round the cavern, coming nearer to the centre every
circuit; while the head of the snake described the same path over the
roof that she did over the floor, for she kept holding it up. And still it
kept slowly oscillating. Round and round the cavern they went, ever
lessening the circuit, till at last the snake made a sudden dart, and clung
to the roof with its mouth.

"That's right, my beauty!" cried the princess; "drain it dry."

She let it go, left it hanging, and sat down on a great stone, with her
black cat, which had followed her all round the cave, by her side. Then
she began to knit and mutter awful words. The snake hung like a huge
leech, sucking at the stone; the cat stood with his back arched, and his

tail like a piece of cable, looking up at the snake; and the old woman
sat and knitted and muttered. Seven days and seven nights they remained thus; when suddenly the serpent dropped from the roof as if
exhausted, and shrivelled up till it was again like a piece of dried
seaweed. The witch started to her feet, picked it up, put it in her
pocket, and looked up at the roof. One drop of water was trembling on
the spot where the snake had been sucking. As soon as she saw that, she
turned and fled, followed by her cat. Shutting the door in a terrible
hurry, she locked it, and having muttered some frightful words, sped to
the next, which also she locked and muttered over; and so with all the
hundred doors, till she arrived in her own cellar. There she sat down on
the floor ready to faint, but listening with malicious delight to the
rushing of the water, which she could hear distinctly through all the
hundred doors.

But this was not enough. Now that she had tasted revenge, she lost
her patience. Without further measures, the lake would be too long in
disappearing. So the next night, with the last shred of the dying old
moon rising, she took some of the water in which she had revived the
snake, put it in a bottle, and set out, accompanied by her cat. Before
morning she had made the entire circuit of the lake, muttering fearful
words as she crossed every stream, and casting into it some of the water
out of her bottle. When she had finished the circuit she muttered yet
again, and flung a handful of water towards the moon. Thereupon every
spring in the country ceased to throb and bubble, dying away like the
pulse of a dying man. The next day there was no sound of falling water
to be heard along the borders of the lake. The very courses were dry;
and the mountains showed no silvery streaks down their dark sides.
And not alone had the fountains of mother Earth ceased to flow; for all
the babies throughout the country were crying dreadfully—only without tears.

XII

Where Is the Prince?

Never since the night when the princess left him so abruptly had the prince had a single interview with her. He had seen her once or twice in the lake; but as far as he could discover, she had not been in it any more at night. He had sat and sung, and looked in vain for his Nereid; while she, like a true Nereid, was wasting away with her lake, sinking as it sank, withering as it dried. When at length he discovered the change that was taking place in the level of the water, he was in great alarm and perplexity. He could not tell whether the lake was dying because the lady had forsaken it; or whether the lady would not come because the lake had begun to sink. But he resolved to know so much at least.

He disguised himself, and, going to the palace, requested to see the lord chamberlain. His appearance at once gained his request; and the lord chamberlain, being a man of some insight, perceived that there was more in the prince's solicitation than met the ear. He felt likewise that no one could tell whence a solution of the present difficulties might arise. So he granted the prince's prayer to be made shoe-black to the princess. It was rather cunning in the prince to request such an easy post, for the princess could not possibly soil as many shoes as other princesses.

He soon learned all that could be told about the princess. He went nearly distracted; but after roaming about the lake for days, and diving in every depth that remained, all that he could do was to put an extra polish on the dainty pair of boots that was never called for.

For the princess kept her room, with the curtains drawn to shut out the dying lake. But could not shut it out of her mind for a moment. It haunted her imagination so that she felt as if the lake were her soul, drying up within her, first to mud, then to madness and death. She thus brooded over the change, with all its dreadful accompaniments, till she was nearly distracted. As for the prince, she had forgotten him. However much she had enjoyed his company in the water, she did not care for him without it. But she seemed to have forgotten her father and mother too.

The lake went on sinking. Small slimy spots began to appear, which glittered steadily amidst the changeful shine of the water. These grew to broad patches of mud, which widened and spread, with rocks here and there, and floundering fishes and crawling eels swarming. The people went everywhere catching these, and looking for anything that might have dropped from the royal boats.

At length the lake was all but gone, only a few of the deepest pools remaining unexhausted.

It happened one day that a party of youngsters found themselves on the brink of one of these pools in the very centre of the lake. It was a rocky basin of considerable depth. Looking in, they saw at the bottom something that shone yellow in the sun. A little boy jumped in and dived for it. It was a plate of gold covered with writing. They carried it to the king.

On one side of it stood these words:—

> "Death alone from death can save.
> Love is death, and so is brave.
> Love can fill the deepest grave.
> Love loves on beneath the wave."

Now this was enigmatical enough to the king and courtiers. But the reverse of the plate explained it a little. Its writing amounted to this:—

"If the lake should disappear, they must find the hole through which the water ran. But it would be useless to try to stop it by any ordinary means. There was but one effectual mode.—The body of a living man should alone stanch the flow. The man must give himself of his own will; and the lake must take his life as it filled. Otherwise the offering would be of no avail. If the nation could not provide one hero, it was time it should perish."

XIII

Here I Am

This was a very disheartening revelation to the king—not that he was unwilling to sacrifice a subject, but that he was hopeless of finding a man willing to sacrifice himself. No time was to be lost, however, for the princess was lying motionless on her bed, and taking no nourishment but lake-water, which was now none of the best. Therefore the king caused the contents of the wonderful plate of gold to be published throughout the country.

No one, however, came forward.

The prince, having gone several days' journey into the forest, to consult a hermit whom he had met there on his way to Lagobel, knew nothing of the oracle till his return.

When he had acquainted himself with all the particulars, he sat down and thought,—

"She will die if I don't do it, and life would be nothing to me without her; so I shall lose nothing by doing it. And life will be as pleasant to her as ever, for she will soon forget me. And there will be so much more beauty and happiness in the world!—To be sure, I shall not see it." (Here the poor prince gave a sigh.) "How lovely the lake will be in the moonlight, with that glorious creature sporting in it like a wild goddess!—It is rather hard to be drowned by inches, though. Let me see—that will be seventy inches of me to drown." (Here he tried to laugh, but could not.) "The longer the better, however," he resumed; "for can I not bargain that the princess shall be beside me all the time? So I shall see her once more, kiss her perhaps,—who knows? and die looking in her eyes. It will be no death. At least, I shall not feel it. And to see the lake filling for the beauty again!—All right! I am ready."

He kissed the princess's boot, laid it down, and hurried to the king's apartment. But feeling, as he went, that anything sentimental would be disagreeable, he resolved to carry off the whole affair with nonchalance. So he knocked at the door of the king's counting-house, where it was all but a capital crime to disturb him.

When the king heard the knock he started up, and opened the door in a rage. Seeing only the shoeblack, he drew his sword. This, I am sorry to say, was his usual mode of asserting his regality when he thought his dignity was in danger. But the prince was not in the least alarmed.

"Please your majesty, I'm your butler," said he.

"My butler! you lying rascal! What do you mean?"

"I mean, I will cork your big bottle."

"Is the fellow mad?" bawled the king, raising the point of his sword.

"I will put a stopper—plug—what you call it, in your leaky lake, grand monarch," said the prince.

The king was in such a rage that before he could speak he had time to cool, and to reflect that it would be great waste to kill the only man who was willing to be useful in the present emergency, seeing that in the end the insolent fellow would be as dead as if he had died by his majesty's own hand.

"Oh!" said he at last, putting up his sword with difficulty, it was so long; "I am obliged to you, you young fool! Take a glass of wine?"

"No, thank you," replied the prince.

"Very well," said the king. "Would you like to run and see your parents before you make your experiment?"

"No, thank you," said the prince.

"Then we will go and look for the hole at once," said his majesty, and proceeded to call some attendants.

"Stop, please your majesty; I have a condition to make," interposed the prince.

"What!" exclaimed the king, "a condition! and with me! How dare you?"

"As you please," returned the prince, coolly. "I wish your majesty a good morning."

"You wretch! I will have you put in a sack, and stuck in the hole."

"Very well, your majesty," replied the prince, becoming a little more respectful, lest the wrath of the king should deprive him of the pleasure of dying for the princess. "But what good will that do your majesty? Please to remember that the oracle says the victim must offer himself."

"Well, you *have* offered yourself," retorted the king.

"Yes, upon one condition."

"Condition again!" roared the king, once more drawing his sword. "Begone! Somebody else will be glad enough to take the honour off your shoulders."

"Your majesty knows it will not be easy to get another to take my place."

"Well, what is your condition?" growled the king, feeling that the prince was right.

"Only this," replied the prince: "that, as I must on no account die before I am fairly drowned, and the waiting will be rather wearisome, the princess, your daughter, shall go with me, feed me with her own hands, and look at me now and then to comfort me; for you must confess it *is* rather hard. As soon as the water is up to my eyes, she may go and be happy, and forget her poor shoeblack."

Here the prince's voice faltered, and he very nearly grew sentimental, in spite of his resolution.

"Why didn't you tell me before what your condition was? Such a fuss about nothing!" exclaimed the king.

"Do you grant it?" persisted the prince.

"Of course I do," replied the king.

"Very well. I am ready."

"Go and have some dinner, then, while I set my people to find the place."

The king ordered out his guards, and gave directions to the officers to find the hole in the lake at once. So the bed of the lake was marked out in divisions and thoroughly examined, and in an hour or so the hole was discovered. It was in the middle of a stone, near the centre of the lake, in the very pool where the golden plate had been found. It was a three-cornered hole of no great size. There was water all round the stone, but very little was flowing through the hole.

XIV

This Is Very Kind of You

The prince went to dress for the occasion, for he was resolved to die like a prince.

When the princess heard that a man had offered to die for her, she was so transported that she jumped off the bed, feeble as she was, and danced about the room for joy. She did not care who the man was; that was nothing to her. The hole wanted stopping; and if only a man would do, why, take one. In an hour or two more everything was ready. Her maid dressed her in haste, and they carried her to the side of the lake. When she saw it she shrieked, and covered her face with her hands. They bore her across to the stone, where they had already placed a little boat for her. The water was not deep enough to float it, but they hoped it would be, before long. They laid her on cushions, placed in the boat wines and fruits and other nice things, and stretched a canopy over all.

In a few minutes the prince appeared. The princess recognized him at once, but did not think it worthwhile to acknowledge him.

"Here I am," said the prince. "Put me in."

"They told me it was a shoeblack," said the princess.

"So I am," said the prince. "I blacked your little boots three times a day, because they were all I could get of you. Put me in."

The courtiers did not resent his bluntness, except by saying to each other that he was taking it out in impudence.

But how was he to be put in? The golden plate contained no instructions on this point. The prince looked at the hole, and saw but one way. He put both his legs into it, sitting on the stone, and, stooping forward, covered the corner that remained open with his two hands. In this uncomfortable position he resolved to abide his fate, and turning to the people, said,—

"Now you can go."

The king had already gone home to dinner.

"Now you can go," repeated the princess after him, like a parrot.

The people obeyed her and went.

Presently a little wave flowed over the stone, and wetted one of the prince's knees. But he did not mind it much. He began to sing, and the song he sang was this:—

> "As a world that has no well,
> Darkly bright in forest dell;
> As a world without the gleam
> Of the downward-going stream;
> As a world without the glance
> Of the ocean's fair expanse;
> As a world where never rain
> Glittered on the sunny plain;—
> Such, my heart, thy world would be,
> If no love did flow in thee.
>
> "As a world without the sound
> Of the rivulets underground;
> Or the bubbling of the spring

Out of darkness wandering;
Or the mighty rush and flowing
Of the river's downward going;
Or the music-showers that drop
On the outspread beech's top;
Or the ocean's mighty voice,
When his lifted waves rejoice;—
Such, my soul, thy world would be,
If no love did sing in thee.

"Lady, keep thy world's delight;
Keep the waters in thy sight.
Love hath made me strong to go,
For thy sake, to realms below,
Where the water's shine and hum
Through the darkness never come:
Let, I pray, one thought of me
Spring, a little well, in thee;
Lest thy loveless soul be found
Like a dry and thirsty ground."

"Sing again, prince. It makes it less tedious," said the princess.

But the prince was too much overcome to sing any more, and a long pause followed.

"This is very kind of you, prince," said the princess at last, quite coolly, as she lay in the boat with her eyes shut.

"I am sorry I can't return the compliment," thought the prince; "but you are worth dying for, after all."

Again a wavelet, and another, and another flowed over the stone, and wetted both the prince's knees; but he did not speak or move. Two—three—four hours passed in this way, the princess apparently asleep, and the prince very patient. But he was much disappointed in his position, for he had none of the consolation he had hoped for.

At last he could bear it no longer.

"Princess!" said he.

But at the moment up started the princess, crying,—

"I'm afloat! I'm afloat!"

And the little boat bumped against the stone.

"Princess!" repeated the prince, encouraged by seeing her wide awake and looking eagerly at the water.

"Well?" said she, without looking round.

"Your papa promised that you should look at me, and you haven't looked at me once."

"Did he? Then I suppose I must. But I am so sleepy!"

"Sleep then, darling, and don't mind me," said the poor prince.

"Really, you are very good," replied the princess. "I think I will go to sleep again."

"Just give me a glass of wine and a biscuit first," said the prince, very humbly.

"With all my heart," said the princess, and gaped as she said it.

She got the wine and the biscuit, however, and leaning over the side of the boat towards him, was compelled to look at him.

"Why, prince," she said, "you don't look well! Are you sure you don't mind it?"

"Not a bit," answered he, feeling very faint indeed. "Only I shall die before it is of any use to you, unless I have something to eat."

"There, then," said she, holding out the wine to him.

"Ah! you must feed me. I dare not move my hands. The water would run away directly."

"Good gracious!" said the princess; and she began at once to feed him with bits of biscuit and sips of wine.

As she fed him, he contrived to kiss the tips of her fingers now and then. She did not seem to mind it, one way or the other. But the prince felt better.

"Now, for your own sake, princess," said he, "I cannot let you go to sleep. You must sit and look at me, else I shall not be able to keep up."

"Well, I will do anything I can to oblige you," answered she, with condescension; and, sitting down, she did look at him, and kept looking at him with wonderful steadiness, considering all things.

The sun went down, and the moon rose, and, gush after gush, the waters were rising up the prince's body. They were up to his waist now.

"Why can't we go and have a swim?" said the princess. "There seems to be water enough just about here."

"I shall never swim more," said the prince.

"Oh, I forgot," said the princess, and was silent.

So the water grew and grew, and rose up and up on the prince. And the princess sat and looked at him. She fed him now and then. The night wore on. The waters rose and rose. The moon rose likewise higher and higher, and shone full on the face of the dying prince. The water was up to his neck.

"Will you kiss me, princess?" said he, feebly. The nonchalance was all gone now.

"Yes, I will," answered the princess, and kissed him with a long, sweet, cold kiss.

"Now," said he, with a sigh of content, "I die happy."

He did not speak again. The princess gave him some wine for the last time: he was past eating. Then she sat down again, and looked at him. The water rose and rose. It touched his chin. It touched his lower lip. It touched between his lips. He shut them hard to keep it out. The princess began to feel strange. It touched his upper lip. He breathed through his nostrils. The princess looked wild. It covered his nostrils. Her eyes looked scared, and shone strange in the moonlight. His head fell back; the water closed over it, and the bubbles of his last breath bubbled up through the water. The princess gave a shriek, and sprang into the lake.

She laid hold first of one leg, and then of the other, and pulled and tugged, but she could not move either. She stopped to take breath, and that made her think that he could not get any breath. She was frantic. She got hold of him, and held his head above the water, which was possible now his hands were no longer on the hole. But it was of no use, for he was past breathing.

Love and water brought back all her strength. She got under the water, and pulled and pulled with her whole might, till at last she got one leg out. The other easily followed. How she got him into the boat she never could tell; but when she did, she fainted away. Coming to herself, she seized the oars, kept herself steady as best she could, and rowed and rowed, though she had never rowed before. Round rocks, and over shallows, and through mud she rowed, till she got to the landing-stairs of the palace. By this time her people were on the shore, for they had heard her shriek. She made them carry the prince to her own room, and lay him in her bed, and light a fire, and send for the doctors.

"But the lake, your highness!" said the chamberlain, who, roused by the noise, came in, in his nightcap.

"Go and drown yourself in it!" she said.

This was the last rudeness of which the princess was ever guilty; and one must allow that she had good cause to feel provoked with the lord chamberlain.

Had it been the king himself, he would have fared no better. But both he and the queen were fast asleep. And the chamberlain went back to his bed. Somehow, the doctors never came. So the princess and her old nurse were left with the prince. But the old nurse was a wise woman, and knew what to do.

They tried everything for a long time without success. The princess was nearly distracted between hope and fear, but she tried on and on, one thing after another, and everything over and over again.

At last, when they had all but given it up, just as the sun rose, the prince opened his eyes.

XV

Look at the Rain!

The princess burst into a passion of tears, and *fell* on the floor. There she lay for an hour, and her tears never ceased. All the pent-up crying of her life was spent now. And a rain came on, such as had never been seen in that country. The sun shone all the time, and the great drops, which fell straight to the earth, shone likewise. The palace was in the heart of a rainbow. It was a rain of rubies, and sapphires, and emeralds, and topazes. The torrents poured from the mountains like molten gold; and if it had not been for its subterraneous outlet, the lake would have overflowed and inundated the country. It was full from shore to shore.

But the princess did not heed the lake. She lay on the floor and wept. And this rain within doors was far more wonderful than the rain out of doors. For when it abated a little, and she proceeded to rise, she found, to her astonishment, that she could not. At length, after many efforts, she succeeded in getting upon her feet. But she tumbled down again directly. Hearing her fall, her old nurse uttered a yell of delight, and ran to her, screaming,—

"My darling child! she's found her gravity!"

"Oh, that's it! is it?" said the princess, rubbing her shoulder and her knee alternately. "I consider it very unpleasant. I feel as if I should be crushed to pieces."

"Hurrah!" cried the prince from the bed. "If you've come round, princess, so have I. How's the lake?"

"Brimful," answered the nurse.

"Then we're all happy."

"That we are indeed!" answered the princess, sobbing.

And there was rejoicing all over the country that rainy day. Even the babies forgot their past troubles, and danced and crowed amazingly. And the king told stories, and the queen listened to them. And he divided the money in his box, and she the honey in her pot, among all the children. And there was such jubilation as was never heard of before.

Of course the prince and princess were betrothed at once. But the princess had to learn to walk, before they could be married with any propriety. And this was not so easy at her time of life, for she could walk no more than a baby. She was always falling down and hurting herself.

"Is this the gravity you used to make so much of?" said she one day to the prince, as he raised her from the floor. "For my part, I was a great deal more comfortable without it."

"No, no, that's not it. This is it," replied the prince, as he took her up, and carried her about like a baby, kissing her all the time. "This is gravity."

"That's better," said she. "I don't mind that so much."

And she smiled the sweetest, loveliest smile in the prince's face. And she gave him one little kiss in return for all his; and he thought them overpaid, for he was beside himself with delight. I fear she complained of her gravity more than once after this, notwithstanding.

It was a long time before she got reconciled to walking. But the pain of learning it was quite counterbalanced by two things, either of which would have been sufficient consolation. The first was, that the prince himself was her teacher; and the second, that she could tumble into the lake as often as she pleased. Still, she preferred to have the prince jump in with her; and the splash they made before was nothing to the splash they made now.

The lake never sank again. In process of time, it wore the roof of the cavern quite through, and was twice as deep as before.

The only revenge the princess took upon her aunt was to tread pretty hard on her gouty toe the next time she saw her. But she was sorry for it the very next day, when she heard that the water had undermined her house, and that it had fallen in the night, burying her in its ruins; whence no one ever ventured to dig up her body. There she lies to this day.

So the prince and princess lived and were happy; and had crowns of gold, and clothes of cloth, and shoes of leather, and children of boys and girls, not one of whom was ever known, on the most critical occasion, to lose the smallest atom of his or her due proportion of gravity.

II

The Giant's Heart

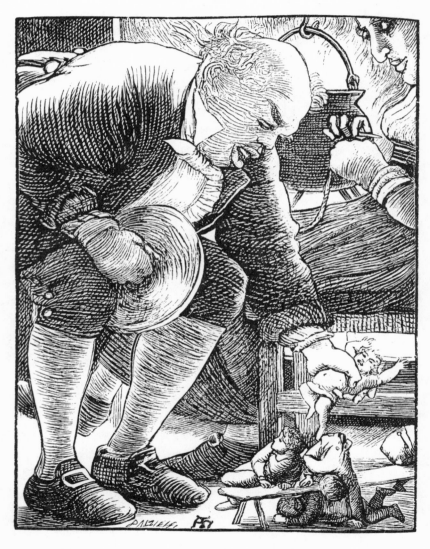

Giant Thunderthump (woodcut by Arthur Hughes; reprinted from *Dealings with the Fairies* [1867]).

There was once a giant who lived on the borders of Giantland where it touched on the country of common people.

Everything in Giantland was so big that the common people saw only a mass of awful mountains and clouds; and no living man had ever come from it, as far as anybody knew, to tell what he had seen in it.

Somewhere near the borders, on the other side, by the edge of a great forest, lived a labourer with his wife and a great many children. One day Tricksey-Wee, as they called her, teased her brother Buffy-Bob, till he could not bear it any longer, and gave her a box on the ear. Tricksey-Wee cried; and Buffy-Bob was so sorry and so ashamed of himself that he cried too, and ran off into the wood. He was so long gone that Tricksey-Wee began to be frightened, for she was very fond of her brother; and she was so distressed that she had first teased him and then cried, that at last she ran into the wood to look for him, though there was more chance of losing herself than of finding him. And, indeed, so it seemed likely to turn out; for, running on without looking, she at length found herself in a valley she knew nothing about. And no wonder; for what she thought was a valley with round, rocky sides, was no other than the space between two of the roots of a great tree that grew on the borders of Giantland. She climbed over the side of it, and went towards what she took for a black, round-topped mountain, far away; but which she soon discovered to be close to her, and to be a hollow place so great that she could not tell what it was hollowed out of. Staring at it, she found that it was a doorway; and going nearer and staring harder, she saw the door, far in, with a knocker of iron upon it, a great many yards above her head, and as large as the anchor of a big ship. Now nobody had ever been unkind to Tricksey-Wee, and therefore she was not afraid of anybody. For Buffy-Bob's box on the ear she did not think worth considering. So spying a little hole at the bottom of the door which had been nibbled by some giant mouse, she crept through it, and found herself in an enormous hall. She could not have

Reprinted from *Illustrated London News,* Christmas Number (1863) entitled "Tell Us a Story."

Tricksey-Wee with the Giantess's Thimble (line drawing by C. Robinson; reprinted from *The Illustrated London News* [1863]).

seen the other end of it at all, except for the great fire that was burning there, diminished to a spark in the distance. Towards this fire she ran as fast as she could, and was not far from it when something fell before her with a great clatter, over which she tumbled, and went rolling on the floor. She was not much hurt, however, and got up in a moment. Then she saw that what she had fallen over was not unlike a great iron bucket. When she examined it more closely, she discovered that it was a thimble; and looking up to see who had dropped it, beheld a huge face, with spectacles as big as the round windows in a church, bending over her, and looking everywhere for the thimble. Tricksey-Wee immediately laid hold of it in both her arms, and lifted it about an inch nearer to the nose of the peering giantess. This movement made the old lady see where it was, and, her finger popping into it, it vanished from the eyes of Tricksey-Wee, buried in the folds of a white stocking like a cloud in the sky, which Mrs. Giant was busy darning. For it was Saturday night, and her husband would wear nothing but white stockings on Sunday. To be sure, he did eat little children, but only *very* little ones; and if ever it crossed his mind that it was wrong to do so, he always said to himself that he wore whiter stockings on Sunday than any other giant in all Giantland.

At the same instant Tricksey-Wee heard a sound like the wind in a tree full of leaves, and could not think what it could be; till, looking up, she found that it was the giantess whispering to her; and when she tried very hard she could hear what she said well enough.

"Run away, dear little girl," she said, "as fast as you can; for my husband will be home in a few minutes."

"But I've never been naughty to your husband," said Tricksey-Wee, looking up in the giantess's face.

"That doesn't matter. You had better go. He is fond of little children, particularly little girls."

"Oh, then he won't hurt me."

"I am not sure of that. He is so fond of them that he eats them up; and I am afraid he couldn't help hurting you a little. He's a very good man, though."

"Oh! then—" began Tricksey-Wee, feeling rather frightened; but before she could finish her sentence she heard the sound of footsteps very far apart and very heavy. The next moment, who should come running towards her, full speed, and as pale as death, but Buffy-Bob. She held out her arms, and he ran into them. But when she tried to kiss him, she only kissed the back of his head; for his white face and round eyes were turned to the door.

"Run, children; run and hide," said the giantess.

"Come, Buffy," said Tricksey; "yonder's a great brake; we'll hide in it."

The brake was a big broom; and they had just got into the bristles of it when they heard the door open with a sound of thunder, and in stalked the giant. You would have thought you saw the whole earth through the door when he opened it, so wide was it; and when he closed it, it was like nightfall.

"Where is that little boy?" he cried, with a voice like the bellowing of a cannon. "He looked a very nice boy indeed. I am almost sure he crept through the mousehole at the bottom of the door. Where is he, my dear?"

"I don't know," answered the giantess.

"But you know it is wicked to tell lies; don't you, my dear?" retorted the giant.

"Now, you ridiculous old Thunderthump!" said his wife, with a smile as broad as the sea in the sun, "how can I mend your white stockings and look after little boys? You have got plenty to last you over Sunday, I am sure. Just look what good little boys they are!"

Tricksey-Wee and Buffy-Bob peered through the bristles, and discovered a row of little boys, about a dozen, with very fat faces and goggle eyes, sitting before the fire, and looking stupidly into it. Thunderthump intended the most of these for pickling, and was feeding them well before salting them. Now and then, however, he could not keep his teeth off them, and would eat one by the bye, without salt.

He strode up to the wretched children. Now what made them very wretched indeed was, that they knew if they could only keep from eating, and grow thin, the giant would dislike them, and turn them out to find their way home; but notwithstanding this, so greedy were they, that they ate as much as ever they could hold. The giantess, who fed them, comforted herself with thinking that they were not real boys and girls, but only little pigs pretending to be boys and girls.

"Now tell me the truth," cried the giant, bending his face down over them. They shook with terror, and every one hoped it was somebody else the giant liked best. "Where is the little boy that ran into the hall just now? Whoever tells me a lie shall be instantly boiled."

"He's in the broom," cried one dough-faced boy. "He's in there, and a little girl with him."

"The naughty children," cried the giant, "to hide from *me!*" And he made a stride towards the broom.

"Catch hold of the bristles, Bobby. Get right into a tuft, and hold on," cried Tricksey-Wee, just in time.

The giant caught up the broom, and seeing nothing under it, set it down again with a force that threw them both on the floor. He then made two strides to the boys, caught the dough-faced one by the neck, took the lid off a great pot that was boiling on the fire, popped him in as if he had been a trussed chicken, put the lid on again, and saying, "There, boys! See what comes of lying!" asked no more questions; for, as he always kept his word, he was afraid he might have to do the same to them all; and he did not like boiled boys. He liked to eat them crisp, as radishes, whether forked or not, ought to be eaten. He then sat down, and asked his wife if his supper was ready. She looked into the pot, and throwing the boy out with the ladle, as if he had been a black beetle that had tumbled in and had had the worst of it, answered that she thought it was. Whereupon he rose to help her; and taking the pot from the fire, poured the whole contents, bubbling and splashing, into a dish like a vat. Then they sat down to supper. The children in the broom could not see what they had; but it seemed to agree with them; for the giant talked like thunder, and the giantess answered like the sea, and they grew chattier and chattier. At length the giant said,—

"I don't feel quite comfortable about that heart of mine." And as he spoke, instead of laying his hand on his bosom, he waved it away towards the corner where the children were peeping from the broom bristles, like frightened little mice.

"Well, you know, my darling Thunderthump," answered his wife, "I always thought it ought to be nearer home. But you know best, of course."

"Ha! ha! You don't know where it is, wife. I moved it a month ago."

"What a man you are, Thunderthump! You trust any creature alive rather than your own wife."

Here the giantess gave a sob which sounded exactly like a wave going flop into the mouth of a cave up to the roof.

"Where have you got it now?" she resumed, checking her emotion.

"Well, Doodlem, I don't mind telling *you*," answered the giant soothingly. "The great she-eagle has got it for a nest egg. She sits on it night and day, and thinks she will bring the greatest eagle out of it that ever sharpened his beak on the rocks of Mount Skycrack. I can warrant no one else will touch it while she has got it. But she is rather capricious, and I confess I am not easy about it; for the least scratch of one of her claws would do for me at once. And she *has* claws."

I refer any one who doubts this part of my story to certain chronicles of Giantland preserved among the Celtic nations. It was quite a common thing for a giant to put his heart out to nurse, because he did not like the trouble and responsibility of doing it himself; although I must confess it was a dangerous sort of plan to take, especially with such a delicate viscus as the heart.

All this time Buffy-Bob and Tricksey-Wee were listening with long ears.

"Oh!" thought Tricksey-Wee, "If I could but find the giant's cruel heart, wouldn't I give it a squeeze!"

The giant and giantess went on talking for a long time. The giantess kept advising the giant to hide his heart somewhere in the house; but he seemed afraid of the advantage it would give her over him.

"You could hide it at the bottom of the flour-barrel," said she.

"That would make me feel chokey," answered he.

"Well, in the coal-cellar. Or in the dust-hole—that's the place! No one would think of looking for your heart in the dust-hole."

"Worse and worse!" cried the giant.

"Well, the water-butt," suggested she.

"No, no; it would grow spongy there," said he.

"Well, what *will* you do with it?"

"I will leave it a month longer where it is, and then I will give it to the Queen of the Kangaroos, and she will carry it in her pouch for me. It is best to change its place, you know, lest my enemies should scent it out. But, dear Doodlem, it's a fretting care to have a heart of one's own to look after. The responsibility is too much for me. If it were not for a bite of a radish now and then, I never could bear it."

Here the giant looked lovingly towards the row of little boys by the fire, all of whom were nodding, or asleep on the floor.

"Why don't you trust it to me, dear Thunderthump?" said his wife. "I would take the best possible care of it."

"I don't doubt it, my love. But the responsibility would be too much for *you*. You would no longer be my darling, light-hearted, airy, laughing Doodlem. It would transform you into a heavy, oppressed woman, weary of life—as I am."

The giant closed his eyes and pretended to go to sleep. His wife got his stockings, and went on with her darning. Soon the giant's pretence became reality, and the giantess began to nod over her work.

"Now, Buffy," whispered Tricksey-Wee, "now's our time. I think it's moonlight, and we had better be off. There's a door with a hole for the cat just behind us."

"All right," said Bob; "I'm ready."

So they got out of the broom-brake and crept to the door. But to their great disappointment, when they got through it, they found themselves in a sort of shed. It was full of tubs and things, and, though it was built of wood only, they could not find a crack.

"Let us try this hole," said Tricksey; for the giant and giantess were sleeping behind them, and they dared not go back.

"All right," said Bob.

He seldom said anything else than *All right*.

Now this hole was in a mound that came in through the wall of the shed, and went along the floor for some distance. They crawled into it, and found it very dark. But groping their way along, they soon came to a small crack, through which they saw grass, pale in the moonshine. As they crept on, they found the hole began to get wider and lead upwards.

"What is that noise of rushing?" said Buffy-Bob.

"I can't tell," replied Tricksey; "for, you see, I don't know what we are in."

The fact was, they were creeping along a channel in the heart of a giant tree; and the noise they heard was the noise of the sap rushing along in its wooden pipes. When they laid their ears to the wall, they heard it gurgling along with a pleasant noise.

"It sounds kind and good," said Tricksey. "It is water running. Now it must be running from somewhere to somewhere. I think we had better go on, and we shall come somewhere."

It was now rather difficult to go on, for they had to climb as if they were climbing a hill; and now the passage was wide. Nearly worn out, they saw light overhead at last, and creeping through a crack into the open air, found themselves on the fork of a huge tree. A great, broad, uneven space lay around them, out of which spread boughs in every

direction, the smallest of them as big as the biggest tree in the country
of common people. Overhead were leaves enough to supply all the trees
they had ever seen. Not much moonlight could come through, but the
leaves would glimmer white in the wind at times. The tree was full of
giant birds. Every now and then, one would sweep through, with a great
noise. But, except an occasional chirp, sounding like a shrill pipe in a
great organ, they made no noise. All at once an owl began to hoot. He
thought he was singing. As soon as he began, other birds replied,
making rare game of him. To their astonishment, the children found
they could understand every word they sang. And what they sang was
something like this:—

> "I will sing a song.
>   I'm the owl."
> "Sing a song, you sing-song
>   Ugly fowl!
> What will you sing about,
> Night in and Day out?"
>
> "Sing about the night;
>   I'm the owl."
> "You could not see for the light,
>   Stupid fowl!"
> "Oh! the moon! and the dew!
> And the shadows!—tu-whoo!"

The owl spread out his silent, soft, sly wings, and lighting between
Tricksey-Wee and Buffy-Bob, nearly smothered them, closing up one
under each wing. It was like being buried in a down bed. But the owl
did not like anything between his sides and his wings, so he opened his
wings again, and the children made haste to get out. Tricksey-Wee
immediately went in front of the bird, and looking up into his huge
face, which was as round as the eyes of the giantess's spectacles, and
much bigger, dropped a pretty courtesy, and said,—

"Please, Mr. Owl, I want to whisper to you."

"Very well, small child," answered the owl, looking important, and
stooping his ear towards her. "What is it?"

"Please tell me where the eagle lives that sits on the giant's heart."

"Oh, you naughty child! That's a secret. For shame!"

Buffy-Bob, Tricksey-Wee, and the Giant Owl (line drawing by C. Robinson; reprinted from *The Illustrated London News* [1863]).

And with a great hiss that terrified them, the owl flew into the tree. All birds are fond of secrets; but not many of them can keep them so well as the owl.

So the children went on because they did not know what else to do. They found the way very rough and difficult, the tree was so full of humps and hollows. Now and then they plashed into a pool of rain; now and then they came upon twigs growing out of the trunk where they had no business, and they were as large as full-grown poplars. Sometimes they came upon great cushions of soft moss, and on one of them they lay down and rested. But they had not lain long before they spied a large nightingale sitting on a branch, with its bright eyes looking up at the moon. In a moment more he began to sing, and the birds about him began to reply, but in a very different tone from that in which they had replied to the owl. Oh, the birds did call the nightingale such pretty names! The nightingale sang, and the birds replied like this: —

> "I will sing a song.
>   I'm the nightingale."
> "Sing a song, long, long,
>   Little Neverfail!
> What will you sing about,
> Light in or light out?"
>
> "Sing about the light
>   Gone away;
> Down, away, and out of sight —
>   Poor lost day!
> Mourning for the day dead,
> O'er his dim bed."

The nightingale sang so sweetly, that the children would have fallen asleep but for fear of losing any of the song. When the nightingale stopped they got up and wandered on. They did not know where they were going, but they thought it best to keep going on, because then they might come upon something or other. They were very sorry they had forgotten to ask the nightingale about the eagle's nest, but his music had put everything else out of their heads. They resolved, however, not to forget the next time they had a chance. So they went on and on, till they were both tired, and Tricksey-Wee said at last, trying to laugh,—

"I declare my legs feel just like a Dutch doll's."

"Then here's the place to go to bed in," said Buffy-Bob.

They stood at the edge of a last year's nest, and looked down with delight into the round, mossy cave. Then they crept gently in, and, lying down in each other's arms, found it so deep, and warm, and comfortable, and soft, that they were soon fast asleep.

Now close beside them, in a hollow, was another nest, in which lay a lark and his wife; and the children were awakened, very early in the morning, by a dispute between Mr. and Mrs. Lark.

"Let me up," said the lark.

"It is not time," said the lark's wife.

"It is," said the lark, rather rudely. "The darkness is quite thin. I can almost see my own beak."

"Nonsense!" said the lark's wife. "You know you came home yesterday morning quite worn out—you had to fly so very high before you saw him. I am sure he would not mind if you took it a little easier. Do be quiet and go to sleep again."

"That's not it at all," said the lark. "He doesn't want me. I want him. Let me up, I say."

He began to sing; and Tricksey-Wee and Buffy-Bob, having now learned the way, answered him:—

> "I will sing a song,
>   I'm the Lark."
> "Sing, sing, Throat-strong,
>   Little Kill-the-dark.
> What will you sing about,
>   Now the night is out?"
>
> "I can only call;
>   I can't think.
> Let me up—that's all.
>   Let me drink!
> Thirsting all the long night
> For a drink of light."

By this time the lark was standing on the edge of his nest and looking at the children.

"Poor little things! You can't fly," said the lark.

"No; but we can look up," said Tricksey.

"Ah, you don't know what it is to see the very first of the sun."

"But we know what it is to wait till he comes. He's no worse for your seeing him first, is he?"

"Oh no, certainly not," answered the lark, with condescension; and then, bursting into his *Jubilate,* he sprang aloft, clapping his wings like a clock running down.

"Tell us where—" began Buffy-Bob.

But the lark was out of sight. His song was all that was left of him. That was everywhere, and he was nowhere.

"Selfish bird!" said Buffy. "It's all very well for larks to go hunting the sun, but they have no business to despise their neighbors, for all that."

"Can I be of any use to you?" said a sweet bird-voice out of the nest.

This was the lark's wife, who stayed at home with the young larks while her husband went to church.

"Oh! thank you. If you please," answered Tricksey-Wee.

And up popped a pretty brown head; and then up came a brown feathery body; and last of all came the slender legs on to the edge of the nest. There she turned, and, looking down into the nest, from which came a whole litany of chirpings for breakfast, said, "Lie still, little ones." Then she turned to the children.

"My husband is King of the Larks," she said.

Buffy-Bob took off his cap, and Tricksey-Wee courtesied very low.

"Oh, it's not me," said the bird, looking very shy. "I am only his wife. It's my husband."

And she looked up after him into the sky, whence his song was still falling like a shower of musical hailstones. Perhaps *she* could see him.

"He's a splendid bird," said Buffy-Bob; "only you know he *will* get up a little too early."

"Oh, no! he doesn't. It's only his way, you know. But tell me what I can do for you."

"Tell us, please, Lady Lark, where the she-eagle lives that sits on Giant Thunderthump's heart."

"Oh! that is a secret."

"Did you promise not to tell?"

"No; but larks ought to be discreet. They see more than other birds."

"But you don't fly up high like your husband, do you?"

"Not often. But it's no matter. I come to know things for all that."

"Do tell me, and I will sing you a song," said Tricksey-Wee.

"Can you sing too?—You have got no wings!"

"Yes. And I will sing you a song I learned the other day about a lark and his wife."

"Please do," said the lark's wife. "Be quiet, children, and listen."

Tricksey-Wee was very glad she happened to know a song which would please the lark's wife, at least, whatever the lark himself might have thought of it, if he had heard it. So she sang:—

> " 'Good-morrow, my lord!' in the sky alone,
> Sang the lark, as the sun ascended his throne.
> 'Shine on me, my lord; I only am come,
> Of all your servants, to welcome you home.
> I have flown a whole hour, right up, I swear,
> To catch the first shine of your golden hair!'

> " 'Must I thank you, then,' said the king, 'Sir Lark,
> For flying so high, and hating the dark?
> You ask a full cup for half a thirst:
> Half is love of me, and half love to be first.
> There's many a bird that makes no haste,
> But waits till I come. That's as much to my taste.'

> "And the king hid his head in a turban of cloud;
> And the lark stopped singing, quite vexed and cowed.
> But he flew up higher, and thought, 'Anon,
> The wrath of the king will be over and gone;
> And his crown, shining out of its cloudy fold,
> Will change my brown feathers to a glory of gold.'

> "So he flew, with the strength of a lark he flew.
> But as he rose the cloud rose too;
> And not a gleam of the golden hair
> Came through the depth of the misty air;

Till, weary with flying, with sighing sore,
The strong sun-seeker could do no more.

"His wings had had no chrism of gold,
And his feathers felt withered and worn and old;
So he quivered and sank, and dropped like a stone.
And there on his nest, where he left her, alone,
Sat his little wife on her little eggs,
Keeping them warm with wings and legs.

"Did I say alone? Ah, no such thing!
Full in her face was shining the king.
'Welcome, Sir Lark! You look tired,' said he.
'*Up* is not always the best way to me.
While you have been singing so high and away,
I've been shining to your little wife all day.'

"He had set his crown all about the nest,
And out of the midst shone her little brown breast;
And so glorious was she in russet gold,
That for wonder and awe Sir Lark grew cold.
He popped his head under her wing, and lay
As still as a stone, till the king was away."

As soon as Tricksey-Wee had finished her song, the lark's wife began
a low, sweet, modest little song of her own; and after she had piped
away for two or three minutes, she said,—
"You dear children, what can I do for you?"
"Tell us where the she-eagle lives, please," said Tricksey-Wee.
"Well, I don't think there can be much harm in telling such wise,
good children," said Lady Lark; "I am sure you don't want to do any
mischief."
"Oh, no; quite the contrary," said Buffy-Bob.
"Then I'll tell you. She lives on the very topmost peak of Mount
Skycrack; and the only way to get up is to climb on the spiders' webs
that cover it from top to bottom."
"That's rather serious," said Tricksey-Wee.
"But you don't want to go up, you foolish little thing! You can't
go. And what do you want to go up for?"

"That is a secret," said Tricksey-Wee.

"Well, it's no business of mine," rejoined Lady Lark, a little offended, and quite vexed that she had told them. So she flew away to find some breakfast for her little ones, who by this time were chirping very impatiently. The children looked at each other, joined hands, and walked off.

In a minute more the sun was up, and they soon reached the outside of the tree. The bark was so knobby and rough, and full of twigs, that they managed to get down, though not without great difficulty. Then, far away to the north they saw a huge peak, like the spire of a church, going right up into the sky. They thought this must be Mount Skycrack, and turned their faces towards it. As they went on, they saw a giant or two, now and then, striding about the fields or through the woods, but they kept out of their way. Nor were they in much danger; for it was only one or two of the border giants that were so very fond of children.

At last they came to the foot of Mount Skycrack. It stood in a plain alone, and shot right up, I don't know how many thousand feet, into the air, a long, narrow, spearlike mountain. The whole face of it, from top to bottom, was covered with a network of spiders' webs, the threads of various sizes, from that of silk to that of whipcord. The webs shook, and quivered, and waved in the sun, glittering like silver. All about ran huge greedy spiders, catching huge silly flies, and devouring them.

Here they sat down to consider what could be done. The spiders did not heed them, but ate away at the flies.—Now at the foot of the mountain, and all round it, was a ring of water, not very broad, but very deep. As they sat watching them, one of the spiders, whose web was woven across this water, somehow or other lost his hold, and fell in on his back. Tricksey-Wee and Buffy-Bob ran to his assistance, and laying hold each of one of his legs, succeeded, with the help of the other legs, which struggled spiderfully, in getting him out upon dry land. As soon as he had shaken himself, and dried himself a little, the spider turned to the children, saying,—

"And now, what can I do for you?"

"Tell us, please," said they, "how we can get up the mountain to the she-eagle's nest."

"Nothing is easier," answered the spider. "Just run up there, and tell them all I sent you, and nobody will mind you."

"But we haven't got claws like you, Mr. Spider," said Buffy.

"Ah! no more you have, poor unprovided creatures! Still, I think we can manage it. Come home with me."

"You won't eat us, will you?" said Buffy.

"My dear child," answered the spider, in a tone of injured dignity, "I eat nothing but what is mischievous or useless. You have helped me, and now I will help you."

The children rose at once, and climbing as well as they could, reached the spider's nest in the centre of the web. Nor did they find it very difficult; for whenever too great a gap came, the spider spinning a strong cord stretched it just where they would have chosen to put their feet next. He left them in his nest, after bringing them two enormous honey-bags, taken from bees that he had caught; but presently about six of the wisest of the spiders came back with him. It was rather horrible to look up and see them all round the mouth of the nest, looking down on them in contemplation, as if wondering whether they would be nice eating. At length one of them said,—"Tell us truly what you want with the eagle, and we will try to help you."

Then Tricksey-Wee told them that there was a giant on the borders who treated little children no better than radishes, and that they had narrowly escaped being eaten by him; that they had found out that the great she-eagle of Mount Skycrack was at present sitting on his heart; and that, if they could only get hold of the heart, they would soon teach the giant better behaviour.

"But," said their host, "if you get at the heart of the giant, you will find it as large as one of your elephants. What can you do with it?"

"The least scratch will kill it," replied Buffy-Bob.

"Ah! but you might do better than that," said the spider.—"Now we have resolved to help you. Here is a little bag of spider-juice. The giants cannot bear spiders, and this juice is dreadful poison to them. We are all ready to go up with you, and drive the eagle away. Then you must put the heart into this other bag, and bring it down with you; for then the giant will be in your power."

"But how can we do that?" said Buffy. "The bag is not much bigger than a pudding-bag."

"But it is as large as you will be able to carry."

"Yes; but what are we to do with the heart?"

"Put it into the bag, to be sure. Only, first, you must squeeze out a drop of the other bag upon it. You will see what will happen."

"Very well; we will do as you tell us," said Tricksey-Wee. "And now, if you please, how shall we go?"

"Oh, that's our business," said the first spider. "You come with me, and my grandfather will take your brother. Get up."

So Tricksey-Wee mounted on the narrow part of the spider's back, and held fast. And Buffy-Bob got on the grandfather's back. And up they scrambled, over one web after another, up and up—so fast! And every spider followed; so that, when Tricksey-Wee looked back, she saw a whole army of spiders scrambling after them.

"What can we want with so many?" she thought; but she said nothing.

The moon was now up, and it was a splendid sight below and around them. All Giantland was spread out under them, with its great hills, lakes, trees, and animals. And all above them was the clear heaven, and Mount Skycrack rising into it, with its endless ladders of spider-webs, glittering like cords made of moonbeams. And up the moon-beams went, crawling and scrambling, and racing, a huge army of spiders.

At length they reached all but the very summit, where they stopped. Tricksey-Wee and Buffy-Bob could see above them a great globe of feathers, that finished off the mountain like an ornamental knob.

"But how shall we drive her off?" said Buffy.

"We'll soon manage that," answered the grandfather-spider. "Come on you, down there."

Up rushed the whole army, past the children, over the edge of the nest, on to the she-eagle, and buried themselves in her feathers. In a moment she became very restless, and went pecking about with her beak. All at once she spread out her wings, with a sound like a whirlwind, and flew off to bathe in the sea; and then the spiders began to drop from her in all directions on their gossamer wings. The children had to hold fast to keep the wind of the eagle's flight from blowing them off. As soon as it was over, they looked into the nest, and there lay the giant's heart—an awful and ugly thing.

"Make haste, child!" said Tricksey's spider.

So Tricksey took her bag, and squeezed a drop out of it upon the heart. She thought she heard the giant give a far-off roar of pain, and she nearly fell from her seat with terror. The heart instantly began to shrink. It shrank and shrivelled till it was nearly gone; and Buffy-Bob caught it up and put it into his bag. Then the two spiders turned and went down again as fast as they could. Before they got to the bottom, they heard the shrieks of the she-eagle over the loss of her egg; but the spiders told them not to be alarmed, for her eyes were too big to see them.—By the time they reached the foot of the mountain, all the spiders had got home, and were busy again catching flies, as if nothing had happened.

After renewed thanks to their friends, the children set off, carrying the giant's heart with them.

"If you should find it at all troublesome, just give it a little more spider-juice directly," said the grandfather, as they took their leave.

Now the giant had given an awful roar of pain the moment they anointed his heart, and had fallen down in a fit, in which he lay so long that all the boys might have escaped if they had not been so fat. One did, and got home in safety. For days the giant was unable to speak. The first words he uttered were,—

"Oh, my heart! my heart!"

"Your heart is safe enough, dear Thunderthump," said his wife. "Really, a man of your size ought not to be so nervous and apprehensive. I am ashamed of you."

"You have no heart, Doodlem," answered he. "I assure you that at this moment mine is in the greatest danger. It has fallen into the hands of foes, though who they are I cannot tell."

Here he fainted again; for Tricksey-Wee, finding the heart beginning to swell a little, had given it the least touch of spider-juice.

Again he recovered, and said,—

"Dear Doodlem, my heart is coming back to me. It is coming nearer and nearer."

After lying silent for hours, he exclaimed,—

"It is in the house, I know!"

And he jumped up and walked about, looking in every corner.

As he rose, Tricksey-Wee and Buffy-Bob came out of the hole in the tree-root, and through the cat-hole in the door, and walked boldly towards the giant. Both kept their eyes busy watching him. Led by the love of his own heart, the giant soon spied them, and staggered furiously towards them.

"I will eat you, you vermin!" he cried. "Here with my heart!"

Tricksey gave the heart a sharp pinch. Down fell the giant on his knees, blubbering, and crying, and begging for his heart.

"You shall have it, if you behave yourself properly," said Tricksey.

"How shall I behave myself properly?" asked he, whimpering.

"Take all those boys and girls, and carry them home at once."

"I'm not able; I'm too ill. I should fall down."

"Take them up directly."

"I can't, till you give me my heart."

"Very well!" said Tricksey; and she gave the heart another pinch.

The giant jumped to his feet, and catching up all the children, thrust some into his waistcoat-pockets, some into his breast-pocket, put two or three into his hat, and took a bundle of them under each arm. Then he staggered to the door.

All this time poor Doodlem was sitting in her arm-chair, crying, and mending a white stocking.

The giant led the way to the borders. He could not go fast but that Buffy and Tricksey managed to keep up with him. When they reached the borders, they thought it would be safer to let the children find their own way home. So they told him to set them down. He obeyed.

"Have you put them all down, Mr. Thunderthump?" asked Tricksey-Wee.

"Yes," said the giant.

"That's a lie!" squeaked a little voice; and out came a head from his waistcoat pocket.

Tricksey-Wee pinched the heart till the giant roared with pain.

"You're not a gentleman. You tell stories," she said.

"He was the thinnest of the lot," said Thunderthump, crying.

"Are you all there now, children?" asked Tricksey.

"Yes, ma'am," returned they, after counting themselves very carefully, and with some difficulty; for they were all stupid children.

"Now," said Tricksey-Wee to the giant, "will you promise to carry off no more children, and never to eat a child again all your life?"

"Yes, yes! I promise," answered Thunderthump, sobbing.

"And you will never cross the borders of Giantland?"

"Never."

"And you shall never again wear white stockings on a Sunday, all your life long.—Do you promise?"

The giant hesitated at this, and began to expostulate; but Tricksey-Wee, believing it would be good for his morals, insisted; and the giant promised.

Then she required of him, that, when she gave him back his heart, he should give it to his wife to take care of for him for ever after. The poor giant fell on his knees, and began again to beg. But Tricksey-Wee giving the heart a slight pinch, he bawled out,—

"Yes, yes! Doodlem shall have it, I swear. Only she must not put it in the flour barrel, or in the dust-hole."

"Certainly not. Make your own bargain with her.—And you promise not to interfere with my brother and me, or to take any revenge for what we have done?"

"Yes, yes, my dear children; I promise everything. Do, pray, make haste and give me back my poor heart."

"Wait there, then, till I bring it to you."

"Yes, yes. Only make haste, for I feel very faint."

Tricksey-Wee began to undo the mouth of the bag. But Buffy-Bob, who had got very knowing on his travels, took out his knife with the pretence of cutting the string; but, in reality, to be prepared for any emergency.

No sooner was the heart out of the bag, than it expanded to the size of a bullock; and the giant, with a yell of rage and vengeance, rushed on the two children, who had stepped sideways from the terrible heart. But Buffy-Bob was too quick for Thunderthump. He sprang to the heart, and buried his knife in it, up to the hilt. A fountain of blood spouted from it; and with a dreadful groan the giant fell dead at the feet of little Tricksey-Wee, who could not help being sorry for him, after all.

III
The Carasoyn

I

The Mountain Stream

Once upon a time, there lived in a valley in Scotland, a boy about twelve years of age, the son of a shepherd. His mother was dead, and he had no sister or brother. His father was out all day on the hills with his sheep; but when he came home at night, he was as sure of finding the cottage neat and clean, the floor swept, a bright fire, and his supper waiting for him, as if he had had wife and daughter to look after his household, instead of only a boy. Therefore, although Colin could only read and write, and knew nothing of figures, he was ten times wiser, and more capable of learning anything, than if he had been at school all his days. He was never at a loss when anything had to be done. Somehow, he always blundered into the straight road to his end, while another would be putting on his shoes to look for it. And yet all the time that he was busiest working, he was busiest building castles in the air. I think the two ought always to go together.

And so Colin was never over-worked, but had plenty of time to himself. In winter he spent it in reading by the fireside, or carving pieces of wood with his pocket knife; and in summer he always went out for a ramble. His great delight was in a little stream which ran down the valley from the mountains above. Up this *burn* he would wander every afternoon, with his hands in his pockets. He never got far, however—he was so absorbed in watching its antics. Sometimes he would sit on a rock, staring at the water as it hurried through the stones, scolding, expostulating, muttering, and always having its own way. Sometimes he would stop by a deep pool, and watch the crimson-spotted trouts, darting about as if their thoughts and not their tails sent them where they wanted to go. And when he stopped at the little

The first part appeared as "The Fairy Fleet" in *Argosy* (1866); the expanded form "The Carasoyn" appeared in *Works* (1871).

cascade, tumbling smooth and shining over a hollowed rock, he seldom got beyond it.

But there was one thing which always troubled him. It was, that when the stream came near the cottage, it could find no other way than through the little yard where stood the cowhouse and the pigsty; and there, not finding a suitable channel, spread abroad in a disconsolate manner, becoming rather a puddle than a brook, all defiled with the treading of the cloven feet of the cow and the pigs. In fact, it looked quite lost and ruined; so that even after it had, with much labour, got out of the yard again, it took a long time to gather itself together, and not quite succeeding, slipped away as if ashamed, with spent forces and poverty-stricken speed; till at length, meeting the friendly help of a rivulet coming straight from the hills, it gathered heart and bounded on afresh.

"It can't be all that the cow drinks that makes the difference," said Colin to himself. "The pigs don't care about it. I do believe it's affronted at being dashed about. The cow isn't dirty, but she's rather stupid and inconsiderate. The pigs are dirty. Something must be done. Let me see."

He reconnoitred the whole ground. Upon the other side of the house all was rock, through which he could not cut; and he was forced to the conclusion that the only other course for the stream to take lay right through the cottage.

To most engineers this would have appeared the one course to be avoided; but Colin's heart danced at the thought of having his dear *burn* running right through the house. How cool it would be all the summer! How convenient for cooking; and how handy at meals! And then the music of it! How it would tell him stories, and sing him to sleep at night! What a companion it would be when his father was away! And then he could bathe in it when he liked. In winter—ah!—to be sure! But winter was a long way off.

The very next day his father went to the fair. So Colin set to work at once.

It was not such a very difficult undertaking; for the walls of the cottage, and the floor as well, were of clay—the former nearly sun-dried into a brick, and the latter trampled hard; but still both assailable by pickaxe and spade. He cut through the walls, and dug a channel along the floor, letting in stones in the bottom and sides. After it got out of the cottage and through the small garden in front, it should find its own way to the channel below, for here the hill was very steep.

The same evening his father came home.

"What have you been about, Colin?" he asked, in great surprise, when he saw the trench in the floor.

"Wait a minute, father," said Colin, "till I have got your supper, and then I'll tell you."

So when his father was seated at the table, Colin darted out, and hurrying up to the stream, broke through the bank just in the place whence a natural hollow led straight to the cottage. The stream dashed out like a wild creature from a cage, faster than he could follow, and shot through the wall of the cottage. His father gave a shout; and when Colin went in, he found him sitting with his spoon half-way to his mouth, and his eyes fixed on the muddy water which rushed foaming through his floor.

"It will soon be clean, father," said Colin, "and then it will be so nice!"

His father made no answer, but continued staring. Colin went on with a long list of the advantages of having a brook running through your house. At length his father smiled and said:—

"You are a curious creature, Colin. But why shouldn't you have your fancies as well as older people? We'll try it awhile, and then we'll see about it."

The fact was, Colin's father had often thought what a lonely life the boy's was. And it seemed hard to take from him any pleasure he could have. So out rushed Colin at the front, to see how the brook would take the shortest way headlong down the hill to its old channel. And to see it go tumbling down that hill was a sight worth living for.

"It is a mercy," said Colin, "it has no neck to break, or it would break twenty times in a minute. It flings itself from rock to rock right down, just as I should like to do, if it weren't for my neck."

All that evening he was out and in without a moment's rest; now up to the beginning of the cut, now following the stream down to the cottage; then through the cottage, and out again at the front door to see it dart across the garden, and dash itself down the hill.

At length his father told him he must go to bed. He took one more peep at the water, which was running quite clear now, and obeyed. His father followed him presently.

II

The Fairy Fleet

The bed was about a couple of yards from the edge of the brook. And as Colin was always first up in the morning, he slept at the front of the bed. So he lay for some time gazing at the faint glimmer of the water in the dull red light from the sod-covered fire, and listening to its sweet music as it hurried through to the night again, till its murmur changed into a lullaby, and sung him fast asleep.

Soon he found that he was coming awake again. He was lying listening to the sound of the busy stream. But it had gathered more sounds since he went to sleep—amongst the rest one of boards knocking together, and a tiny chattering and sweet laughter, like the tinkling of heather-bells. He opened his eyes. The moon was shining along the brook, lighting the smoky rafters above with its reflection from the water, which had been dammed back at its outlet from the cottage, so that it lay bank-full and level with the floor. But its surface was hardly to be seen, save by an occasional glimmer, for the crowded boats of a fairy fleet which had just arrived. The sailors were as busy as sailors could be, mooring along the banks, or running their boats high and dry on the shore. Some had little sails which glimmered white in the moonshine—half-lowered, or blowing out in the light breeze that crept down the course of the stream. Some were pulling about through the rest, oars flashing, tiny voices calling, tiny feet running, tiny hands hauling at ropes that ran through blocks of shining ivory. On the shore stood groups of fairy ladies in all colours of the rainbow, green predominating, waited upon by gentlemen all in green, but with red and yellow feathers in their caps. The queen had landed on the side next to Colin, and in a few minutes more twenty dances were going at once along the shores of the fairy river. And there lay great Colin's face, just above the bed-clothes, *glowering* at them like an ogre.

At last, after a few dances, he heard a clear, sweet, ringing voice say,

"I've had enough of this. I'm tired of doing like the big people. Let's have a game of Hey Cockolorum Jig!"

That instant every group sprang asunder, and every fairy began a frolic on his own account. They scattered all over the cottage, and Colin lost sight of most of them.

While he lay watching the antics of two of those near him, who behaved more like clowns at a fair than the gentlemen they had been a little while before, he heard a voice close to his ear; but though he looked everywhere about his pillow, he could see nothing. The voice stopped the moment he began to look, but began again as soon as he gave it up.

"You can't see me. I'm talking to you through a hole in the head of your bed."

"Don't look," said the voice. "If the queen sees me I shall be pinched. Oh, please don't."

The voice sounded as if its owner would cry presently. So Colin took good care not to look. It went on:

"Please, I am a little girl, not a fairy. The queen stole me the minute I was born, seven years ago, and I can't get away. I don't like the fairies. They are so silly. And they never grow any wiser. I grow wiser every year. I want to get back to my own people. They won't let me. They make me play at being somebody else all night long, and sleep all day. That's what they do themselves. And I should so like to be myself. The queen says that's not the way to be happy at all; but I do want very much to be a little girl. Do take me."

"How am I to get you?" asked Colin in a whisper, which sounded, after the sweet voice of the changeling, like the wind in a field of dry beans.

"The queen is so pleased with you that she is sure to offer you something. Choose me. Here she comes."

Immediately he heard another voice, shriller and stronger, in front of him; and, looking about, saw standing on the edge of the bed a lovely little creature, with a crown glittering with jewels, and a rush for a sceptre in her hand, the blossom of which shone like a bunch of garnets.

"You great staring creature!" she said. "Your eyes are much too big to see with. What clumsy hobgoblins you thick folk are!"

So saying, she laid her wand across Colin's eyes.

"Now, then, stupid!" she said; and that instant Colin saw the room like a huge barn, full of creatures about two feet high. The beams overhead were crowded with fairies, playing all imaginable tricks,

scrambling everywhere, knocking each other over, throwing dust and
soot in each other's faces, grinning from behind corners, dropping on
each other's necks, and tripping up each other's heels. Two had got
hold of an empty egg-shell, and coming behind one sitting on the edge
of the table, and laughing at some one on the floor, tumbled it right
over him, so that he was lost in the cavernous hollow. But the lady-
fairies mingled in none of these rough pranks. Their tricks were always
graceful, and they had more to say than to do.

But the moment the queen had laid her wand across his eyes, she
went on:

"Know, son of a human mortal, that thou hast pleased a queen of
the fairies. Lady as I am over the elements, I cannot have everything I
desire. One thing thou hast given me. Years have I longed for a path
down this rivulet to the ocean below. Your horrid farm-yard, ever since
your great-grandfather built this cottage, was the one obstacle. For we
fairies hate dirt, not only in houses, but in fields and woods as well, and
above all in running streams. But I can't talk like this any longer. I tell
you what, you are a dear good boy, and you shall have what you please.
Ask me for anything you like."

"May it please your majesty," said Colin, very deliberately, "I want
a little girl that you carried away some seven years ago the moment she
was born. May it please your majesty, I want her."

"It does not please my majesty," cried the queen, whose face had
been growing very black. "Ask for something else."

"Then, whether it pleases your majesty or not," said Colin, bravely,
"I hold your majesty to your word. I want that little girl, and that little
girl I *will* have, and nothing else."

"You dare to talk so to me, you thick!"

"Yes, your majesty."

"Then you sha'n't have her."

"Then I'll turn the brook right through the dunghill," said Colin.
"Do you think I'll let you come into my cottage to play at high jinks
when you please, if you behave to me like this?"

And Colin sat up in bed, and looked the queen in the face. And as
he did so he caught sight of the loveliest little creature peeping round
the corner at the foot of the bed. And he knew she was the little girl,
because she was quiet, and looked frightened, and was sucking her
thumb.

Then the queen, seeing with whom she had to deal, and knowing that queens in Fairyland are bound by their word, began to try another plan with him. She put on her sweetest manner and looks; and as she did so, the little face at the foot of the bed grew more troubled, and the little head shook itself, and the little thumb dropped out of the little mouth.

"Dear Colin," said the queen, "you shall have the girl. But you must do something for me first."

The little girl shook her head as fast as ever she could, but Colin was taken up with the queen.

"To be sure I will. What is it?" he said.

And so he was bound by a new bargain, and was in the queen's power.

"You must fetch me a bottle of Carasoyn," said she.

"What is that?" asked Colin.

"A kind of wine that makes people happy."

"Why, are you not happy already?"

"No, Colin," answered the queen, with a sigh.

"You have everything you want."

"Except the Carasoyn," returned the queen.

"You do whatever you like, and go wherever you please."

"That's just it. I want something that I neither like nor please—that I don't know anything about. I want a bottle of Carasoyn."

And here she cried like a spoilt child, not like a sorrowful woman.

"But how am I to get it?"

"I don't know. You must find out."

"Oh! that's not fair," cried Colin.

But the queen burst into a fit of laughter that sounded like the bells of a hundred frolicking sheep, and bounding away to the side of the river, jumped on board of her boat. And like a swarm of bees gathered the courtiers and sailors; two creeping out of the bellows, one at the nozzle and the other at the valve; three out of the basket-hilt of the broadsword on the wall; six all white out of the meal-tub; and so from all parts of the cottage to the river-side. And amongst them Colin spied the little girl creeping on board the queen's boat, with her pinafore to her eyes; and the queen was shaking her fist at her. In five minutes more they had all scrambled into the boats, and the whole fleet was in motion down the stream. In another moment the cottage was empty, and everything had returned to its usual size.

"They'll be all dashed to pieces on the rocks," cried Colin, jumping up, and running into the garden. When he reached the fall, there was nothing to be seen but the swift plunge and rush of the broken water in the moonlight. He thought he heard cries and shouts coming up from below, and fancied he could distinguish the sobs of the little maiden whom he had so foolishly lost. But the sounds might be only those of the water, for to the different voices of a running stream there is no end. He followed its course all the way to its old channel, but saw nothing to indicate any disaster. Then he crept back to his bed, where he lay thinking what a fool he had been, till he cried himself to sleep over the little girl who would never grow into a woman.

III

The Old Woman and Her Hen

In the morning, however, his courage had returned; for the word Carasoyn was always saying itself in his brain.

"People in fairy stories," he said, "always find what they want. Why should not I find this Carasoyn? It does not seem likely. But the world doesn't go round by *likely*. So I will try."

But how was he to begin?

When Colin did not know what to do, he always did something. So as soon as his father was gone to the hill, he wandered up the stream down which the fairies had come.

"But I needn't go on so," he said, "for if the Carasoyn grew in the fairies' country, the queen would know how to get it."

All at once he remembered how he had lost himself on the moor when he was a little boy; and had gone into a hut and found there an old woman spinning. And she had told him such stories! and shown him the way home. So he thought she might be able to help him now; for he remembered that she was very old then, and must be older and still wiser now. And he resolved to go and look for the hut, and ask the old woman what he was to do.

So he left the stream, and climbed the hill, and soon came upon a desolate moor. The sun was clouded and the wind was cold, and everything looked dreary. And there was no sign of a hut anywhere. He wandered on, looking for it; and all at once found that he had forgotten the way back. At the same instant he saw the hut right before him. And then he remembered it was when he had lost himself that he saw it the former time.

"It seems the way to find some things is to lose yourself," said he to himself.

He went up to the cottage, which was like a large beehive built of turf, and knocked at the door.

"Come in, Colin," said a voice; and he entered, stooping low.

The old woman sat by a little fire, spinning, after the old fashion, with a distaff and spindle. She stopped the moment he went in.

"Come and sit down by the fire," she said, "and tell me what you want."

Then Colin saw that she had no eyes.

"I am very sorry you are blind," he said.

"Never you mind that, my dear. I see more than you do for all my blindness. Tell me what you want, and I shall see at least what I can do for you."

"How do you know I want anything?" asked Colin.

"Now that's what I don't like," said the old woman. "Why do you waste words? Words should not be wasted any more than crumbs."

"I beg your pardon," returned Colin. "I will tell you all about it."

And so he told her the whole story.

"Oh those children! those children!" said the old woman. "They are always doing some mischief. They never know how to enjoy themselves without hurting somebody or other. I really must give that queen a bit of my mind. Well, my dear, I like you; and I will tell you what must be done. You shall carry the silly queen her bottle of Carasoyn. But she won't like it when she gets it, I can tell her. That's my business, however. —First of all, Colin, you must dream three days without sleeping. Next, you must work three days without dreaming. And last, you must work and dream three days together."

"How am I to do all that?"

"I will help you all I can, but a great deal will depend on yourself. In the meantime you must have something to eat."

So saying, she rose, and going to a corner behind her bed, returned with a large golden-coloured egg in her hand. This she laid on the hearth, and covered over with hot ashes. She then chatted away to

Colin about his father, and the sheep, and the cow, and the housework, and showed that she knew all about him. At length she drew the ashes off the egg, and put it on a plate.

"It shines like silver now," said Colin.

"That is a sign it is quite done," said she, and set it before him.

Colin had never tasted anything half so nice. And he had never seen such a quantity of meat in an egg. Before he had finished it he had made a hearty meal. But, in the meantime, the old woman said,—

"Shall I tell you a story while you have your dinner?"

"Oh, yes, please do," answered Colin. "You told me such stories before!"

"Jenny," said the old woman, "my wool is all done. Get me some more."

And from behind the bed out came a sober-coloured, but large and beautifully-shaped hen. She walked sedately across the floor, putting down her feet daintily, like a prim matron as she was, and stopping by the door, gave a *cluck, cluck*.

"Oh, the door is shut, is it?" said the old woman.

"Let me open it," said Colin.

"Do, my dear."

"What are all those white things?" he asked, for the cottage stood in the middle of a great bed of grass with white tops.

"Those are my sheep," said the old woman. "You will see."

Into the grass Jenny walked, and stretching up her neck, gathered the white woolly stuff in her beak. When she had as much as she could hold, she came back and dropped it on the floor; then picked the seeds out and swallowed them, and went back for more. The old woman took the wool, and fastening it on her distaff, began to spin, giving the spindle a twirl, and then dropping it and drawing out the thread from the distaff. But as soon as the spindle began to twirl, it began to sparkle all the colours of the rainbow, that it was a delight to see. And the hands of the woman, instead of being old and wrinkled, were young and long-fingered and fair, and they drew out the wool, and the spindle spun and flashed, and the hen kept going out and in, bringing wool and swallowing the seeds, and the old woman kept telling Colin one story after another, till he thought he could sit there all his life and listen. Sometimes it seemed the spindle that was flashing them, sometimes the long fingers that were spinning them, and sometimes the hen that was gathering them off the heads of the long dry grass and bringing them in her beak and laying them down on the floor.

All at once the spindle grew slower, and gradually ceased turning; the fingers stopped drawing out the thread, the hen retreated behind the bed, and the voice of the blind woman was silent.

"I suppose it is time for me to go," said Colin.

"Yes, it is," answered his hostess.

"Please tell me, then, how I am to dream three days without sleeping."

"That's over," said the old woman. "You've just finished that part. I told you I would help you all I could."

"Have I been here three days, then?" asked Colin, in astonishment.

"And nights too. And I and Jenny and the spindle are quite tired and want to sleep. Jenny has got three eggs to lay besides. Make haste, my boy."

"Please, then, tell me what I am to do next."

"Jenny will put you in the way. When you come where you are going, you will tell them that the old woman with the spindle desires them to lift Cumberbone Crag a yard higher, and to send a flue under Stonestarvit Moss. Jenny, show Colin the way."

Jenny came out with a surly *cluck* and led him a good way across the heath by a path only a hen could have found. But she turned suddenly and walked home again.

IV

The Goblin Blacksmith

Colin could just perceive something suggestive of a track, which he followed till the sun went down. Then he saw a dim light before him, keeping his eye upon which, he came at last to a smithy, where, looking in at the open door, he saw a huge, humpbacked smith working a forehammer in each hand.

He grinned out of the middle of his breast when he saw Colin, and said, "Come in; come in: my youngsters will be glad of you."

He was an awful looking creature, with a great hare lip, and a red ball for a nose. Whatever he did—speak, or laugh, or sneeze—he did not stop working one moment. As often as the sparks flew in his face, he snapped at them with his eyes (which were the colour of a half-dead coal), now with this one, now with that; and the more sparks they got into them the brighter his eyes grew. The moment Colin entered, he took a huge bar of iron from the furnace, and began laying on it so with his two forehammers that he disappeared in a cloud of sparks, and Colin had to shut his eyes and be glad to escape with a few burns on his face and hands. When he had beaten the iron till it was nearly black, the smith put it in the fire again, and called out a hundred odd names:

"Here Gob, Shag, Latchit, Licker, Freestone, Greywhackit, Mouse-trap, Potatoe-pot, Blob, Blotch, Blunker——"

And ever as he called, one dwarf after another came tumbling out of the chimney in the corner of which the fire was roaring. They crowded about Colin and began to make hideous faces and spit fire at him. But he kept a bold countenance. At length one pinched him, and he could not stand that, but struck him hard on the head. He thought he had knocked his own hand to pieces, it gave him such a jar; and the head rung like an iron pot.

"Come, come, young man?" cried the smith; "you keep your hands off my children."

"Tell them to keep their hands off me, then," said Colin.

And calling to mind his message, just as they began to crowd about him again with yet more spiteful looks, he added—

"Here, you imps! I won't stand it longer. Get to your work directly. The old woman with the spindle says you're to lift Cumberbone Crag a yard higher, and to send a flue under Stonestarvit Moss."

In a moment they had vanished in the chimney. In a moment more the smithy rocked to its foundations. But the smith took no notice, only worked more furiously than ever. Then came a great crack and a shock that threw Colin on the floor. The smith reeled, but never lost hold of his hammers of missed a blow on the anvil.

"Those boys will do themselves a mischief," he said; then turning to Colin, "Here, you sir, take that hammer. This is no safe place for idle people. If you don't work you'll be knocked to pieces in no time."

The same moment there came a wind from the chimney that blew all the fire into the middle of the smithy. The smith dashed up upon the forge, and rushed out of sight. Presently he returned with one of the goblins under his arm kicking and screaming, laid his ugly head down on the anvil, where he held him by the neck, and hit him a great blow with his hammer above the ear. The hammer rebounded, the goblin gave a shriek, and the smith flung him into the chimney, saying—

"That's the only way to serve *him*. You'll be more careful for one while, I guess, Slobberkin."

And thereupon he took up his other hammer and began to work again, saying to Colin,

"Now, young man, as long as you get a blow with your hammer in for every one of mine, you'll be quite safe; but if you stop, or lose the beat, I won't be answerable to the old woman with the spindle for the consequences."

Colin took up the hammer and did his best. But he soon found that he had never known what it was to work. The smith worked a hammer in each hand, and it was all Colin could do to work his little hammer with both his hands; so it was a terrible exertion to put in blow for blow with the smith. Once, when he lost the time, the smith's fore-hammer came down on the head of his, beat it flat on the anvil, and flung the handle to the other end of the smithy, where it struck the wall like the report of a cannon.

"I told you," said the smith. "There's another. Make haste, for the boys will be in want of you and me too before they get Cumberbone Crag half a foot higher."

Presently in came the biggest-headed of the family, out of the chimney.

"Six-foot wedges, and a three-yard crowbar!" he said; "or Cumberbone will cumber our bones presently."

The smith rushed behind the bellows, brought out a bar of iron three inches thick or so, cut off three yards, put the end in the fire, blew with might and main, and brought it out as white as paper. He and Colin then laid upon it till the end was flattened to an edge, which the smith turned up a little. He then handed the tool to the imp.

"Here, Gob," he said; "run with it, and the wedges will be ready by the time you come back."

Then to the wedges they set. And Colin worked like three. He never knew how he could work before. Not a moment's pause, except when the smith was at the forge for another glowing mass! And yet, to Colin's amazement, the more he worked, the stronger he seemed to grow. Instead of being worn out, the moment he had got his breath he wanted to be at it again; and he felt as if he had grown twice the size since he took hammer in hand. And the goblins kept running in and out all the time, now for one thing, now for another. Colin thought if they made use of all the tools they fetched, they must be working very hard indeed: And the convulsions felt in the smithy bore witness to their exertions somewhere in the neighbourhood.

And the longer they worked together, the more friendly grew the smith. At length he said—his words always adding energy to his blows—

"What does the old woman want to improve Stonestarvit Moss for?"

"I didn't know she did want to improve it," returned Colin.

"Why, anybody may see that. First, she wants Cumberbone Crag a yard higher—just enough to send the north-east blast over the Moss without touching it. Then she wants a hot flue passed under it. Plain as a fore-hammer!—What did you ask her to do for you? She's always doing things for people and making my bones ache."

"You don't seem to mind it much, though, sir," said Colin.

"No more I do," answered the smith, with a blow that drove the anvil half way into the earth, from which it took him some trouble to drag it out again. "But I want to know what she is after now."

So Colin told him all he knew about it, which was merely his own story.

"I see, I see," said the smith. "It's all moonshine; but we must do as she says notwithstanding. And now it is my turn to give you a lift, for you have worked well.—As soon as you leave the smithy, go straight to Stonestarvit Moss. Get on the highest part of it; make a circle three yards across, and dig a trench round it. I will give you a spade. At the end of the first day you will see a vine break the earth. By the end of the second, it will be creeping all over the circle. And by the end of the third day, the grapes will be ripe. Squeeze them one by one into a bottle—I will give you a bottle—till it is full. Cork it up tight, and by the time the queen comes for it, it will be Carasoyn."

"Oh, thank you, thank you," cried Colin. "When am I to go?"

"As soon as the boys have lifted Cumberbone Crag, and bored the flue under the Moss. It is of no use till then."

"Well, I'll go on with my work," said Colin, and struck away at the anvil.

In a minute or two in came the same goblin whose head his father had hammered, and said, respectfully,

"It's all right, sir. The boys are gathering their tools, and will be home to supper directly."

"Are you sure you have lifted the Crag a yard?" said the smith.

"Slumkin says it's a half inch over the yard. Grungle says it's three-quarters. But that won't matter—will it?"

"No. I dare say not. But it is much better to be accurate. Is the flue done?"

"Yes, we managed that partly in lifting the crag."

"Very well. How's your head?"

"It rings a little."

"Let it ring you a lesson, then, Slobberkin, in future."

"Yes, sir."

"Now, master, you may go when you like," said the smith to Colin. "We've nothing here you can eat, I am sorry to say."

"Oh, I don't mind that. I'm not very hungry. But the old woman with the spindle said I was to work three days without dreaming."

"Well, you haven't been dreaming—have you?"

And the smith looked quite furious as he put the question, lifting his forehammer as if he would serve Colin like Slobberkin.

"No, that I haven't," answered Colin. "You took good care of that, sir."

The smith actually smiled.

"Then go along," he said. "It is all right."

"But I've only worked—"

"Three whole days and nights," interrupted the smith. "Get along with you. The boys will bother you if you don't. Here's your spade and here's your bottle."

V

The Moss Vineyard

Colin did not need a hint more, but was out of the smithy in a moment. He turned, however, to ask the way: there was nothing in sight but a great heap of peats which had been dug out of the moss, and

was standing there to dry. Could he be on Stonestarvit Moss already?
The sun was just setting. He would look out for the highest point at
once. So he kept climbing, and at last reached a spot whence he could
see all round him for a long way. Surely that must be Cumberbone Crag
looking down on him! And there at his feet lay one of Jenny's eggs, as
bright as silver. And there was a little path trodden and scratched by
Jenny's feet, inclosing a circle just the size the smith told him to make.
He set to work at once, ate Jenny's egg, and then dug the trench.

Those three days were the happiest he had ever known. For he
understood everything he did himself, and all that everything was doing
round about him. He saw what the rushes were, and why the blossom
came out at the side, and why it was russet-coloured, and why the pith
was white, and the skin green. And he said to himself, "If I were a rush
now, that's just how I should make a point of growing." And he knew
how the heather felt with its cold roots, and its head of purple bells;
and the wise-looking cotton-grass, which the old woman called her
sheep, and the white beard of which she spun into thread. And he knew
what she spun it for: namely, to weave it into lovely white cloth of
which to make nightgowns for all the good people that were like to die;
for one with one of these nightgowns upon him never died, but was laid
in a beautiful white bed, and the door was closed upon him, and no
noise came near him, and he lay there, dreaming lovely cool dreams, till
the world had turned round, and was ready for him to get up again and
do something.

He felt the wind playing with every blade of grass in his charmed
circle. He felt the rays of heat shooting up from the hot flue beneath
the moss. He knew the moment when the vine was going to break from
the earth, and he felt the juices gathering and flowing from the roots
into the grapes. And all the time he seemed at home, tending the cow,
or making his father's supper, or reading a fairy tale as he sat waiting
for him to come home.

At length the evening of the third day arrived. Colin squeezed the
rich red grapes into his bottle, corked it, shouldered his spade, and
turned homewards, guided by a peak which he knew in the distance.
After walking all night in the moonlight, he came at length upon a place
which he recognized, and so down upon the brook, which he followed
home.

He met his father going out with his sheep. Great was his delight to
see Colin again, for he had been dreadfully anxious about him. Colin

told him the whole story; and as at that time marvels were much easier
to believe than they are now, Colin's father did not laugh at him, but
went away to the hills thinking, while Colin went on to the cottage,
where he found plenty to do, having been nine days gone. He laid the
bottle carefully away with his Sunday clothes, and set about everything
just as usual.

But though the fairy brook was running merrily as ever through the
cottage, and although Colin watched late every night, and latest when
the moon shone, no fairy fleet came glimmering and dancing in along
the stream. Autumn was there at length, and cold fogs began to rise in
the cottage, and so Colin turned the brook into its old course, and filled
up the breaches in the walls and the channel along the floor, making all
close against the blasts of winter. But he had never known such a weary
winter before. He could not help constantly thinking how cold the little
girl must be, and how she would be saying to herself, "I wish Colin
hadn't been so silly and lost me."

VI

The Consequences

But at last the spring came, and after the spring the summer. And the
very first warm day, Colin took his spade and pickaxe, and down
rushed the stream once more, singing and bounding into the cottage.
Colin was even more delighted than he had been the first time. And he
watched late into the night, but there came neither moon nor fairy
fleet. And more than a week passed thus.

At length, on the ninth night, Colin, who had just fallen asleep,
opened his eyes with sudden wakefulness, and behold! the room was all
in a glimmer with moonshine and fairy glitter. The boats were rocking
on the water, and the queen and her court had landed, and were
dancing merrily on the earthen floor. He lost no time.

"Queen! queen!" he said, "I've got your bottle of Carasoyn."

The dance ceased in a moment, and the queen bounded upon the
edge of his bed.

I can't bear the look of your great, glaring, ugly eyes," she said. "I must make you less before I can talk to you."

So once more she laid her rush wand across his eyes, whereupon Colin saw them all six times the size they were before, and the queen went on:

"Where is the Carasoyn? Give it me."

"It is in my box under the bed. If your majesty will stand out of the way, I will get it for you."

The queen jumped on the floor, and Colin, leaning from the bed, pulled out his little box, and got out the bottle.

"There it is, your majesty," he said, but not offering it to her.

"Give it me directly," said the queen, holding out her hand.

"First give me my little girl," returned Colin, boldly.

"Do you dare to bargain with me?" said the queen, angrily.

"Your majesty deigned to bargain with me first," said Colin.

"But since then you tried to break all our necks. You made a wicked cataract out there on the other side of the garden. Our boats were all dashed to pieces, and we had to wait till our horses were fetched. If I had been killed, you couldn't have held me to my bargain, and I won't hold to it now."

"If you chose to go down my cataract—" began Colin.

"*Your* cataract!" cried the queen. "All the waters that run from Loch Lonely are mine, I can tell you—all the way to the sea."

"Except where they run through farmyards, your majesty."

"I'll rout you out of the country," said the queen.

"Meantime I'll put the bottle in the chest again," returned Colin.

The queen bit her lips with vexation.

"Come here, Changeling," she cried at length, in a flattering tone.

And the little girl came slowly up to her, and stood staring at Colin, with the tears in her eyes.

"Give me your hand, little girl," said he, holding out his.

She did so. It was cold as ice.

"Let go her hand," said the queen.

"I won't," said Colin. "She's mine."

"Give me the bottle then," said the queen.

"Don't," said the child.

But it was too late. The queen had it.

"Keep your girl," she cried, with an ugly laugh.

"Yes, keep me," cried the child.

The cry ended in a hiss.

Colin felt something slimy wriggling in his grasp, and looking down, saw that instead of a little girl he was holding a great writhing worm. He had almost flung it from him, but recovering himself, he grasped it tighter.

"If it's a snake, I'll choke it," he said. "If it's a girl, I'll keep her."

The same instant it changed to a little white rabbit, which looked him piteously in the face, and pulled to get its little forefoot out of his hand. But, though he tried not to hurt it, Colin would not let it go. Then the rabbit changed to a great black cat, with eyes that flashed green fire. She sputtered and spit and swelled her tail, but all to no purpose. Colin held fast. Then it was a wood pigeon, struggling and fluttering in terror to get its wing out of his hold. But Colin still held fast.

All this time the queen had been getting the cork out. The moment it yielded she gave a scream and dropped the bottle. The Carasoyn ran out, and a strange odour filled the cottage. The queen stood shivering and sobbing beside the bottle, and all her court came about her and shivered and sobbed too, and their faces grew ancient and wrinkled. Then the queen, bending and tottering like an old woman, led the way to the boats, and her courtiers followed her, limping and creeping and distorted. Colin stared in amazement. He saw them all go aboard, and he heard the sound of them like a far-off company of men and women crying bitterly. And away they floated down the stream, the rowers dipping no oar, but bending weeping over them, and letting the boats drift along the stream. They vanished from his sight, and the rush of the cataract came up on the night-wind louder than he had ever heard it before.—But alas! when he came to himself, he found his hand relaxed, and the dove flown. Once more there was nothing left but to cry himself asleep, as he well might.

In the morning he rose very wretched. But the moment he entered the cowhouse, there, beside the cow, on the milking stool, sat a lovely little girl, with just one white garment on her, crying bitterly.

"I am so cold," she said, sobbing.

He caught her up, ran with her into the house, put her into the bed, and ran back to the cow for a bowl of warm milk. This she drank eagerly, laid her head down, and fell fast asleep. Then Colin saw that though she must be eight years old by her own account, her face was scarcely older than that of a baby of as many months.

When his father came home you may be sure he stared to see the child in the bed. Colin told him what had happened. But his father said he had met a troop of gipsies on the hill that morning.

"And you were always a dreamer, Colin, even before you could speak."

"But don't you smell the Carasoyn still?" said Colin.

"I do smell something very pleasant, to be sure," returned his father; "but I think it is the wallflower on the tope of the garden-wall. What a blossom there is of it this year! I am sure there is nothing sweeter in all Fairyland, Colin."

Colin allowed that.

The little girl slept for three whole days. And for three days more she never said another word than "I am so cold!" But after that she began to revive a little, and to take notice of things about her. For three weeks she would taste nothing but milk from the cow, and would not move from the chimney-corner. By degrees, however, she began to help Colin a little with his house-work, and as she did so, her face gathered more and more expression; and she made such progress, that by the end of three months she could do everything as well as Colin himself, and certainly more neatly. Whereupon he gave up his duties to her, and went out with his father to learn the calling of a shepherd.

Thus things went on for three years. And Fairy, as they called her, grew lovelier every day, and looked up to Colin more and more every day.

At the end of the three years, his father sent him to an old friend of his, a schoolmaster. Before he left, he made Fairy promise never to go near the brook after sundown. He had turned it into its old channel the very day she came to them. And he begged his father especially to look after her when the moon was high, for then she grew very restless and strange, and her eyes looked as if she saw things other people could not see.

When the end of the other three years had come, the schoolmaster would not let Colin go home, but insisted on sending him to college. And there he remained for three years more.

When he returned at the end of that time, he found Fairy so beautiful and so wise, that he fell dreadfully in love with her. And Fairy found out that she had been in love with him since ever so long—she did not know how long. And Colin's father agreed that they should be married as soon as Colin should have a house to take her to. So Colin went away to London, and worked very hard, till at last he managed to get a little cottage in Devonshire to live in. Then he went back to Scotland and married Fairy. And he was very glad to get her away from the neighbourhood of a queen who was not to be depended upon.

VII

The Banished Fairies

Those fairies had for a long time been doing wicked things. They had played many ill-natured pranks upon the human mortals; had stolen children upon whom they had no claim; had refused to deliver them up when they were demanded of them; had even terrified infants in their cradles; and, final proof of moral declension in fairies, had attempted to get rid of the obligations of their word, by all kinds of trickery and false logic.

It was not till they had sunk thus low that their queen began to long for the Carasoyn. She, no more than if she had been a daughter of Adam, could be happy while going on in that way; and, therefore, having heard of its marvellous virtues, and thinking it would stop her growing misery, she tried hard to procure it. For a hundred years she had tried in vain. Not till Colin arose did she succeed. But the Carasoyn was only for really good people, and therefore when the iron bottle which contained it was uncorked, she, and all her attendants, were, by the vapours thereof, suddenly changed into old men and women fairies. They crowded away weeping and lamenting, and Colin had as yet seen them no more.

For when the wickedness of any fairy tribe reaches its climax, the punishment that falls upon them is, that they are compelled to leave that part of the country where they and their ancestors have lived for more years than they can count, and wander away, driven by an inward restlessness, ever longing after the country they have left, but never able to turn round and go back to it, always thinking they will do so to-morrow, but when to-morrow comes, saying *to-morrow* again, till at last they find, not their old home, but the place of their doom—that is,

a place where their restlessness leaves them, and they find they can
remain. This partial repose, however, springs from no satisfaction with
the place; it is only that their inward doom ceases to drive them
further. They sit down to weep, and to long after the country they have
left.

    This is not because the country to which they have been driven is
ugly and inclement—it may or may not be such: it is simply because it
is not *their* country. If it would be, and it must be, torture to the fairy
of a harebell to go and live in a hyacinth—a torture quite analogous to
which many human beings undergo from their birth to their death, and
some of them longer, for anything I can tell—think what it must be for
a tribe of fairies to have to go and live in a country quite different from
that in and for which they were born. To the whole tribe the country is
what the flower is to the individual; and when a fairy is born to whom
the whole country is what the individual flower is to the individual
fairy, then the fairy is king or queen of the fairies, and always makes a
new nursery rhyme for the young fairies, which is never forgotten.
When, therefore, a tribe is banished, it is long before they can settle
themselves into their new quarters. Their clothes do not fit them, as it
were. They are constantly wriggling themselves into harmony with their
new circumstances—which is only another word for clothes—and never
quite succeeding. It is their punishment—and something more. Consequently their temper is not always of the evenest; indeed, and in a
word, they are as like human mortals as may well be, considering the
differences between them.

    In the present case, you would say it was surely no great hardship
to be banished from the heathy hills, the bare rocks, the wee trotting
burnies of Scotland, to the rich valleys, the wooded shores, the great
rivers, the grand ocean of the south of Devon. You may say they could
not have been very wicked when this was all their punishment. If you
do, you must have studied the human mortals to no great purpose. You
do not believe that a man may be punished by being made very rich? I
do. Anyhow, these fairies were not of your opinion, *for they were in it*.
In the splendour of their Devon banishment, they sighed for their bare
Scotland. Under the leafy foliage of the Devonshire valleys, with the
purple and green ocean before them, that had seen ships of a thousand
builds, or on the shore rich with shells and many-coloured creatures,
they longed for the clear, cold, pensive, open sides of the far-stretching
heathy sweeps, to which a gray, wild, torn sea, with memories only of

Norsemen, whales, and mermaids, cried aloud. For the big rivers, on which reposed great old hulks scarred with battle, they longed after the rocks and stones and rowan and birch-trees of the solitary burns. The country they had left might be an ill-favoured thing, but it was their own.

Now that which happens to the aspect of a country when the fairies leave it, is that a kind of deadness falls over the landscape. The traveller feels the wind as before, but it does not seem to refresh him. The child sighs over his daisy chain, and cannot find a red-tipped one amongst all that he has gathered. The cowslips have not half the honey in them. The wasps outnumber the bees. The horses come from the plough more tired at night, hanging their heads to their very hoofs as they plod homewards. The youth and the maiden, though perfectly happy when they meet, find the road to and from the trysting-place unaccountably long and dreary. The hawthorn-blossom is neither so white nor so red as it used to be, and the dark rough bark looks through and makes it ragged. The day is neither so warm nor the night so friendly as before. In a word, that something which no one can describe or be content to go without is missing. Everything is common-place. Everything falls short of one's expectations.

But it does not follow that the country to which the fairies are banished is so much richer and more beautiful for their presence. If that country has its own fairies, it needs no more, and Devon in especial has been rich in fairies from the time of the Phoenicians, and ever so long before that. But supposing there were no aborigines left to quarrel with, it takes centuries before the new immigration can fit itself into its new home. Until this comes about, the queerest things are constantly happening. For however could a convolvulus grow right with the soul of a Canterbury-bell inside it, for instance? The banished fairies are forced to do the best they can, and take the flowers the nearest they can find.

VIII

Their Revenge

When Colin and his wife settled then in their farm-house, the same tribe of fairies was already in the neighbourhood, and was not long in discovering who had come after them. An assembly was immediately called. Something must be done; but what, was disputed. Most of them thought only of revenge—to be taken upon the children. But the queen hesitated. Perhaps her sufferings had done her good. She suggested that before coming to any conclusion they should wait and watch the household.

In consequence of this resolution they began to frequent the house constantly, and sometimes in great numbers. But for a long time they could do the children no mischief. Whatever they tried turned out to their amusement. They were three, two girls and a boy; the girls nine and eight, and the boy three years old.

When they succeeded in enticing them beyond the home-boundaries, they would at one time be seized with an unaccountable panic, and turn and scurry home without knowing why; at another, a great butterfly or dragon fly, or some other winged and lovely creature, would dart past them, and away towards the house, and they after it, scampering; or the voice of their mother would be heard calling from the door. But at last their opportunity arrived.

One day the children were having such a game! The sisters had blindfolded their little brother, and were carrying him now on their backs, now in their arms, all about the place; now up stairs, talking about the rugged mountain paths they were climbing; now down again, filling him with the fancy that they were descending into a narrow valley; then they would set the tap of a rain-water barrel running, and represent that they were travelling along the bank of a rivulet. Now they were threading the depths of a great forest: and when the low of a cow reached them from a nigh field, that was the roaring of a lion or a tiger. At length they reached a lake into which the rivulet ran, and then it was necessary to take off his shoes and socks, that he might skim over the water on his bare feet, which they dipped and dabbled now in this tub, now in that, standing for farm and household purposes by the water-butt. The sisters kept their own imaginations alive by carrying him through all the strange places inside and outside of the house. When they told him they were ascending a precipice, they were, in fact, climbing a rather difficult ladder up to the door of the hayloft; when they told him they were traversing a pathless desert, they were, in fact, in a waste, empty place, a wide floor, used sometimes as a granary, with the rafters of the roof coming down to it on both sides, a place abundantly potent in their feelings to the generation of the desert in his; when they were wandering through a trackless forest, they were, in fact, winding about amongst the trees of a large orchard, which, in the moonlight, was vast enough for the fancy of any child. Had they uncovered his eyes at any moment, he would only have been seized with a wonder and awe of another sort, more overwhelming because more real, and more strange because not even in part bodied forth from his own brain.

In the course of the story, and while they bore the bare-footed child through the orchard, telling him they saw the fairies gliding about everywhere through the trees, not thinking that he believed every word they told him, they set him down, and the child suddenly opened his eyes. His sisters were gone. The moon was staring at him out of the sky, through the mossy branches of the apple-trees, which he thought looked like old women all about him, they were so thin and bony.

When the sisters, who had only for a moment run behind some of the trees, that they might cause him additional amazement, returned, he was gone. There was terrible lamentation in the house; but his father and mother, who were experienced in such matters, knew that the fairies must be in it, and cherished a hope that their son would yet be restored to them, though all their endeavours to find him were unavailing.

IX

The Fairy Fiddler

The father thought over many plans, but never came upon the right one. He did not know that they were the same tribe which had before carried away his wife when she was an infant. If he had, they might have done something sooner.

At length, one night, towards the close of seven years, about twelve o'clock, Colin suddenly opened his eyes, for he had been fast asleep and dreaming, and saw a few grotesque figures which he thought he must have seen before, dancing on the floor between him and the nearly extinguished fire. One of them had a violin, but when Colin first saw him he was not playing. Another of them was singing, and thus keeping the dance in time. This was what he sang, evidently addressed to the fiddler, who stood in the centre of the dance:—

> "Peterkin, Peterkin, tall and thin,
> What have you done with his cheek and his chin?
> What have you done with his ear and his eye?
> Hearken, hearken, and hear him cry."

Here Peterkin put his fiddle to his neck, and drew from it a wail just like the cry of a child, at which the dancers danced more furiously. Then he went on playing the tune the other had just sung, in accompaniment to his own reply:—

> "Silversnout, Silversnout, short and stout,
> I have cut them off and plucked them out,
> And salted them down in the Kelpie's Pool,
> Because papa Colin is such a fool."

Then the fiddle cried like a child again, and they danced more wildly than ever.

Colin, filled with horror, although he did not more than half believe what they were saying, sat up in bed and stared at them with fierce eyes, waiting to hear what they would say next. Silversnout now resumed his part:—

> "Ho, ho! Ho! ho! and if he don't know,
> And fish them out of the pool, so—so,"—

here they all pretended to be hauling in a net as they danced.

> "Before the end of the seven long years,
> Sweet babe will be left without eyes or ears."

Then Peterkin replied:—

> "Sweet babe will be left without cheek or chin,
> Only a hole to put porridge in;
> Porridge and milk, and haggis, and cakes:
> Sweet babe will gobble till his stomach aches."

From this last verse, Colin knew that they must be Scotch fairies, and all at once recollected their figures as belonging to the multitude he had once seen frolicking in his father's cottage. It was now Silversnout's turn. He began:—

> "But never more shall Colin see
> Sweet babe again upon his knee,
> With or without his cheek or chin,
> Except——"

Here Silversnout caught sight of Colin's face staring at him from the bed, and with a shriek of laughter they all vanished, the tones of Peterkin's fiddle trailing after them through the darkness like the train of a shooting star.

X

The Old Woman and Her Hen

Now Colin had got the better of these fairies once, not by his own skill, but by the help that other powers had afforded him. What were those powers? First the old woman on the heath. Indeed, he might attribute it all to her. He would go back to Scotland and look for her and find her. But the old woman was never found except by the seeker losing himself. It could not be done otherwise. She would cease to be the old woman, and become her own hen, if ever the moment arrived when any one found her without losing himself. And Colin since that time had wandered so much all over the moor, wide as it was, that lay above his father's cottage, that he did not believe he was able to lose himself there any more. He had yet to learn that it did not so much matter where he lost himself, provided only he was lost.

Just at this time Colin's purse was nearly empty, and he set out to borrow the money of a friend who lived on the other side of Dartmoor. When he got there, he found that he had gone from home. Unable to rest, he set out again to return.

It was almost night when he started, and before he had got many miles into the moor, it was dark, for there was no moon, and it was so cloudy that he could not see the stars. He thought he knew the way quite well, but as the track even in daylight was in certain places very indistinct, it was no wonder that he strayed from it, and found that he had lost himself. The same moment that he became aware of this, he saw a light away to the left. He turned towards it and found it proceeded from a little hive-like hut, the door of which stood open. When he was within a yard or two of it, he heard a voice say—

"Come in, Colin; I'm waiting for you."

Colin obeyed at once, and found the old woman seated with her spindle and distaff, just as he had seen her when he was a boy on the moor above his father's cottage.

"How do you do, mother?" he said.

"I am always quite well. Never ask me that question."

"Well, then, I won't any more," returned Colin. "But I thought you lived in Scotland?"

"I don't live anywhere; but those that will do as I tell them, will always find me when they want me."

"Do you see yet, mother?"

"See! I always see so well that it is not worth while to burn eyelight. So I let them go out. They were expensive."

Where her eyes should have been, there was nothing but wrinkles.

"What do you want?" she resumed.

"I want my child. The fairies have got him."

"I know that."

"And they have taken out his eyes."

"I can make him see without them."

"And they've cut off his ears," said Colin.

"He can hear without them."

"And they've salted down his cheek and his chin."

"Now I don't believe that," said the old woman.

"I heard them say so myself," returned Colin.

"Those fairies are worse liars than any I know. But something must be done. Sit down and I'll tell you a story."

"There's only nine days of the seven years left," said Colin, in a tone of expostulation.

"I know that as well as you," answered the old woman. "Therefore, I say, there is no time to be lost. Sit down and listen to my story. Here, Jenny."

The hen came pacing solemnly out from under the bed.

"Off to the sheep-shearing, Jenny, and make haste, for I must spin faster than usual. There are but nine days left."

Jenny ran out at the door with her head on a level with her tail, as if the kite had been after her. In a few moments she returned with a bunch of wool, as they called it, though it was only cotton from the cotton-grass that grew all about the cottage, nearly as big as herself, in her bill, and then darted away for more. The old woman fastened it on her distaff, drew out a thread to her spindle, and then began to spin. And as she spun she told her story—fast, fast; and Jenny kept scampering out and in; and by the time Colin thought it must be midnight, the story was told, and seven of the nine days were over.

"Colin," said the old woman, "now that you know all about it, you must set off at once."

"I am ready," answered Colin, rising.

"Keep on the road Jenny will show you till you come to the

cobbler's. Tell him the old woman with the distaff requests him to give you a lump of his wax."

"And what am I to do with it?"

"The cobbler always knows what his wax is for."

And with this answer, the old woman turned her face towards the fire, for, although it was summer, it was cold at night on the moor. Colin, moved by sudden curiosity, instead of walking out of the hut after Jenny, as he ought to have done, crept round by the wall, and peeped in the old woman's face. There, instead of wrinkled blindness, he saw a pair of flashing orbs of light, which were rather reflected on the fire than had the fire reflected in them. But the same instant the hut and all that was in it vanished, he felt the cold fog of the moor blowing upon him, and fell heavily to the earth.

XI

The Goblin Cobbler

When he came to himself he lay on the moor still. He got up and gazed around. The moon was up, but there was no hut to be seen. He was sorry enough now that he had been so foolish. He called, "Jenny, Jenny," but in vain. What was he to do? To-morrow was the eighth of the nine days left, and if before twelve at night the following day he had not rescued his boy, nothing could be done, at least for seven years more. True, the year was not quite out till about seven the following evening, but the fairies, instead of giving days of grace, always take them. He could do nothing but begin to walk, simply because that gave him a shadow more of a chance of finding the cobbler's than if he sat still, but there was no possibility of choosing one direction rather than another.

He wandered the rest of that night and the next day. He could not go home before the hour when the cobbler could no longer help him. Such was his anxiety, that although he neither ate nor drank, he never thought of the cause of his gathering weakness.

As it grew dark, however, he became painfully aware of it, and was

just on the point of sitting down exhausted upon a great white stone
that looked inviting, when he saw a faint glimmering in front of him.
He was erect in a moment, and making towards the place. As he drew
near he became aware of a noise made up of many smaller noises, such
as might have proceeded from some kind of factory. Not till he was
close to the place could he see that it was a long low hut, with one
door, and no windows. The light shone from the door, which stood
wide upen. He approached, and peeped in. There sat a multitude of
cobblers, each on his stool, with his candle stuck in the hole in the seat,
cobbling away. They looked rather little men, though not at all of
fairy-size. The most remarkable thing about them was, that at any given
moment they were all doing precisely the same thing, as if they had
been a piece of machinery. When one drew the threads in stitching,
they all did the same. If Colin saw one wax his thread, and looked up,
he saw that they were all waxing their thread. If one took to hammering on his lapstone, they did not follow his example, but all together
with him they caught up their lapstones and fell to hammering away, as
if nothing but hammering could ever be demanded of them. And when
he came to look at them more closely, he saw that every one was blind
of an eye, and had a nose turned up like an awl. Every one of them,
however, looked different from the rest, notwithstanding a very close
resemblance in their features.

The moment they caught sight of him, they rose as one man,
pointed their awls at him, and advanced towards him like a closing bush
of aloes, glittering with spikes.

"Fine upper-leathers," said one and all, with a variety of accordant
grimaces.

"Top of his head—good paste-bowl," was the next general remark.

"Coarse hair—good ends," followed.

"Sinews—good thread."

"Bones and blood—good paste for seven-leaguers."

"Ears—good loops to pull 'em on with. Pair short now."

"Soles—same for queen's slippers."

And so on they went, portioning out his body in the most irrever-
ent fashion for the uses of their trade, till having come to his teeth, and
said—

"Teeth—good brads,"—they all gave a shriek like the whisk of the
waxed threads through the leather, and sprung upon him with their
awls drawn back like daggers. There was no time to lose.

"The old woman with the spindle— —" said Colin.

"Don't know her," shrieked the cobblers.

"The old woman with the distaff," said Colin, and they all scurried back to their seats and fell to hammering vigorously.

"She desired me," continued Colin, "to ask the cobbler for a lump of his wax."

Every one of them caught up his lump of wrought rosin, and held it out to Colin. He took the one offered by the nearest, and found that all their lumps were gone; after which they sat motionless and stared at him.

"But what am I to do with it?" asked Colin.

"I will walk a little way with you," said the one nearest, "and tell you all about it. The old woman is my grandmother, and a very worthy old soul she is."

Colin stepped out at the door of the workshop, and the cobbler followed him. Looking round, Colin saw all the stools vacant, and the place as still as an old churchyard. The cobbler, who now in his talk, gestures, and general demeanour appeared a very respectable, not to say conventional, little man, proceeded to give him all the information he required, accompanying it with the present of one of his favourite awls.

They walked a long way, till Colin was amazed to find that his strength stood out so well. But at length the cobbler said—

"I see, sir, that the sun is at hand. I must return to my vocation. When the sun is once up you will know where you are."

He turned aside a few yards from the path, and entered the open door of a cottage. In a moment the place resounded with the soft hammering of three hundred and thirteen cobblers, each with his candle stuck in a hole in the stool on which he sat. While Colin stood gazing in wonderment, the rim of the sun crept up above the horizon; and there the cottage stood white and sleeping, while the cobblers, their lights, their stools, and their tools had all vanished. Only there was still the sound of the hammers ringing in his head, where it seemed to shape itself into words something like these: a good deal had to give way to the rhyme, for they were more particular about their rhymes than their etymology:

> "Dub-a-dub, dub-a-dub,
> Cobbler's man

Hammer it, stitch it,
As fast as you can.
The week-day ogre
Is wanting his boots;
The trip-a-trap fairy
Is going bare-foots.
Dream-daughter has worn out
Her heels and her toeses,
For want of cork slippers
To walk over noses.
Spark-eye, the smith,
May shoe the nightmare,
The kelpie and pookie,
The nine-footed bear:
We shoe the mermaids—
The tips of their tails—
Stitching the leather
On to their scales.
We shoe the brownie,
Clumsy and toeless,
And then he goes quiet
As a mole or a moless.
There is but one creature
That we cannot shoe,
And that is the Boneless,
All made of glue."

A great deal of nonsense of this sort went through Colin's head before the sounds died away. Then he found himself standing in the field outside his own orchard.

XII

The Wax and the Awl

The evening arrived. The sun was going down over the sea, cloudless, casting gold from him lavishly, when Colin arrived on the shore at some distance from his home. The tide was falling, and a good space of sand was uncovered, and lay glittering in the setting sun. This sand lay between some rocks and the sea; and from the rocks innumerable runnels of water that had been left behind in their hollows were hurrying back to their mother. These occasionally spread into little shallow lakes, resting in hollows in the sand. These lakes were in a constant ripple from the flow of the little streams through them; and the sun shining on these multitudinous ripples, the sand at the bottom shone like brown silk watered with gold, only that the golden lines were flitting about like living things, never for a moment in one place.

Now Colin had no need of fairy ointment to anoint his eyes and make him able to see fairies. Most people need this; but Colin was naturally gifted. Therefore, as he drew near a certain high rock, which he knew very well, and from which many streams were flowing back into the sea, he saw that the little lakes about it were crowded with fairies, playing all kinds of pranks in the water. It was a lovely sight to see them thus frolicking in the light of the setting sun, in their gay dresses, sparkling with jewels, or what looked like jewels, flashing all colours as they moved. But Colin had not much time to see them; for the moment they saw him, knowing that this was the man whom they had wronged by stealing his child, and knowing too that he saw them, they fled at once up the high rock and vanished. This was just what Colin wanted. He went all round and round the rock, looked in every direction in which there might be a pool, found more fairies, here and there, who fled like the first up the rock and disappeared. When he had thus driven them all from the sands, he approached the rock, taking the lump of cobbler's wax from his pocket as he went. He scrambled up the rock, and, without showing his face, put his hand on the uppermost edge of it, and began drawing a line with the wax all along. He went creeping round the rock, still drawing the wax along the edge, till he had completed the circuit. Then he peeped over.

Now in the heart of this rock, which was nearly covered at high-water, there was a big basin, known as the Kelpie's Pool, filled with sea-water and the loveliest sea-weed and many little sea-animals; and this was a favourite resort of the fairies. It was now, of course, crowded. When they saw his big head come peeping over, they burst into a loud fit of laughter, and began mocking him and making game of him in a hundred ways. Some made the ugliest faces they could, some queer gestures of contempt; others sung bits of songs, and so on; while the queen sat by herself on a projecting corner of the rock, with her feet in the water, and looked at him sulkily. Many of them kept on plunging and swimming and diving and floating, while they mocked him; and Colin would have enjoyed the sight much if they had not spoiled their beauty and their motions by their grimaces and their gestures.

"I want my child," said Colin.

"Give him his child," cried one.

Thereupon a dozen of them dived, and brought up a huge sea-slug—a horrid creature, like a lump of blubber—and held it up to him, saying—

"There he is; come down and fetch him."

Others offered him a blue lobster, struggling in their grasp; others, a spider-crab; others, a whelk; while some of them sung mocking verses, each capping the line the other gave. At length they lifted a dreadful object from the bottom. It was like a baby with his face half eaten away by the fishes, only that he had a huge nose, like the big toe of a lobster. But Colin was not to be taken in.

"Very well, good people," he said, "I will try something else."

He crept down the rock again, took out the little cobbler's awl, and began boring a hole. It went through the rock as if it had been butter, and as he drew it out the water followed in a far-reaching spout. He bored another, and went on boring till there were three hundred and thirteen spouts gushing from the rock, and running away in a strong little stream towards the sea. He then sat down on a ledge at the foot of the rock and waited.

By-and-by he heard a clamour of little voices from the basin. They had found that the water was getting very low. But when they discovered the holes by which it was escaping, "He's got Dottlecob's awl! He's got Dottlecob's awl!" they cried with one voice of horror.

When he heard this, Colin climbed the rock again to enjoy their confusion. But here I must explain a little.

In the former part of this history I showed how fond these fairies were of water. But the fact was, they were far too fond of it. It had grown a thorough dissipation with them. Their business had been chiefly to tend and help the flowers in which they lived, and to do good offices for every thing that had any kind of life about them. Hence their name of Good People. But from finding the good the water did to the flowers, and from sharing in the refreshment it brought them, flowing up to them in tiny runnels through the veins of the plants, they had fallen in love with the water itself, for its own sake, or rather for the pleasure it gave to them, irrespective of the good it was to the flowers which lived upon it. So they neglected their business, and took to sailing on the streams, and plunging into every pool they could find. Hence the rapidity of their decline and fall.

Again, on coming to the sea-coast, they had found that the salt water did much to restore the beauty they had lost by partaking of the Carasoyn. Therefore they were constantly on the shore, bathing for ever in the water, especially that left in this pool by the ebbing tide, which was particularly to their taste; till at last they had grown entirely dependent for comfort on the sea-water, and, they thought, entirely dependent on it for existence also, at least such existence as was in the least worth possessing.

Therefore when they saw the big face of Colin peering once more over the ledge, they rushed at him in a rage, scrambling up the side of the rock like so many mad beetles. Colin drew back and let them come on. The moment the foremost put his foot on the line that Colin had drawn around the rock, he slipped and tumbled backwards head over heels into the pool, shrieking—

"He's got Dottlecob's wax!"

"He's got Dottlecob's wax!" screamed the next, as he fell backwards after his companion, and this took place till no one would approach the line. In fact no fairy could keep his footing on the wax, and the line was so broad—for as Colin rubbed it, it had melted and spread—that not one of them could spring over it. The queen now rose.

"What do you want, Colin?" she said.

"I want my child, as you know very well," answered Colin.

"Come and take him," returned the queen, and sat down again, not now with her feet in the water, for it was much too low for that.

But Colin knew better. He sat down on the edge of the basin. Unfortunately, the tail of his coat crossed the line. In a moment half-a-dozen of the fairies were out of the circle. Colin rose instantly, and there was not much harm done, for the multitude was still in prison. The water was nearly gone, beginning to leave the very roots of the long tangles uncovered. At length the queen could bear it no longer.

"Look here, Colin," she said; "I wish you well."

And as she spoke she rose and descended the side of the rock towards the water now far below her. She had to be very cautious too, the stones were so slippery, though there was none of Dottlecob's wax there. About half-way below where the surface of the pool had been, she stopped, and pushed a stone aside. Colin saw what seemed the entrance to a cave inside the rock. The queen went in. A few moments after she came out wringing her hands.

"Oh dear! oh dear! What shall I do?" she cried. "You horrid thick people will grow so. He's grown to such a size that I *can't* get him out."

"Will you let him go if I get him out?" asked Colin.

"I will, I will. We shall all be starved to death for want of sea-water if I don't," she answered.

"Swear by the cobbler's awl and the cobbler's wax," said Colin.

"I swear," said the queen.

"By the cobbler's awl and the cobbler's wax," insisted Colin.

"I swear by the cobbler's awl and the cobbler's wax," returned the queen.

"In the name of your people?"

"In the name of my people," said the queen, "that none of us here present will ever annoy you or your family hereafter."

"Then I'll come down," said Colin, and jumped into the basin. With the cobbler's awl he soon cleared a big opening into the rock, for it bored and cut it like butter. Then out crept a beautiful boy of about ten years old, into his father's arms, with eyes, and ears, and chin, and cheek all safe and sound. And he carried him home to his mother.

It was a disappointment to find him so much of a baby at his age; but that fault soon began to mend. And the house was full of jubilation. And little Colin told them the whole story of his sojourn among the fairies. And it did not take so long as you would think, for he fancied he had been there only about a week.

IV
The Gray Wolf

One evening-twilight in spring, a young English student, who had wandered northwards as far as the outlying fragments of Scotland called the Orkney and Shetland islands, found himself on a small island of the latter group, caught in a storm of wind and hail, which had come on suddenly. It was in vain to look about for any shelter; for not only did the storm entirely obscure the landscape, but there was nothing around him save a desert moss.

At length, however, as he walked on for mere walking's sake, he found himself on the verge of a cliff, and saw, over the brow of it, a few feet below him, a ledge of rock, where he might find some shelter from the blast, which blew from behind. Letting himself down by his hands, he alighted upon something that crunched beneath his tread, and found the bones of many small animals scattered about in front of a little cave in the rock, offering the refuge he sought. He went in, and sat upon a stone. The storm increased in violence, and as the darkness grew he became uneasy, for he did not relish the thought of spending the night in the cave. He had parted from his companions on the opposite side of the island, and it added to his uneasiness that they must be full of apprehension about him. At last there came a lull in the storm, and the same instant he heard a footfall, stealthy and light as that of a wild beast, upon the bones at the mouth of the cave. He started up in some fear, though the least thought might have satisfied him that there could be no very dangerous animals upon the island. Before he had time to think, however, the face of a woman appeared in the opening. Eagerly the wanderer spoke. She started at the sound of his voice. He could not see her well, because she was turned towards the darkness of the cave.

"Will you tell me how to find my way across the moor to Shielness?" he asked.

"You cannot find it to-night," she answered, in a sweet tone, and with a smile that bewitched him, revealing the whitest of teeth.

"What am I to do then?" he asked.

"My mother will give you shelter, but that is all she has to offer."

Reprinted from *Works of Fancy and Imagination* (1871).

"And that is far more than I expected a minute ago," he replied. "I shall be most grateful."

She turned in silence and left the cave. The youth followed.

She was barefooted, and her pretty brown feet went catlike over the sharp stones, as she led the way down a rocky path to the shore. Her garments were scanty and torn, and her hair blew tangled in the wind. She seemed about five and twenty, lithe and small. Her long fingers kept clutching and pulling nervously at her skirts as she went. Her face was very gray in complexion, and very worn, but delicately formed, and smooth-skinned. Her thin nostrils were tremulous as eyelids, and her lips, whose curves were faultless, had no colour to give sign of indwelling blood. What her eyes were like he could not see, for she had never lifted the delicate films of her eyelids.

At the foot of the cliff they came upon a little hut leaning against it, and having for its inner apartment a natural hollow within it. Smoke was spreading over the face of the rock, and the grateful odour of food gave hope to the hungry student. His guide opened the door of the cottage; he followed her in, and saw a woman bending over a fire in the middle of the floor. On the fire lay a large fish broiling. The daughter spoke a few words, and the mother turned and welcomed the stranger. She had an old and very wrinkled, but honest face, and looked troubled. She dusted the only chair in the cottage, and placed it for him by the side of the fire, opposite the one window, whence he saw a little patch of yellow sand over which the spent waves spread themselves out listlessly. Under this window there was a bench, upon which the daughter threw herself in an unusual posture, resting her chin upon her hand. A moment after, the youth caught the first glimpse of her blue eyes. They were fixed upon him with a strange look of greed, amounting to craving, but as if aware that they belied or betrayed her, she dropped them instantly. The moment she veiled them, her face, notwithstanding its colourless complexion, was almost beautiful.

When the fish was ready, the old woman wiped the deal table, steadied it upon the uneven floor, and covered it with a piece of fine table-linen. She then laid the fish on a wooden platter, and invited the guest to help himself. Seeing no other provision, he pulled from his pocket a hunting knife, and divided a portion from the fish, offering it to the mother first.

"Come, my lamb," said the old woman; and the daughter

approached the table. But her nostrils and mouth quivered with disgust.

The next moment she turned and hurried from the hut.

"She doesn't like fish," said the old woman, "and I haven't anything else to give her."

"She does not seem in good health," he rejoined.

The woman answered only with a sigh, and they ate their fish with the help of a little rye-bread. As they finished their supper, the youth heard the sound as of the pattering of a dog's feet upon the sand close to the door; but ere he had time to look out of the window, the door opened and the young woman entered. She looked better, perhaps from having just washed her face. She drew a stool to the corner of the fire opposite him. But as she sat down, to his bewilderment, and even horror, the student spied a single drop of blood on her white skin within her torn dress. The woman brought out a jar of whisky, put a rusty old kettle on the fire, and took her place in front of it. As soon as the water boiled, she proceeded to make some toddy in a wooden bowl.

Meantime the youth could not take his eyes off the young woman, so that at length he found himself fascinated, or rather bewitched. She kept her eyes for the most part veiled with the loveliest eyelids fringed with darkest lashes, and he gazed entranced; for the red glow of the little oil-lamp covered all the strangeness of her complexion. But as soon as he met a stolen glance out of those eyes unveiled, his soul shuddered within him. Lovely face and craving eyes alternated fascination and repulsion.

The mother placed the bowl in his hands. He drank sparingly, and passed it to the girl. She lifted it to her lips, and as she tasted—only tasted it—looked at him. He thought the drink must have been drugged and have affected his brain. Her hair smoothed itself back, and drew her forehead backwards with it; while the lower part of her face projected towards the bowl, revealing, ere she sipped, her dazzling teeth in strange prominence. But the same moment the vision vanished; she returned the vessel to her mother, and rising, hurried out of the cottage.

Then the old woman pointed to a bed of heather in one corner with a murmured apology; and the student, wearied both with the fatigues of the day and the strangeness of the night, threw himself upon it, wrapped in his cloak. The moment he lay down, the storm began afresh, and the wind blew so keenly through the crannies of the hut, that it was only by drawing his cloak over his head that he could protect himself from its currents. Unable to sleep, he lay listening to the uproar, which grew in violence, till the spray was dashing against the window. At length the door opened, and the young woman came in, made up the fire, drew the bench before it, and lay down in the same strange posture, with her chin propped on her hand and elbow, and her face turned towards the youth. He moved a little; she dropped her head, and lay on her face, with her arms crossed beneath her forehead. The mother had disappeared.

Drowsiness crept over him. A movement of the bench roused him, and he fancied he saw some four-footed creature as tall as a large dog trot quietly out of the door. He was sure he felt a rush of cold wind. Gazing fixedly through the darkness, he thought he saw the eyes of the damsel encountering his, but a glow from the falling together of the remnants of the fire, revealed clearly enough that the bench was vacant. Wondering what could have made her go out in such a storm, he fell fast asleep.

In the middle of the night he felt a pain in his shoulder, came broad awake, and saw the gleaming eyes and grinning teeth of some animal close to his face. Its claws were in his shoulder, and its mouth in the act of seeking his throat. Before it had fixed its fangs, however, he had its throat in one hand, and sought his knife with the other. A terrible struggle followed; but regardless of the tearing claws, he found and opened his knife. He had made one futile stab, and was drawing it for a surer, when, with a spring of the whole body, and one wildly-contorted effort, the creature twisted its neck from his hold, and with something betwixt a scream and a howl, darted from him. Again he heard the door open; again the wind blew in upon him, and it continued blowing; a sheet of spray dashed across the floor, and over his face. He sprung from his couch and bounded to the door.

It was a wild night—dark, but for the flash of whiteness from the waves as they broke within a few yards of the cottage; the wind was raving, and the rain pouring down the air. A gruesome sound as of mingled weeping and howling came from somewhere in the dark. He turned again into the hut and closed the door, but could find no way of securing it.

The lamp was nearly out, and he could not be certain whether the form of the young woman was upon the bench or not. Overcoming a strong repugnance, he approached it, and put out his hands—there was nothing there. He sat down and waited for the daylight: he dared not sleep any more.

When the day dawned at length, he went out yet again, and looked around. The morning was dim and gusty and gray. The wind had fallen, but the waves were tossing wildly. He wandered up and down the little strand, longing for more light.

At length he heard a movement in the cottage. By and by the voice of the old woman called to him from the door.

"You're up early, sir. I doubt you didn't sleep well."

"Not very well," he answered. "But where is your daughter?"

"She's not awake yet," said the mother. "I'm afraid I have but a poor breakfast for you. But you'll take a dram and a bit of fish. It's all I've got."

Unwilling to hurt her, though hardly in good appetite, he sat down at the table. While they were eating, the daughter came in, but turned her face away and went to the further end of the hut. When she came forward after a minute or two, the youth saw that her hair was drenched, and her face whiter than before. She looked ill and faint, and when she raised her eyes, all their fierceness had vanished, and sadness had taken its place. Her neck was now covered with a cotton handkerchief. She was modestly attentive to him, and no longer shunned his gaze. He was gradually yielding to the temptation of braving another night in the hut, and seeing what would follow, when the old woman spoke.

"The weather will be broken all day, sir," she said. "You had better be going, or your friends will leave without you."

Ere he could answer, he saw such a beseeching glance on the face of the girl, that he hesitated, confused. Glancing at the mother, he saw the flash of wrath in her face. She rose and approached her daughter, with her hand lifted to strike her. The young woman stooped her head with a cry. He darted round the table to interpose between them. But the mother had caught hold of her; the handkerchief had fallen from her neck; and the youth saw five blue bruises on her lovely throat—the marks of the four fingers and the thumb of a left hand. With a cry of horror he darted from the house, but as he reached the door he turned. His hostess was lying motionless on the floor, and a huge gray wolf came bounding after him.

There was no weapon at hand; and if there had been, his inborn chivalry would never have allowed him to harm a woman even under the guise of a wolf. Instinctively, he set himself firm, leaning a little forward, with half outstretched arms, and hands curved ready to clutch again at the throat upon which he had left those pitiful marks. But the creature as she sprung eluded his grasp, and just as he expected to feel her fangs, he found a woman weeping on his bosom, with her arms around his neck. The next instant, the gray wolf broke from him, and bounded howling up the cliff. Recovering himself as he best might, the youth followed, for it was the only way to the moor above, across which he must now make his way to find his companions.

All at once he heard the sound of a crunching of bones—not as if a creature was eating them, but as if they were ground by the teeth of rage and disappointment; looking up, he saw close above him the mouth of the little cavern in which he had taken refuge the day before. Summoning all his resolution, he passed it slowly and softly. From within came the sounds of a mingled moaning and growling.

Having reached the top, he ran at full speed for some distance across the moor before venturing to look behind him. When at length he did so, he saw, against the sky, the girl standing on the edge of the cliff, wringing her hands. One solitary wail crossed the space between. She made no attempt to follow him, and he reached the opposite shore in safety.

V
The Cruel Painter

Among the young men assembled at the University of Prague, in the year 159-, was one called Karl von Wolkenlicht. A somewhat careless student, he yet held a fair position in the estimation of both professors and men, because he could hardly look at a proposition without understanding it. Where such proposition, however, had to do with anything relating to the deeper insights of the nature, he was quite content that, for him, it should remain a proposition; which, however, he laid up in one of his mental cabinets, and was ready to reproduce at a moment's notice. This mental agility was more than matched by the corresponding corporeal excellence, and both aided in producing results in which his remarkable strength was equally apparent. In all games depending upon the combination of muscle and skill, he had scarce rivalry enough to keep him in practice. His strength, however, was embodied in such a softness of muscular outline, such a rare Greek-like style of beauty, and associated with such gentleness of manner and behaviour, that, partly from the truth of the resemblance, partly from the absurdity of the contrast, he was known throughout the university by the diminutive of the feminine form of his name, and was always called Lottchen.

"I say, Lottchen," said one of his fellow-students, called Richter, across the table in a wine-cellar they were in the habit of frequenting, "do you know, Heinrich Höllenrachen here says that he saw this morning, with mortal eyes, whom do you think?—Lilith."

"Adam's first wife?" asked Lottchen, with an attempt at carelessness, while his face flushed like a maiden's.

"None of your chaff!" said Richter. "Your face is honester than you tongue, and confesses what you cannot deny, that you would give your chance of salvation—a small one to be sure, but all you've got—for one peep at Lilith. Wouldn't you now, Lottchen?"

"Go to the devil!" was all Lottchen's answer to his tormentor; but he turned to Heinrich, to whom the students had given the surname above mentioned, because of the enormous width of his jaws, and said

Reprinted from *Adela Cathcart* (1864).

with eagerness and envy, disguising them as well as he could, under the appearance of curiosity:

"You don't mean it, Heinrich? You've been taking the beggar in! Confess now."

"Not I. I saw her with my two eyes."

"Notwithstanding the different planes of their orbits," suggested Richter.

"Yes, notwithstanding the fact that I can get a parallax to any of the fixed stars in a moment, with only the breadth of my nose for the base," answered Heinrich, responding at once to the fun, and careless of the personal defect insinuated. "She was near enough for even me to see her perfectly."

"When? Where? How?" asked Lottchen.

"Two hours ago. In the churchyard of St. Stephen's. By a lucky chance. Any more little questions, my child?" answered Höllenrachen.

"What could have taken her there, who is seen nowhere?" said Richter.

"She was seated on a grave. After she left, I went to the place; but it was a new-made grave. There was no stone up. I asked the sexton about her. He said he supposed she was the daughter of the woman buried there last Thursday week. I knew it was Lilith."

"Her mother dead?" said Lottchen, musingly. Then he thought with himself—"She will be going there again, then!" But he took care that this ghost-thought should wander unembodied. "But how did you know her, Heinrich? You never saw her before."

"How do you come to be over head and ears in love with her, Lottchen, and you haven't seen her at all?" interposed Richter.

"Will you or will you not go to the devil?" rejoined Lottchen, with a comic *crescendo;* to which the other replied with a laugh.

"No one could miss knowing her," said Heinrich.

"Is she so very like, then?"

"It is always herself, her very self."

A fresh flask of wine, turning out to be not up to the mark, brought the current of conversation against itself; not much to the dissatisfaction of Lottchen, who had already resolved to be in the churchyard of St. Stephen's at sun-down the following day, in the hope that he too might be favoured with a vision of Lilith.

This resolution he carried out. Seated in a porch of the church, not knowing in what direction to look for the apparition he hoped to see, and desirous as well of not seeming to be on the watch for one, he was gazing at the fallen rose-leaves of the sunset, withering away upon the sky; when, glancing aside by an involuntary movement, he saw a woman seated upon a new-made grave, not many yards from where he sat, with her face buried in her hands, and apparently weeping bitterly. Karl was in the shadow of the porch, and could see her perfectly, without much danger of being discovered by her; so he sat and watched her. She raised her head for a moment, and the rose-flush of the west fell over it, shining on the tears with which it was wet, and giving the whole a bloom which did not belong to it, for it was always pale, and now pale as death. It was indeed the face of Lilith, the most celebrated beauty of Prague.

Again she buried her face in her hands; and Karl sat with a strange feeling of helplessness, which grew as he sat; and the longing to help her whom he could not help, drew his heart towards her with a trembling reverence which was quite new to him. She wept on. The western roses withered slowly away, and the clouds blended with the sky, and the stars gathered like drops of glory sinking through the vault of night, and the trees about the church yard grew black, and Lilith almost vanished in the wide darkness. At length she lifted her head, and seeing the night around her, gave a little broken cry of dismay. The minutes had swept over her head, not through her mind, and she did not know that the dark had come.

Hearing her cry, Karl rose and approached her. She heard his footsteps, and started to her feet. Karl spoke—

"Do not be frightened," he said. "Let me see you home. I will walk behind you."

"Who are you?" she rejoined.

"Karl Wolkenlicht."

"I have heard of you. Thank you. I can go home alone."

Yet, as if in a half-dreamy, half-unconscious mood, she accepted his offered hand to lead her through the graves, and allowed him to walk beside her, till, reaching the corner of a narrow street, she suddenly bade him good-night and vanished. He thought it better not to follow her, so he returned her good-night and went home.

How to see her again was his first thought the next day; as, in fact, how to see her at all had been his first thought for many days. She went nowhere that ever he heard of; she knew nobody that he knew; she was never seen at church, or at market; never seen in the street. Her home had a dreary, desolate aspect. It looked as if no one ever went out or in. It was like a place on which decay had fallen because there was no indwelling spirit. The mud of years was baked upon its door, and no faces looked out of its dusty windows.

How then could she be the most celebrated beauty of Prague? How, then, was it that Heinrich Höllenrachen knew her the moment he saw her? Above all, how was it that Karl Wolkenlicht had, in fact, fallen in love with her before ever he saw her? It was thus:

Her father was a painter. Belonging thus to the public, it had taken the liberty of re-naming him. Every one called him Teufelsbürst, or Devilsbrush. It was a name with which, to judge from the nature of his representations, he could hardly fail to be pleased. For, not as a nightmare-dream, which may alternate with the loveliest visions, but as his ordinary every-day work, he delighted to represent human suffering.

Not an aspect of human woe or torture, as expressed in countenance or limb, came before his willing imagination, but he bore it straightway to his easel. In the moments that precede sleep, when the black space before the eyes of the poet teems with lovely faces, or dawns into a spirit-landscape, face after face of suffering, in all varieties of expression, would crowd, as if compelled by the accompanying fiends, to present themselves, in awful levée, before the inner eye of the expectant master. Then he would rise, light his lamp, and, with rapid hand, make notes of his visions; recording with swift successive sweeps of his pencil, every individual face which had rejoiced his evil fancy. Then he would return to his couch, and, well satisfied, fall asleep, to dream yet further embodiments of human ill.

What wrong could man or mankind have done him, to be thus fearfully pursued by the vengeance of the artist's hate?

Another characteristic of the faces and forms which he drew was, that they were all beautiful in the original idea. The lines of each face, however distorted by pain, would have been, in rest, absolutely beautiful; and the whole of the execution bore witness to the fact that upon this original beauty the painter had directed the artillery of anguish, to bring down the sky-soaring heights of its divinity to the level of a hated existence. To do this, he worked in perfect accordance with artistic law, falsifying no line of the original forms. It was the suffering, rather than his pencil, that wrought the change. The latter was the willing instrument to record what the imagination conceived with a cruelty composed enough to be correct.

To enhance the beauty he had thus distorted, and so to enhance yet further the suffering that produced the distortion, he would often represent attendant demons, whom he made as ugly as his imagination could compass; avoiding, however, all grotesqueness beyond what was sufficient to indicate that they were demons, and not men. Their ugliness rose from hate, envy, and all evil passions; amongst which he especially delighted to represent a gloating exultation over human distress. And often in the midst of his clouds of demon faces, would some one who knew him recognise the painter's own likeness, such as the mirror might have presented it to him when he was busiest over the incarnation of some exquisite torture.

But, apparently with the wish to avoid being supposed to choose such representations for their own sakes, he always found a story, often in the histories of the church, whose name he gave to the painting, and which he pretended to have inspired the pictorial conception. No one, however, who looked upon his suffering martyrs, could suppose for a moment that he honoured their martyrdom. They were but the vehicles for his hate of humanity. He was the torturer, and not Diocletian or Nero.

But, stranger yet to tell, there was no picture, whatever its subject, into which he did not introduce one form of placid and harmonious loveliness. In this, however, his fierceness was only more fully displayed. For in no case did this form manifest any relation either to the actors or the endurers in the picture. Hence its very loveliness became almost hateful to those who beheld it. Not a shade crossed the still sky of that brow, not a ripple disturbed the still sea of that cheek. She did not hate, she did not love the sufferers: the painter would not have her hate, for that would be to the injury of her loveliness; would not have her love, for he hated. Sometimes she floated above, as a still, unobservant angel, her gaze turned upward, dreaming along, careless as a white summer cloud, across the blue. If she looked down on the scene below, it was only that the beholder might see that she saw and did not care— that not a feather of her outspread pinions would quiver at the sight. Sometimes she would stand in the crowd, as if she had been copied there from another picture, and had nothing to do with this one, nor any right to be in it at all. Or when the red blood was trickling drop by drop from the crushed limb, she might be seen standing nearest, smiling over a primrose or the bloom on a peach. Some had said that she was the painter's wife; that she had been false to him; that he had killed her;

and, finding that that was no sufficing revenge, thus half in love, and half in deepest hate, immortalized his vengeance. But it was now universally understood that it was his daughter, of whose loveliness extravagant reports went abroad; though all said, doubtless reading this from her father's pictures, that she was a beauty without a heart. Strange theories of something else supplying its place were rife among the anatomical students. With the girl in the pictures, the wild imagination of Lottchen, probably in part from her apparently absolute unattainableness and her undisputed heartlessness, had fallen in love, as far as the mere imagination can fall in love.

But again, how was he to see her? He haunted the house night after night. Those blue eyes never met his. No step responsive to his came from that door. It seemed to have been so long unopened that it had grown as fixed and hard as the stones that held its bolts in their passive clasp. He dared not watch in the day-time, and with all his watching at night, he never saw father or daughter or domestic cross the threshold. Little he thought that, from a shot-window near the door, a pair of blue eyes, like Lilith's, but paler and colder, were watching him, just as a spider watches the fly that is likely ere long to fall into his toils. And into those toils Karl soon fell. For her form darkened the page; her form stood on the threshold of sleep; and when, overcome with watching, he did enter its precincts, her form entered with him, and walked by his side. He must find her; or the world might go to the bottomless pit for him. But how?

Yes. He would be a painter. Teufelsbürst would receive him as a humble apprentice. He would grind his colours, and Teufelsbürst would teach him the mysteries of the science which is the handmaiden of art. Then he might see *her,* and that was all his ambition.

In the clear morning light of a day in autumn, when the leaves were beginning to fall seared from the hand of that Death which has his dance in the chapels of nature as well as in the cathedral aisles of men—he walked up and knocked at the dingy door. The spider painter opened it himself. He was a little man, meagre and pallid, with those faded blue eyes, a low nose in three distinct divisions, and thin, curveless, cruel lips. He wore no hair on his face; but long grey locks, long as a woman's, were scattered over his shoulders, and hung down on his breast. When Wolkenlicht had explained his errand, he smiled a smile in which hypocrisy could not hide the cunning, and, after many difficulties, consented to receive him as a pupil, on condition that he would become an inmate of his house. Wolkenlicht's heart bounded with delight, which he tried to hide: the second smile of Teufelsbürst might have shown him that he had ill succeeded. The fact that he was not a native of Prague, but, coming from a distant part of the country, was entirely his own master in the city, rendered this condition perfectly easy to fulfil; and that very afternoon, he entered the studio of Teufelsbürst as his scholar and servant.

It was a great room, filled with the appliances and results of art. Many pictures, festooned with cobwebs, were hung carelessly on the dirty walls. Others, half finished, leaned against them, on the floor. Several, in different stages of progress, stood upon easels. But all spoke the cruel bent of the artist's genius. In one corner a lay-figure was extended on a couch, covered with a pall of black velvet. Through its folds, the form beneath was easily discernible; and one hand and fore-arm protruded from beneath it, at right angles to the rest of the frame. Lottchen could not help shuddering when he saw it. Although he overcame the feeling in a moment, he felt a great repugnance to seating himself with his back towards it, as the arrangement of an easel, at which Teufelsbürst wished him to draw, rendered necessary. He contrived to edge himself round, so that when he lifted his eyes he should see the figure, and be sure that it could not rise without his being aware of it. But his master saw and understood his altered position; and under some pretence about the light, compelled him to resume the position in which he had placed him at first; after which he sat watching, over the top of his picture, the expression of his countenance as he tried to draw; reading in it the horrid fancy that the figure under the pall had risen, and was stealthily approaching to look over his shoulder. But Lottchen resisted the feeling, and, being already no contemptible draughtsman, was soon interested enough to forget it. And then, any moment, *she* might enter.

Now began a system of slow torture, for the chance of which the painter had been long on the watch—especially since he had first seen Karl lingering about the house. His opportunities of seeing physical suffering were nearly enough even for the diseased necessities of his art; but now he had one in his power, on whom, his own will fettering him, he could try any experiments he pleased for the production of a kind of suffering, in the observation of which he did not consider that he had yet had sufficient experience. He would hold the very heart of the youth in his hand, and wring it and torture it to his own content. And lest Karl should be strong enough to prevent those expressions of pain for which he lay on the watch, he would make use of further means, known to himself, and known to few besides.

All that day Karl say nothing of Lilith; but he heard her voice once—and that was enough for one day. The next, she was sitting to her father the greater part of the day, and he could see her as often as he dared glance up from his drawing. She had looked at him when she entered, but had shown no sign of recognition; and all day long she took no further notice of him. He hoped, at first, that this came of the intelligence of love; but he soon began to doubt it. For he saw that, with the holy shadow of sorrow, all that distinguished the expression of her countenance from that which the painter so constantly reproduced, had vanished likewise. It was the very face of the unheeding angel whom, as often as he lifted his eyes higher than hers, he saw on the wall above her, playing on a psaltery in the smoke of the torment ascending for ever from burning Babylon.—The power of the painter had not merely wrought for the representation of the woman of his imagination: it had had scope as well in realizing her.

Karl soon began to see that communication, other than of the eyes, was all but hopeless; and to any attempt in that way she seemed altogether indisposed to respond. Nor, if she had wished it, would it have been safe; for as often as he glanced towards her, instead of hers, he met the blue eyes of the painter, gleaming upon him like winter-lightning. His tones, his gestures, his words, seemed kind: his glance and his smile refused to be disguised.

The first day he dined alone in the studio, waited upon by an old woman; the next he was admitted to the family table, with Teufelsbürst and Lilith. The room offered a strange contrast to the study. As far as handicraft, directed by a sumptuous taste, could construct a house-paradise, this was one. But it seemed rather a paradise of demons; for the walls were covered with Teufelsbürst's paintings. During the dinner. Lilith's gaze scarcely met that of Wolkenlicht; and once or twice, when their eyes did meet, her glance was so perfectly unconcerned, that Karl wished he might look at her for ever without the fear of her looking at him again. She seemed like one whose love had rushed out glowing with seraphic fire, to be frozen to death in a more than wintry cold: she now walked lonely without her love. In the evenings, he was expected to continue his drawing by lamp-light; and at night he was conducted by Teufelsbürst to his chamber. Not once did he leave him there without locking and bolting the door on the outside. But he felt nothing except the coldness of Lilith.

Day after day she sat to her father, in every variety of costume that could best show the variety of her beauty. How much greater that beauty might be, if it ever blossomed into a beauty of soul, Wolkenlicht never imagined; for he soon loved her enough to attribute to her all the possibilities of her face as actual possessions of her being. To account for everything that seemed to contradict this perfection, his brain was prolific in inventions; till he was compelled at last to see that she was in the condition of a rose-bud, which, on the point of blossoming, has been chilled into a changeless bud by the cold of an untimely frost. For one day, after the father and daughter had become a little more accustomed to his silent presence, a conversation began between them, which went on until he saw that Teufelsbürst believed in nothing except his art. How much of his feeling for that could be dignified by the name of belief, seeing its objects were such as they were, might have been questioned. It seemed to Wolkenlicht to amount only to this: that, amidst a thousand distastes, it was a pleasant thing to re-produce on the canvas the forms he beheld around him, modifying them to express the prevailing feelings of his own mind.

A more desolate communication between souls than that which then passed between father and daughter could hardly be imagined. The father spoke of humanity and all its experiences in a tone of the bitterest scorn. He despised men and himself amongst them; and re-joiced to think that the generations rose and vanished, brood after brood, as the crops of corn grew and disappeared. Lilith, who listened to it all unmoved, taking only an intellectual interest in the question, remarked that even the corn had more life than that; for, after its death, it rose again in the new crop. Whether she meant that the corn was therefore superior to man, forgetting that the superior can produce being without losing its own, or only advanced an objection to her father's argument, Wolkenlicht could not tell. But Teufelsbürst laughed like the sound of a saw, and said: "Follow out the analogy, my Lilith, and you will see that man is like the corn that springs again after it is buried; but unfortunately the only result we know of is a vampire."

Wolkenlicht looked up, and saw a shudder pass through the frame, and over the pale thin face of the painter. This he could not account for. But Teufelsbürst could have explained it, for there were strange whis-pers abroad, and they had reached his ear; and his philosophy was not quite enough for them. But the laugh with which Lilith met this frightful attempt at wit, grated dreadfully on Wolkenlicht's feeling. With her, too, however, a reaction seemed to follow. For, turning round a moment after, and looking at the picture on which her father was working, the tears rose in her eyes, and she said: "Oh! father, how like my mother you have made me this time!" "Child!" retorted the painter with a cold fierceness, "you have no mother. That which is gone out is gone out. Put no name in my hearing on that which is not. Where no substance is, how can there be a name?"

Lilith rose and left the room. Wolkenlicht now understood that Lilith was a frozen bud, and could not blossom into a rose. But pure love lives by faith. It loves the vaguely beheld and unrealized ideal. It dares believe that the loved is not all that she ever seemed. It is in virtue of this that love lives on. And it was in virtue of this, that Wolkenlicht loved Lilith yet more after he discovered what a grave of misery her unbelief was digging for her within her own soul. For her sake he would bear anything—bear even with calmness the torments of his own love; he would stay on, hoping and hoping.—The text, that we know not what a day may bring forth, is just as true of good things as of evil things; and out of Time's womb the facts must come.

But with the birth of this resolution to endure, his suffering abated; his face grew more calm; his love, no less earnest, was less imperious; and he did not look up so often from his work when Lilith was present. The master could see that his pupil was more at ease, and that he was making rapid progress in his art. This did not suit his designs, and he would betake himself to his further schemes.

For this purpose he proceeded first to simulate a friendship for Wolkenlicht, the manifestations of which he gradually increased, until, after a day or two, he asked him to drink wine with him in the evening. Karl readily agreed. The painter produced some of his best; but took care not to allow Lilith to taste it; for he had cunningly prepared and mingled with it a decoction of certain herbs and other ingredients, exercising specific actions upon the brain, and tending to the inordinate excitement of those portions of it which are principally under the rule of the imagination. By the reaction of the brain during the operation of these stimulants, the imagination is filled with suggestions and images. The nature of these is determined by the prevailing mood of the time. They are such as the imagination would produce of itself; but increased in number and intensity. Teufelsbürst, without philosophizing about it, called his preparation simply a love-philtre, a concoction well known by name, but the composition of which was the secret of only a few. Wolkenlicht had, of course, not the least suspicion of the treatment to which he was subjected.

Teufelsbürst was, however, doomed to fresh disappointment. Not that his potion failed in the anticipated effect; for now Karl's real sufferings began; but that such was the strength of Karl's will, and his fear of doing anything that might give a pretext for banishing him from the presence of Lilith, that he was able to conceal his feelings far too successfully for the satisfaction of Teufelsbürst's art. Yet he had to fetter himself with all the restraints that self-exhortation could load him with, to refrain from falling at the feet of Lilith and kissing the hem of her garment. For that, as the lowliest part of all that surrounded her, itself kissing the earth, seemed to come nearest within the reach of his ambition, and therefore to draw him the most.

No doubt the painter had experience and penetration enough to preceive that he was suffering intensely; but he wanted to see the suffering embodied in outward signs, bringing it within the region over which his pencil held sway. He kept on, therefore, trying one thing after another, and rousing the poor youth to agony; till to his other sufferings were added, at length, those of failing health; a fact which notified itself evidently enough even for Teufelsbürst, though its signs were not of the sort he chiefly desired. But Karl endured all bravely.

Meantime, for various reasons, he scarcely ever left the house.

I must now interrupt the course of my story to introduce another element.

A few years before the period of my tale, a certain shoemaker of the city had died under circumstances more than suggestive of suicide. He was buried, however, with such precautions, that six weeks elapsed before the rumour of the facts broke out; upon which rumour, not before, the most fearful reports began to be circulated, supported by what seemed to the people of Prague incontestable evidence.—A *spectrum* of the deceased appeared to multitudes of persons, playing horrible pranks, and occasioning indescribable consternation throughout the whole town. This went on till at last, about eight months after his burial, the magistrates caused his body to be dug up; when it was found in just the condition of the bodies of those who in the eastern countries of Europe are called *vampires*. They buried the corpse under the gallows; but neither the digging up nor the re-burying were of avail to banish the spectre. Again the spade and pick-axe were set to work, and the dead man, being found considerably improved in *condition* since his last interment, was, with various horrible indignities, burnt to ashes, "after which the *spectrum* was never seen more."

And a second epidemic of the same nature had broken out a little before the period to which I have brought my story.

About midnight, after a calm frosty day, for it was now winter, a terrible storm of wind and snow came on. The tempest howled frightfully about the house of the painter, and Wolkenlicht found some solace in listening to the uproar, for his troubled thoughts would not allow him to sleep. It raged on all the next three days, till about noon on the fourth day, when it suddenly fell, and all was calm. The following night, Wolkenlicht, lying awake, heard unaccountable noises in the next house, as of things thrown about, of kicking and fighting horses, and of opening and shutting gates. Flinging wide his lattice and looking out, the noise of howling dogs came to him from every quarter of the town. The moon was bright and the air was still. In a little while he heard the sounds of a horse going at full gallop round the house, so that it shook as if it would fall; and flashes of light shone into his room. How much of this may have been owing to the effect of the drugs on poor Lottchen's brain, I leave my readers to determine. But when the family met at breakfast in the morning, Teufelsbürst, who had been already out of doors, reported that he had found the marks of strange feet in the snow, all about the house and through the garden at the back; stating, as his belief, that the tracks must be continued over the roofs, for there was no passage otherwise. There was a wicked gleam in his eye as he spoke; and Lilith believed that he was only trying an experiment on Karl's nerves. He persisted that he had never seen any footprints of the sort before. Karl informed him of his experiences during the night; upon which Teufelsbürst looked a little graver still, and proceeded to tell them that the storm, whose snow was still covering the ground, had arisen the very moment that their next door neighbour died, and had ceased as suddenly the moment he was buried, though it had raved furiously all the time of the funeral, so that "it made men's bodies quake and their teeth chatter in their heads." Karl had heard that the man, whose name was John Kuntz, was dead and buried. He knew that he had been a very wealthy, and therefore most respectable, alderman of the town; that he had been very fond of horses; and that he had died in consequence of a kick received from one of his own, as he was looking at his hoof. But he had not heard that, just before he died, a black cat "opened the casement with her nails, ran to his bed, and violently scratched his face and the bolster, as if she endeavoured by force to remove him out of the place where he lay. But the cat afterwards was suddenly gone, and she was no sooner gone, but he breathed his last."

So said Teufelsbürst, as the reporter of the town-talk. Lilith looked very pale and terrified; and it was perhaps owing to this that the painter brought no more tales home with him. There were plenty to bring, but he heard them all and said nothing. The fact was that the philosopher himself could not resist the infection of the fear that was literally raging in the city; and perhaps the reports that he himself had sold himself to the devil, had sufficient response from his own evil conscience to add to the influence of the epidemic upon him. The whole place was infested with the presence of the dead Kuntz, till scarce a man or woman would dare to be alone. He strangled old men; insulted women; squeezed children to death; knocked out the brains of dogs against the ground; pulled up posts; turned milk into blood; nearly killed a worthy clergy-man by beathing upon him the intolerable airs of the grave, cold and malignant and noisome; and, in short, filled the city with a perfect madness of fear, so that every report was believed without the smallest doubt or investigation.

Though Teufelsbürst brought home no more of the town-talk, the old servant was a faithful purveyor, and frequented the news-mart assiduously. Indeed she had some nightmare experiences of her own that she was proud to add to the stock of horrors which the city enjoyed with such a hearty community of goods. For those regions were not far removed from the very birth-place and home of the vampire. The belief in vampires is the quintessential concentration and embodiment of all the passion of fear in Hungary and the adjacent regions. Nor of all the other inventions of the human imagination, has there ever been one so perfect in crawling terror as this. Lilith and Karl were quite familiar with the popular ideas on the subject. It did not require to be explained to them, that a vampire was a body retaining a kind of animal life after the soul had departed. If any relation con-tinued between it and the vanished ghost, it was only sufficient to make it restless in its grave. Possessed of vitality enough to keep it uncor-rupted and pliant, its only instinct was a blind hunger for the sole food which could keep its awful life persistent—living human blood. Hence

it, or if not it, a sort of semi-material exhalation of essence of it,
retaining its form and material relations, crept from its tomb, and went
roaming about till it found some one asleep, towards whom it had an
attraction, founded on old affection. It sucked the blood of this
unhappy being, transferring so much of its life to itself as a vampire
could assimilate. Death was the certain consequence. If suspicion con-
jectured aright, and they opened the proper grave, the body of the
vampire would be found perfectly fresh and plump, sometimes indeed
of rather florid complexion;—with grown hair, eyes half open, and the
stains of recent blood about its greedy leech-like lips. Nothing remained
but to consume the corpse to ashes, upon which the vampire would
show itself no more. But what added infinitely to the horror was the
certainty that whoever died from the mouth of the vampire, wrinkled
grandsire, or delicate maiden, must in turn rise from the grave, and go
forth a vampire, to suck the blood of the dearest left behind. This was
the generation of the vampire brood. Lilith trembled at the very name
of the creature. Karl was too much in love to be afraid of anything. Yet
the evident fear of the unbelieving painter took a hold of his imagination; and, under the influence of the potions of which he still partook
unwittingly—when he was not thinking about Lilith, he was thinking
about the vampire.

Meantime, the condition of things in the painter's household continued much the same for Wolkenlicht—work all day; no communication between the young people; the dinner and the wine; silent reading
when work was done, with stolen glances many over the top of the
book, glances that were never returned; the cold good night; the locking
of the door; the wakeful night and the drowsy morning. But at length a
change came, and sooner than any of the party had expected. For,
whether it was that the impatience of Teufelsbürst had urged him to
yet more dangerous experiments, or that the continuance of those he
had been so long employing had overcome at length the vitality of
Wolkenlicht—one afternoon, as he was sitting at his work, he suddenly
dropped from his chair, and his master hurrying to him in some alarm,
found him rigid and apparently lifeless. Lilith was not in the study
when this took place. In justice to Teufelsbürst, it must be confessed
that he employed all the skill he was master of, which for beneficent
purposes was not very great, to restore the youth; but without avail. At
last, hearing the footsteps of Lilith, he desisted in some consternation;
and that she might escape being shocked by the sight of a dead body

where she had been accustomed to see a living one, he removed the lay
figure from the couch, and laid Karl in its place, covering him with the
black velvet pall. He was just in time. She started at seeing no one in
Karl's place, and said:

"Where is your pupil, father?"

"Gone home," he answered, with a kind of convulsive grin.

She glanced round the room, caught sight of the lay figure where it
had not been before, looked at the couch, and saw the pall yet heaved
up from beneath, opened her eyes till the entire white sweep around
the iris suggested a new expression of consternation to Teufelsbürst,
though from a quarter whence he did not desire or look for it; and
then, without a word, sat down to a drawing she had been busy upon
the day before. But her father, glancing at her now, as Wolkenlicht had
used to do, could not help seeing that she was frightfully pale. She
showed no other sign of uneasiness. As soon as he released her, she
withdrew, with one more glance, as she passed, at the couch and the
figure blocked out in black upon it. She hastened to her chamber, shut
and locked the door, sat down on the side of the couch, and fell, not
a-weeping, but a-thinking. Was he dead? What did it matter? They
would all be dead soon. Her mother was dead already. It was only that
earth could not bear more children, except she devoured those to
whom she had already given birth. But what if they had to come back
in another form, and live another sad, hopeless, loveless life over
again?—And so she went on questioning, and receiving no replies; while
through all her thoughts passed and repassed the eyes of Wolkenlicht,
which she had often felt to be upon her when she did not see them,
wild with repressed longing, the light of their love shining through the
veil of diffused tears, ever gathering and never overflowing. Then came
the pale face, so worshipping, so distant in its self-withdrawn devotion,
slowly dawning out of the vapours of her reverie. When it vanished, she
tried to see it again. It would not come when she called it; but when her
thoughts left knocking at the door of the lost and wandered away, out
came the pale, troubled, silent face again, gathering itself up from some
unknown nook in her world of phantasy, and once more, when she
tried to steady it by the fixedness of her own regard, fading back into
the mist. So the phantasm of the dead drew near and wooed, as the
living had never dared.—What if there were any good in loving? What if
men and women did not die all out, but some dim shade of each, like
that pale, mind-ghost of Wolkenlicht, floated through the eternal vapours

of chaos? And what if they might sometimes cross each other's path, meet, know that they met, love on? Would not that revive the withered memory, fix the fleeting ghost, give a new habitation, a body even, to the poor, unhoused wanderers, frozen by the eternal frosts, no longer thinking beings, but thoughts wandering through the brain of the "Melancholy Mass"? Back with the thought came the face of the dead Karl, and the maiden threw herself on her bed in a flood of bitter tears. She could have loved him if he had only lived: she did love him, for he was dead. But even in the midst of the remorse that followed,—for had she not killed him?—life seemed a less hard and hopeless thing than before. For it is love itself and not its responses or results that is the soul of life and its pleasures.

Two hours passed ere she could again show herself to her father, from whom she seemed in some new way divided by the new feeling in which he did not, and could not share. But at last, lest he should seek her, and finding her, should suspect her thoughts, she descended and sought him.—For there is a maidenliness in sorrow, that wraps her garments close around her.—But he was not to be seen; the door of the study was locked. A shudder passed through her as she thought of what her father, who lost no opportunity of furthering his all but perfect acquaintance with the human form and structure, might be about with the figure which she knew lay dead beneath that velvet pall, but which had arisen to haunt the hollow caves and cells of her living brain. She rushed away, and up once more to her silent room, through the darkness which had now settled down in the house; threw herself again on her bed, and lay almost paralysed with horror and distress.

But Teufelsbürst was not about anything so rightful as she supposed, though something frightful enough. I have already implied that Wolkenlicht was, in form, as fine an embodiment of youthful manhood as any old Greek republic could have provided one of its sculptors with as model for an Apollo. It is true, that to the eye of a Greek artist he would not have been more acceptable in consequence of the regimen he had been going through for the last few weeks; but the emaciation of Wolkenlicht's frame, and the consequent prominence of the muscles, indicating the pain he had gone through, were peculiarly attractive to Teufelsbürst.—He was busy preparing to take a cast of the body of his dead pupil, that it might aid to the perfection of his future labours.

He was deep in the artistic enjoyment of a form, at the same time so beautiful and strong, yet with the lines of suffering in every limb and feature, when his daughter's hand was laid on the latch. He started, flung the velvet drapery over the body, and went to the door. But Lilith had vanished. He returned to his labours. The operation took a long time, for he performed it very carefully. Towards midnight, he had finished encasing the body in a close-clinging shell of plaster, which, when broken off, and fitted together, would be the matrix to the form of the dead Wolkenlicht. Before leaving it to harden till the morning, he was just proceeding to strengthen it with an additional layer all over, when a flash of lightning, reflected in all its dazzle from the snow without, almost blinded him. A peal of long-drawn thunder followed; the wind rose; and just such a storm came on as had risen some time before at the death of Kuntz, whose spectre was still tormenting the city. The gnomes of terror, deep hidden in the caverns of Teufelsbürst's nature, broke out jubilant. With trembling hands he tried to cast the pall over the awful white chrysalis,—failed, and fled to his chamber. And there lay the studio naked to the eyes of the lightning, with its tortured forms throbbing out of the dark, and quivering, as with life, in the almost continuous palpitations of the light; while on the couch lay the motionless mass of whiteness, gleaming blue in the lightning, almost more terrible in its crude indications of the human form, than that which it enclosed. It lay there as if dropped from some tree of chaos, haggard with the snows of eternity—a huge mis-shapen nut, with a corpse for its kernel.

But the lightning would soon have revealed a more terrible sight still, had there been any eyes to behold it. At midnight, while a peal of thunder was just dying away in the distance, the crust of death flew asunder, rending in all directions; and, pale as his investiture, staring with ghastly eyes, the form of Karl started up sitting on the couch. Had he not been far beyond ordinary men in strength, he could not thus have rent his sepulchre. Indeed, had Teufelsbürst been able to finish his task by the additional layer of gypsum which he contemplated, he must have died the moment life revived; although, so long as the trance lasted, neither the exclusion from the air, nor the practical solidification of the walls of his chest, could do him any injury. He had lain unconscious throughout the operations of Teufelsbürst, but now the catalepsy had passed away, possibly under the influence of the electric condition of the atmosphere. Very likely the strength he now put forth was intensified by a convulsive reaction of all the powers of life, as is not unfrequently the case in sudden awakenings from similar interruptions of vital activity. The coming to himself and the bursting of his case were simultaneous. He sat staring about him, with, of all his mental faculties, only his imagination awake, from which the thoughts that occupied it when he fell senseless had not yet faded. These thoughts had been compounded of feelings about Lilith, and speculations about the vampire that haunted the neighbourhood; and the fumes of the last drug of which he had partaken, still hovering in his brain, combined with these thoughts and fancies to generate the delusion that he had just broken from the embrace of his coffin, and risen, the last-born of the vampire-race. The sense of unavoidable obligation to fulfil his doom, was yet mingled with a faint flutter of joy, for he knew that he must go to Lilith. With a deep sigh, he rose, gathered up the pall of black velvet, flung it around him, stepped from the couch, and left the study to find her.

Meantime, Teufelsbürst had sufficiently recovered to remember that he had left the door of the studio unfastened, and that anyone entering would discover in what he had been engaged, which, in the case of his getting into any difficulty about the death of Karl, would tell powerfully against him. He was at the farther end of a long passage, leading from the house to the studio, on his way to make all secure, when Karl appeared at the door, and advanced towards him. The painter, seized with invincible terror, turned and fled. He reached his room, and fell senseless on the floor. The phantom held on its way, heedless.

Lilith, on gaining her room the second time, had thrown herself on her bed as before, and had wept herself into a troubled slumber. She lay dreaming—and dreadful dreams. Suddenly she awoke in one of those peals of thunder which tormented the high regions of the air, as a storm billows the surface of the ocean. She lay awake and listened. As it died away, she thought she heard, mingling with its last muffled murmurs, the sound of moaning. She turned her face towards the room in keen terror. But she saw nothing. Another light, long-drawn sigh reached her ear, and at the same moment a flash of lightning illumined the room. In the corner farthest from her bed, she spied a white face, nothing more. She was dumb and motionless with fear. Utter darkness followed, a darkness that seemed to enter into her very brain. Yet she felt that the face was slowly crossing the black gulf of the room, and drawing near to where she lay. The next flash revealed, as it bended over her, the ghastly face of Karl, down which flowed fresh tears. The rest of his form was lost in blackness. Lilith did not faint, but it was the very force of her fear that seemed to keep her alive. It became for the moment the atmosphere of her life. She lay trembling and staring at the spot in the darkness where she supposed the face of Karl still to be. But the next flash showed her the face far off, looking at her through the panes of her lattice-window.

For Lottchen, as soon as he saw Lilith, seemed to himself to go through a second stage of awaking. Her face made him doubt whether he could be a vampire after all; for instead of wanting to bite her arm and suck the blood, he all but fell down at her feet in a passion of speechless love. The next moment he became aware that his presence must be at least very undesirable to her; and in an instant he had reached her window, which he knew looked upon a lower roof that extended between two different parts of the house, and before the next flash came, he had stepped through the lattice and closed it behind him.

Believing his own room to be attainable from this quarter, he proceeded along the roof in the direction he judged best. The cold winter air by degrees restored him entirely to his right mind, and he soon comprehended the whole of the circumstances in which he found himself. Peeping through a window he was passing, to see whether it belonged to his room, he spied Teufelsbürst, who, at the very moment, was lifting his head from the faint into which he had fallen at the first sight of Lottchen. The moon was shining clear, and in its light the painter saw, to his horror, the pale face staring in at his window. He thought it had been there ever since he had fainted, and dropped again in a deeper swoon than before. Karl saw him fall, and the truth flashed upon him that the wicked artist took him for what he had believed himself to be when first he recovered from his trance—namely, the vampire of the former Karl Wolkenlicht. The moment he comprehended it, he resolved to keep up the delusion if possible. Meantime he was innocently preparing a new ingredient for the popular dish of horrors to be served at the ordinary of the city the next day. For the old servant's were not the only eyes that had seen him besides those of Teufelsbürst. What could be more like a vampire, dragging his pall after him, than this apparition of poor, half-frozen Lottchen, crawling across the roof? Karl remembered afterwards that he had heard the dogs howling awfully in every direction, as he crept along; but this was hardly necessary to make those who saw him conclude that it was the same phantasm of John Kuntz, which had been infesting the whole

city, and especially the house next door to the painter's, which had
been the dwelling of the respectable alderman who had degenerated
into this most disreputable of moneyless vagabonds. What added to the
consternation of all who heard of it, was the sickening conviction that
the extreme measures which they had resorted to in order to free the
city from the ghoul, beyond which nothing could be done, had been
utterly unavailing, successful as they had proved in every other known
case of the kind. For, urged as well by various horrid signs about his
grave, which not even its close proximity to the altar could render a
place of repose, they had opened it, had found in the body every
peculiarity belonging to a vampire, had pulled it out with the greatest
difficulty on account of a quite supernatural ponderosity; which rendered the horse which had killed him—a strong animal—all but unable
to drag it along, and had at last, after cutting it in pieces, and expending
on the fire two hundred and sixteen great billets, succeeded in con-
quering its incombustibleness, and reducing it to ashes. Such, at least,
was the story which had reached the painter's household, and was
believed by many; and if all this did not compel the perturbed corpse to
rest, what more could be done?

When Karl had reached his room, and was dressing himself, the
thought struck him that something might be made of the report of the
extreme weight of the body of old Kuntz, to favour the continuance of
the delusion of Teufelsbürst, although he hardly knew yet to what use
he could turn this delusion. He was convinced that he would have made
no progress however long he might have remained in his house; and that
he would have more chance of favour with Lilith if he were to meet her
in any other circumstances whatever, than those in which he invariably
saw her—namely, surrounded by her father's influences, and watched
by her father's cold blue eyes.

As soon as he was dressed, he crept down to the studio, which was
now quiet enough, the storm being over, and the moon filling it with
her steady shine. In the corner lay in all directions the fragments of the
mould which his own body had formed and filled. The bag of plaster
and the bucket of water which the painter had been using stood beside.
Lottchen gathered all the pieces together, and then making his way to
an out-house where he had seen various odds and ends of rubbish lying,
chose from the heap as many pieces of old iron and other metal as he
could find. To these he added a few large stones from the garden. When
he had got all into the studio, he locked the door, and proceeded to fit

together the parts of the mould, filling up the hollow as he went on
with the heaviest things he could get into it, and solidifying the whole
by pouring in plaster; till, having at length completed it, and obliter-
ated, as much as possible, the marks of joining, he left it to harden,
with the conviction that now it would make a considerable impression
on Teufelsbürst's imagination, as well as on his muscular sense. He
then left everything else as nearly undisturbed as he could; and, knowing all the ways of the house, was soon in the street, without leaving
any signs of his exit.

Karl soon found himself before the house in which his friend
Höllenrachen resided. Knowing his studious habits, he had hoped to see
his light still burning, nor was he disappointed. He contrived to bring
him to his window, and a moment after, the door was cautiously
opened.

"Why, Lottchen, where do you come from?"

"From the grave, Heinrich, or next door to it."

"Come in, and tell me all about it. We thought the old painter had
made a model of you, and tortured you to death."

"Perhaps you were not far wrong. But get me a horn of ale, for even
a vampire is thirsty, you know."

"A vampire!" exclaimed Heinrich, retreating a pace, and involuntarily putting himself upon his guard.

Karl laughed.

"My hand was warm, was it not, old fellow?" he said. "Vampires
are cold, all but the blood."

"What a fool I am!" rejoined Heinrich. "But you know we have
been hearing such horrors lately that a fellow may be excused for
shuddering a little when a pale-faced apparition tells him at two o'clock
in the morning that he is a vampire, and thirsty, too."

Karl told him the whole story; and the mental process of regarding
it for the sake of telling it, revealed to him pretty clearly some of the
treatment of which he had been unconscious at the time. Heinrich was
quite sure that his suspicions were correct. And now the question was,
what was to be done next.

"At all events," said Heinrich, "we must keep you out of the way
for some time. I will represent to my landlady that you are in hiding
from enemies, and her heart will rule her tongue. She can let you have a
garret-room, I know; and I will do as well as I can to bear you
company. We shall have time then to invent some plan of operation."

To this proposal Karl agreed with hearty thanks, and soon all was arranged. The only conclusion they could yet arrive at was, that somehow or other the old demon-painter must be tamed.

Meantime, how fared it with Lilith? She too had no doubt that she had seen the body-ghost of poor Karl, and that the vampire had, according to rule, paid her the first visit because he loved her best. This was horrible enough if the vampire were not really the person he represented; but if in any sense it were Karl himself, at least it gave some expectation of a more prolonged existence than her father had taught her to look for; and if love anything like her mother's still lasted, even along with the habits of a vampire, there was something to hope for in the future. And then, though he had visited her, he had not, as far as she was aware, deprived her of a drop of blood. She could not be certain that he had not bitten her, for she had been in such a strange condition of mind that she might not have felt it, but she believed that he had restrained the impulses of his vampire nature, and had left her, lest he should yet yield to them. She fell fast asleep; and, when morning came, there was not, as far as she could judge, one of those triangular leech-like perforations to be found upon her whole body. Will it be believed that the moment she was satisfied of this, she was seized by a terrible jealousy, lest Karl should have gone and bitten someone else? Most people will wonder that she should not have gone out of her senses at once; but there was all the difference between a visit from a real vampire and a visit from a man she had begun to love, even although she took him for a vampire. All the difference does *not* lie in a name. They were very different causes, and the effects must be very different.

When Teufelsbürst came down in the morning, he crept into the studio like a murderer. There lay the awful white block, seeming to his eyes just the same as he had left it. What was to be done with it? He dared not open it. Mould and model must go together. But whither? If inquiry should be made after Wolkenlicht, and this were discovered anywhere on his premises, would it not be enough to bring him at once to the gallows? Therefore it would be dangerous to bury it in the garden; or in the cellar.

"Besides," thought he, with a shudder, "that would be to fix the vampire as a guest for ever." —And the horrors of the past night rushed back upon his imagination with renewed intensity. What would it be to have the dead Karl crawling about his house for ever, now inside, now out, now sitting on the stairs, now staring in at the windows?

He would have dragged it to the bottom of his garden, past which the Moldau flowed, and plunged it into the stream; but then, should the spectre continue to prove troublesome, it would be almost impossible to reach the body so as to destroy it by fire; besides which, he could not do it without assistance, and the probability of discovery. If, however, the apparition should turn out to be no vampire, but only a respectable ghost, they might manage to endure its presence. till it should be weary of haunting them.

He resolved at last to convey the body for the meantime into a concealed cellar in the house, seeing something must be done before his daughter came down. Proceeding to remove it, his consternation was greatly increased when he discovered how the body had grown in weight since he had thus disposed of it, leaving on his mind scarcely a hope that it could turn out not to be a vampire after all. He could scarcely stir it, and there was but one whom he could call to his assistance—the old woman who acted as his housekeeper and servant.

He went to her room, roused her, and told her the whole story. Devoted to her master for many years, and not quite so sensitive to fearful influences as when less experienced in horrors, she showed immediate readiness to render him assistance. Utterly unable, however, to lift the mass between them, they could only drag and push it along; and such a slow toil was it that there was no time to remove the traces of its track, before Lilith came down and saw a broad white line leading from the door of the studio down the cellar-stairs. She knew in a moment what it meant; but not a word was uttered about the matter, and the name of Karl Wolkenlicht seemed to be entirely forgotten.

But how could the affairs of a house go on all the same when every one of the household knew that a dead body lay in the cellar?—nay more, that, although it lay still and dead enough all day, it would come half alive at nightfall, and, turning the whole house into a sepulchre by its presence, go creeping about like a cat all over it in the dark—perhaps with phosphorescent eyes? So it was not surprising that the painter abandoned his studio early, and that the three found themselves together in the gorgeous room formerly described, as soon as twilight began to fall.

Already Teufelsbürst had begun to experience a kind of shrinking from the horrid faces in his own pictures, and to feel disgusted at the abortions of his own mind. But all that he and the old woman now felt was an increasing fear as the night drew on, a kind of sickening and paralysing terror. The thing down there would not lie quiet—at least its phantom in the cellars of their imagination would not. As much as possible, however, they avoided alarming Lilith, who, knowing all they knew, was as silent as they. But her mind was in a strange state of excitement, partly from the presence of a new sense of love, the pleasure of which all the atmosphere of grief into which it grew could not totally quench. It comforted her somehow, as a child may comfort when his father is away.

Bedtime came, and no one made a move to go. Without a word spoken on the subject, the three remained together all night; the elders nodding and slumbering occasionally, and Lilith getting some share of repose on a couch. All night the shape of death might be somewhere about the house; but it did not disturb them. They heard no sound, saw no sight; and when the morning dawned, they separated, chilled and stupid, and for the time beyond fear, to seek repose in their private chambers. There they remained equally undisturbed.

But when the painter approached his easel a few hours after, looking more pale and haggard still than he was wont, from the fears of the night, a new bewilderment took possession of him. He had been busy with a fresh embodiment of his favourite subject, into which he had sketched the form of the student as the sufferer. He had repre- sented poor Wolkenlicht as just beginning to recover from a trance, while a group of surgeons, unaware of the signs of returning life, were absorbed in a minute dissection of one of the limbs. At an open door he had painted Lilith passing, with her face buried in a bunch of sweet- peas. But when he came to the picture, he found, to his astonishment and terror, that the face of one of the group was now turned towards that of the victim, regarding his revival with demoniac satisfaction, and taking pains to prevent the others from discovering it. The face of this prince of torturers was that of Teufelsbürst himself. Lilith had alto- gether vanished, and in her place stood the dim vampire reiteration of the body that lay extended on the table, staring greedily at the assembled company. With trembling hands the painter removed the picture from the easel, and turned its face to the wall.

Of course this was the work of Lottchen. When he left the house, he took with him the key of a small private door, which was so seldom used that, while it remained closed, the key would not be missed, perhaps for many months. Watching the windows, he had chosen a safe time to enter, and had been hard at work all night on these alterations. Teufelsbürst attributed them to the vampire, and left the picture as he found it, not daring to put brush to it again.

The next night was passed much after the same fashion. But the fear had begun to die away a little in the hearts of the women, who did not know what had taken place in the study on the previous night. It burrowed, however, with gathered force in the vitals of Teufelsbürst. But this night likewise passed in peace; and before it was over, the old woman had taken to speculating in her own mind as to the best way of disposing of the body, seeing it was not at all likely to be troublesome. But when the painter entered his study in trepidation the next morning, he found that the form of the lovely Lilith was painted out of every picture in the room. This could not be concealed; and Lilith and the servant became aware that the studio was the portion of the house in haunting which the vampire left the rest in peace.

Karl recounted all the tricks he had played to his friend Heinrich, who begged to be allowed to bear him company the following night. To this Karl consented, thinking it would be considerably more agreeable to have a companion. So they took a couple of bottles of wine and some provisions with them, and before midnight found themselves snug in the study. They sat very quiet for some time, for they knew that if they were seen, two vampires would not be so terrible as one, and might occasion discovery. But at length Heinrich could bear it no longer.

"I say, Lottchen, let's go and look for your dead body. What has the old beggar done with it?"

"I think I know. Stop; let me peep out. All right! Come along."

With a lamp in his hand, he led the way to the cellars, and after searching about a little, they discovered it.

"It looks horrid enough," said Heinrich, "but I think a drop or two of wine would brighten it up a little."

So he took a bottle from his pocket, and after they had had a glass apiece, he dropped a third in blots all over the plaster. Being red wine, it had the effect Höllenrachen desired.

"When they visit it next, they will know that the vampire can find the food he prefers," said he.

In a corner close by the plaster, they found the clothes Karl had worn.

"Hillo!" said Heinrich, "we'll make something of this find."

So he carried them with him to the study. There he got hold of the lay-figure.

"What are you about, Heinrich?"

"Going to make a scarecrow to keep the ravens off old Teufel's pictures," answered Heinrich, as he went on dressing the lay-figure in Karl's clothes. He next seated the creature at an easel with its back to the door, so that it should be the first thing the painter should see when he entered. Karl meant to remove this before he went, for it was too comical to fall in with the rest of his proceedings. But the two sat down to their supper, and by the time they had finished the wine, they thought they should like to go to bed. So they got up and went home, and Karl forgot the lay-figure, leaving it in busy motionlessness all night before the easel.

When Teufelsbürst saw it, he turned and fled with a cry that brought his daughter to his help. He rushed past her, able only to articulate:

"The vampire! The vampire! Painting!"

Far more courageous than he, because her conscience was more peaceful, Lilith passed on to the studio. She too recoiled a step or two when she saw the figure; but with the sight of the back of Karl, as she supposed it to be, came the longing to see the face that was on the other side. So she crept round and round by the wall, as far off as she could. The figure remained motionless. It was a strange kind of shock that she experienced when she saw the face, disgusting from its inanity. The absurdity next struck her; and with the absurdity flashed into her mind the conviction that this was not the doing of a vampire; for of all creatures under the moon, he could not be expected to be a humourist. A wild hope sprang up in her mind that Karl was not dead. Of this she soon resolved to make herself sure.

She closed the door of the studio; in the strength of her new hope, undressed the figure, put it in its place, concealed the garments—all the work of a few minutes; and then, finding her father just recovering from the worst of his fear, told him there was nothing in the studio but what ought to be there, and persuaded him to go and see. He not only saw no one, but found that no further liberties had been taken with his pictures. Reassured, he soon persuaded himself that the spectre in this case had been the offspring of his own terror-haunted brain. But he had no spirit for painting now. He wandered about the house, himself haunting it like a restless ghost.

When night came, Lilith retired to her own room. The waters of fear had begun to subside in the house; but the painter and his old attendant did not yet follow her example.

As soon, however, as the house was quite still, Lilith glided noiselessly down the stairs, went into the studio, where as yet there assuredly was no vampire, and concealed herself in a corner.

As it would not do for an earnest student like Heinrich to be away from his work very often, he had not asked to accompany Lottchen this time. And indeed Karl himself, a little anxious about the result of the scarecrow, greatly preferred going alone.

While she was waiting for what might happen, the conviction grew upon Lilith, as she reviewed all the past of the story, that these phenomena were the work of the real Karl, and of no vampire. In a few moments she was still more sure of this. Behind the screen where she had taken refuge, hung one of the pictures out of which her portrait had been painted the night before last. She had taken a lamp with her into the study, with the intention of extinguishing it the moment she heard any sign of approach; but as the vampire lingered, she began to occupy herself with examining the picture beside her. She had not looked at it long, before she wetted the tip of her forefinger, and began to rub away at the obliteration. Her suspicions were instantly confirmed: the substance employed was only a gummy wash over the paint. The delight she experienced at the discovery threw her into a mischievous humour.

"I will see," she said to herself, "whether I cannot match Karl Wolkenlicht at this game."

In a closet in the room hung a number of costumes, which Lilith had at different times worn for her father. Among them was a large white drapery, which she easily disposed as a shroud. With the help of some chalk, she soon made herself ghastly enough, and then placing her lamp on the floor behind the screen, and setting a chair over it, so that it should throw no light in any direction, she waited once more for the vampire. Nor had she much longer to wait. She soon heard a door move, the sound of which she hardly knew, and then the studio door opened. Her heart beat dreadfully, not with fear lest it should be a vampire after all, but with hope that it was Karl. To see him once more was too great joy. Would she not make up to him for all her coldness! But would he care for her now? Perhaps he had been quite cured of his longing for a hard heart like her. She peeped. It was he sure enough, looking as handsome as ever. He was holding his light to look at her last work, and the expression of his face, even in regarding her handiwork, was enough to let her know that he loved her still. If she had not seen this, she dared not have shown herself from her hiding-place. Taking the lamp in her hand, she got upon the chair, and looked over the screen, letting the light shine from below upon her face. She then made a slight noise to attract Karl's attention. He looked up, evidently rather startled, and saw the face of Lilith in the air. He gave a stifled cry, threw himself on his knees, with his arms stretched towards her, and moaned—

"I have killed her! I have killed her!"

Lilith descended, and approached him noiselessly. He did not move. She came close to him and said:

"Are you Karl Wolkenlicht?"

His lips moved, but no sound came.

"If you are a vampire, and I am a ghost," she said—but a low happy laugh alone concluded the sentence.

Karl sprang to his feet. Lilith's laugh changed into a burst of sobbing and weeping, and in another moment the ghost was in the arms of the vampire.

Lilith had no idea how far her father had wronged Karl, and though, from thinking over the past, he had no doubt that the painter had drugged him, he did not wish to pain her by imparting this conviction. But Lilith was afraid of a reaction of rage and hatred in her father after the terror was removed; and Karl saw that he might thus be deprived of all further intercourse with Lilith, and all chance of softening the old man's heart towards him; while Lilith would not hear of forsaking him who had banished all the human race but herself. They managed at length to agree upon a plan of operation.

The first thing they did was to go to the cellar where the plaster mass lay, Karl carrying with him a great axe used for cleaving wood. Lilith shuddered when she saw it, stained as it was with the wine Heinrich had spilt over it, and almost believed herself the midnight companion of a vampire after all, visiting with him the terrible corpse in which he lived all day. But Karl soon reassured her; and a few good blows of the axe revealed a very different core to that which Teufels-bürst supposed to be in it. Karl broke it into pieces, and with Lilith's

help, who insisted on carrying her share, the whole was soon at the
bottom of the Moldau, and every trace of its ever having existed
removed. Before morning, too, the form of Lilith had dawned anew in
every picture. There was no time to restore to its former condition the
one Karl had first altered; for in it the changes were all that they
seemed; nor indeed was he capable of restoring it in the master's style;
but they put it quite out of the way, and hoped that sufficient time
might elapse before the painter thought of it again.

When they had done, and Lilith, for all his entreaties, would remain
with him no longer, Karl took his former clothes with him, and having
spent the rest of the night in his old room, dressed in them in the
morning. When Teufelsbürst entered his studio next day, there sat Karl,
as if nothing had happened, finishing the drawing on which he had been
at work when the fit of insensibility came upon him. The painter
started, stared, rubbed his eyes, thought it was another spectral illusion,
but was on the point of yielding to his terror, when Karl rose, and
approached him with a smile. The healthy, sunshiny countenance of
Karl, let him be ghost or goblin, could not fail to produce somewhat of
a tranquillizing effect on Teufelsbürst. He took his offered hand me-
chanically, his countenance utterly vacant with idiotic bewilderment.
Karl said:

"I was not well, and thought it better to pay a visit to a friend for a
few days; but I shall soon make up for lost time, for I am all right
now."

He sat down at once, taking no notice of his master's behaviour,
and went on with his drawing. Teufelsbürst stood staring at him for
some minutes without moving, then suddenly turned and left the room.
Karl heard him hurrying down the cellar stairs. In a few moments he
came up again. Karl stole a glance at him. There he stood in the same
spot, no doubt more full of bewilderment than ever; but it was not
possible that his face should express more. At last he went to his easel,
and sat down with a long-drawn sigh as if of relief. But though he sat at
his easel, he painted none that day; and as often as Karl ventured a
glance, he saw him still staring at him. The discovery that his pictures
were restored to their former condition aided, no doubt, in leading him
to the same conclusion as the other facts, whatever that conclusion
might be—probably that he had been the sport of some evil power, and
had been for the greater part of a week utterly bewitched. Lilith had
taken care to instruct the old woman, with whom she was all-powerful;

and as neither of them showed the smallest traces of the astonishment
which seemed to be slowly vitrifying his own brain, he was at last
perfectly satisfied that things had been going on all right everywhere
but in his inner man; and in this conclusion he certainly was not far
wrong in more senses than one. But when all was restored again to the
old routine, it became evident that the peculiar direction of his art in
which he had hitherto indulged had ceased to interest him. The shock
had acted chiefly upon that part of his mental being which had been so
absorbed. He would sit for hours without doing anything, apparently
plunged in meditation. —Several weeks elapsed without any change, and
both Lilith and Karl were getting dreadfully anxious about him. Karl
paid him every attention; and the old man, for he now looked much
older than before, submitted to receive his services as well as those of
Lilith. At length, one morning, he said in a slow thoughtful tone:

"Karl Wolkenlicht, I should like to paint you."

"Certainly, sir," answered Karl, jumping up, "where would you like
me to sit?"

So the ice of silence and inactivity was broken, and the painter
drew and painted; and the spring of his art flowed once more; and he
made a beautiful portrait of Karl—a portrait without evil or suffering.
And as soon as he had finished Karl, he began once more to paint
Lilith; and when he had painted her, he composed a picture for the very
purpose of introducing them together; and in this picture there was
neither ugliness nor torture, but human feeling and human hope instead. Then Karl knew that he might speak to him of Lilith; and he
spoke, and was heard with a smile. But he did not dare to tell him the
truth of the vampire story till one day that Teufelsbürst was lying on
the floor of a room in Karl's ancestral castle, half smothered in
grand-children; when the only answer it drew from the old man was a
kind of shuddering laugh, and the words—"Don't speak of it, Karl, my
boy!"

VI
The Broken Swords

The eyes of three, two sisters and a brother, gazed for the last time on a great pale-golden star, that followed the sun down the steep west. It went down to arise again; and the brother about to depart might return, but more than the usual doubt hung upon his future. For between the white dresses of the sisters, shone his scarlet coat and golden sword-knot, which he had put on for the first time, more to gratify their pride than his own vanity. The brightening moon, as if prophetic of a future memory, had already begun to dim the scarlet and the gold, and to give them a pale, ghostly hue. In her thoughtful light the whole group seemed more like a meeting in the land of shadows, than a parting in the substantial earth.—But which should be called the land of realities?—the region where appearance, and space, and time drive between, and stop the flowing currents of the soul's speech? or that region where heart meets heart, and appearance has become the slave to utterance, and space and time are forgotten?

Through the quiet air came the far-off rush of water, and the near cry of the land-rail. Now and then a chilly wind blew unheeded through the startled and jostling leaves that shaded the ivy-seat. Else, there was calm everywhere, rendered yet deeper and more intense by the dusky sorrow that filled their hearts. For, far away, hundreds of miles beyond the hearing of their ears, roared the great war-guns; next week their brother must sail with his regiment to join the army; and to-morrow he must leave his home.

The sisters looked on him tenderly, with vague fears about his fate. Yet little they divined it. That the face they loved might lie pale and bloody, in a heap of slain, was the worst image of it that arose before them; but this, had they seen the future, they would, in ignorance of the further future, have infinitely preferred to that which awaited him. And even while they looked on him, a dim feeling of the unsuitableness of his lot filled their minds. For, indeed, to all judgments it must have seemed unsuitable that the home-boy, the loved of his mother, the pet of his sisters, who was happy, womanlike (as Coleridge says), if he

Reprinted from *Monthly Christian Spectator* (1854).

possessed the signs of love, having never yet sought for its proofs—that he should be sent amongst soldiers, to command and be commanded; to kill, or perhaps to be himself crushed out of the fair earth in the uproar that brings back for the moment the reign of Night and Chaos. No wonder that to his sisters it seemed strange and sad. Yet such was their own position in the battle of life, in which their father had died with doubtful conquest, that when their old military uncle sent the boy an ensign's commission, they did not dream of refusing the only path open, as they thought, to an honourable profession, even though it might lead to the trench-grave. They heard it as the voice of destiny, wept, and yielded.

If they had possessed a deeper insight into his character, they would have discovered yet further reason to doubt the fitness of the profession chosen for him; and if they had ever seen him at school, it is possible the doubt of fitness might have strengthened into a certainty of incongruity. His comparative inactivity amongst his schoolfellows, though occasioned by no dulness of intellect, might have suggested the necessity of a quiet life, if inclination and liking had been the arbiters in the choice. Nor was this inactivity the result of defective animal spirits either, for sometimes his mirth and boyish frolic were unbounded; but it seemed to proceed from an over-activity of the inward life, absorbing, and in some measure checking, the outward manifestation. He had so much to do in his own hidden kingdom, that he had not time to take his place in the polity and strife of the commonwealth around him. Hence, while other boys were acting, he was thinking. In this point of difference, he felt keenly the superiority of many of his companions; for another boy would have the obstacle overcome, or the adversary subdued, while he was meditating on the propriety, or on the means, of effecting the desired end. He envied their promptitude, while they never saw reason to envy his wisdom; for his conscience, tender and not strong, frequently transformed slowness of determination into irresolution: while a delicacy of the sympathetic nerves tended to distract him from any predetermined course, by the diversity of their vibrations, responsive to influences from all quarters, and destructive to unity of purpose.

Of such a one, the *a priori* judgment would be, that he ought to be left to meditate and grow for some time, before being called upon to produce the fruits of action. But add to these mental conditions a vivid imagination, and a high sense of honour, nourished in childhood by the reading of the old knightly romances, and then put the youth in a position in which action is imperative, and you have elements of strife sufficient to reduce that fair kingdom of his to utter anarchy and madness. Yet so little do we know ourselves, and so different are the symbols with which the imagination works its algebra, from the realities which those symbols represent, that as yet the youth felt no uneasiness, but contemplated his new calling with a glad enthusiasm and some vanity; for all his prospect lay in the glow of the scarlet and the gold. Nor did this excitement receive any check till the day before his departure, on which day I have introduced him to my readers, when, accidentally taking up a newspaper of a week old, his eye fell on these words—"*Already crying women are to be met in the streets.*" With this cloud afar on his horizon, which, though no bigger than a man's hand, yet cast a perceptible shadow over his mind, he departed next morning. The coach carried him beyond the consecrated circle of home laws and impulses, out into the great tumult, above which rises ever and anon the cry of Cain, "Am I my brother's keeper?"

Every tragedy of higher order, constructed in Christian times, will correspond more or less to the grand drama of the Bible; wherein the first act opens with a brilliant sunset vision of Paradise, in which childish sense and need are served with all the profusion of the indulgent nurse. But the glory fades off into grey and black, and night settles down upon the heart which, rightly uncontent with the childish, and not having yet learned the childlike, seeks knowledge and manhood as a thing denied by the Maker, and yet to be gained by the creature; so sets forth alone to climb the heavens, and instead of climbing, falls into the abyss. Then follows the long dismal night of feverish efforts and delirious visions, or, it may be, helpless despair; till at length a deeper stratum of the soul is heaved to the surface; and amid the first dawn of morning, the youth says within him, "I have sinned against my *Maker*—I will arise and go to my *Father.*" More or less, I say, will Christian tragedy correspond to this—a fall and a rising again; not a rising only, but a victory; not a victory merely, but a triumph. Such, in its way and degree, is my story. I have shown, in one passing scene, the home paradise; now I have to show a scene of a far differing nature.

The young ensign was lying in his tent, weary, but wakeful. All day long the cannon had been bellowing against the walls of the city, which now lay with wide, gaping breach, ready for the morrow's storm, but covered yet with the friendly darkness. His regiment was ordered to be

ready with the earliest dawn to march up to the breach. That day, for
the first time, there had been blood on his sword—there the sword lay,
a spot on the chased hilt still. He had cut down one of the enemy in a
skirmish with a sally party of the besieged, and the look of the man as
he fell, haunted him. He felt, for the time, that he dared not pray to the
Father, for the blood of a brother had rushed forth at the stroke of his
arm, and there was one fewer of living souls on the earth because he
lived thereon. And to-morrow he must lead a troop of men up to that
poor disabled town, and turn them loose upon it, not knowing what
might follow in the triumph of enraged and victorious foes, who for
weeks had been subjected, by the constancy of the place, to the
greatest privations. It was true the general had issued his commands
against all disorder and pillage; but if the soldiers once yielded to
temptation, what might not be done before the officers could reclaim
them! All the wretched tales he had read of the sack of cities rushed
back on his memory. He shuddered as he lay. Then his conscience
began to speak, and to ask what right he had to be there.—Was the war
a just one?—He could not tell; for this was a bad time for settling nice
questions. But there he was, right or wrong, fighting and shedding
blood on God's earth, beneath God's heaven.

Over and over he turned the question in his mind; again and again
the spouting blood of his foe, and the death-look in his eye, rose before
him; and the youth who at school could never fight with a companion
because he was not sure that he was in the right, was alone in the midst
of undoubting men of war, amongst whom he was driven helplessly
along, upon the waves of a terrible necessity. What wonder that in the
midst of these perplexities his courage should fail him! What wonder
that the consciousness of fainting should increase the faintness! or that
the dread of fear and its consequences should hasten and invigorate its
attacks! To crown all, when he dropped into a troubled slumber at
length, he found himself hurried, as on a storm of fire, through the
streets of the captured town, from all the windows of which looked
forth familiar faces, old and young, but distorted from the memory of
his boyhood by fear and wild despair. On one spot lay the body of his
father, with his face to the earth; and he woke at the cry of horror and
rage that burst from his own lips, as he saw the rough, bloody hand of a
soldier twisted in the loose hair of his elder sister, and the younger
fainting in the arms of a scoundrel belonging to his own regiment.

He slept no more. As the grey morning broke, the troops appointed for the attack assembled without sound of trumpet or drum, and were silently formed in fitting order. The young ensign was in his place, weary and wretched after his miserable night. Before him he saw a great, broad-shouldered lieutenant, whose brawny hand seemed almost too large for his sword-hilt, and in any one of whose limbs played more animal life than in the whole body of the pale youth. The firm-set lips of this officer, and the fire of his eye, showed a concentrated resolution, which, by the contrast, increased the misery of the ensign, and seemed, as if the stronger absorbed the weaker, to draw out from him the last fibres of self-possession: the sight of unattainable determination, while it increased the feeling of the arduousness of that which required such determination, threw him into the great gulf which lay between him and it. In this disorder of his nervous and mental condition, with a doubting conscience and a shrinking heart, is it any wonder that the terrors which lay before him at the gap in those bristling walls, should draw near, and, making sudden inroad upon his soul, overwhelm the government of a will worn out by the tortures of an unassured spirit? What share fear contributed to unman him, it was impossible for him, in the dark, confused conflict of differing emotions, to determine; but doubtless a natural shrinking from danger, there being no excitement to deaden its influence, and no hope of victory to encourage to the struggle, seeing victory was dreadful to him as defeat, had its part in the sad result. Many men who have courage, are dependent on ignorance and a low state of the moral feeling for that courage; and a further progress towards the development of the higher nature would, for a time at least, entirely overthrow it. Nor could such loss of courage be rightly designated by the name of cowardice.

But, alas! the colonel happened to fix his eyes upon him as he passed along the file; and this completed his confusion. He betrayed such evident symptoms of perturbation, than that officer ordered him under arrest; and the result was, that, chiefly for the sake of example to the army, he was, upon trial by court-martial, expelled from the service, and had his sword broken over his head. Alas for the delicate-minded youth! Alas for the home-darling!

Long after, he found at the bottom of his chest the pieces of the broken sword, and remembered that, at the time, he had lifted them from the ground and carried them away. But he could not recall under what impulse he had done so. Perhaps the agony he suffered, passing the bounds of mortal endurance, had opened for him a vista into the

eternal, and had shown him, if not the injustice of the sentence passed
upon him, yet his freedom from blame, or, endowing him with dim
prophetic vision, had given him the assurance that some day the stain
would be wiped from his soul, and leave him standing clear before the
tribunal of his own honour. Some feeling like this, I say, may have
caused him, with a passing gleam of indignant protest, to lift the
fragments from the earth, and carry them away; even as the friends of a
so-called traitor may bear away his mutilated body from the wheel. But
if such was the case, the vision was soon overwhelmed and forgotten in
the succeeding anguish. He could not see that, in mercy to his doubting
spirit, the question which had agitated his mind almost to madness, and
which no results of the impending conflict could have settled for him,
was thus quietly set aside for the time; nor that, painful as was the
dark, dreadful existence that he was now to pass in self-torment and
moaning, it would go by, and leave his spirit clearer far, than if, in his
apprehension, it had been stained with further blood-guiltiness, instead
of the loss of honour. Years after, when he accidentally learned that on
that very morning the whole of his company, with parts of several
more, had, or ever they began to mount the breach, been blown to
pieces by the explosion of a mine, he cried aloud in bitterness, "Would
God that my fear had not been discovered before I reached that spot!"
But surely it is better to pass into the next region of life having reaped
some assurance, some firmness of character, determination of effort,
and consciousness of the worth of life, in the present world; so
approaching the future steadily and faithfully, and if in much darkness
and ignorance, yet not in the oscillations of moral uncertainty.

Close upon the catastrophe followed a torpor, which lasted he did
not know how long, and which wrapped in a thick fog all the succeeding events. For some time he can hardly be said to have had any
conscious history. He awoke to life and torture when half-way across
the sea towards his native country, where was no home any longer for
him. To this point, and no farther, could his thoughts return in after
years. But the misery which he then endured is hardly to be understood, save by those of like delicate temperament with himself. All day
long he sat silent in his cabin; nor could any effort of the captain, or
others on board, induce him to go on deck till night came on, when,
under the starlight, he ventured into the open air. The sky soothed him
then, he knew not how. For the face of nature is the face of God, and
must bear expressions that can influence, though unconsciously to

them, the most ignorant and hopeless of His children. Often did he watch the clouds in hope of a storm, his spirit rising and falling as the sky darkened or cleared; he longed, in the necessary selfishness of such suffering, for a tumult of waters to swallow the vessel; and only the recollection of how many lives were involved in its safety besides his own, prevented him from praying to God for lightning and tempest, borne on which he might dash into the haven of the other world. One night, following a sultry calm day, he thought that Mercy had heard his unuttered prayer. The air and sea were intense darkness, till a light as intense for one moment annihilated it, and the succeeding darkness seemed shattered with the sharp reports of the thunder that cracked without reverberation. He who had shrunk from battle with his fellow-men, rushed to the mainmast, threw himself on his knees, and stretched forth his arms in speechless energy of supplication; but the storm passed away overhead, and left him kneeling still by the uninjured mast. At length the vessel reached her port. He hurried on shore to bury himself in the most secret place he could find. *Out of sight* was his first, his only thought. Return to his mother he would not, he could not; and, indeed, his friends never learned his fate, until it had carried him far beyond their reach.

For several weeks he lurked about like a malefactor, in low lodging-houses in narrow streets of the seaport to which the vessel had borne him, heeding no one, and but little shocked at the strange society and conversation with which, though only in bodily presence, he had to mingle. These formed the subjects of reflection in after times; and he came to the conclusion that, though much evil and much misery exist, sufficient to move prayers and tears in those who love their kind, yet there is less of both than those looking down from a more elevated social position upon the weltering heap of humanity, are ready to imagine; especially if they regard it likewise from the pedestal of self-congratulation on which a meagre type of religion has elevated them. But at length his little stock of money was nearly expended, and there was nothing that he could do, or learn to do, in this seaport. He felt impelled to seek manual labour, partly because he thought it more likely he could obtain that sort of employment, without a request for reference as to his character, which would lead to inquiry about his previous history; and partly, perhaps, from an instinctive feeling that hard bodily labour would tend to lessen his inward suffering.

He left the town, therefore, at nightfall of a July day, carrying a

little bundle of linen, and the remains of his money, somewhat aug-
mented by the sale of various articles of clothing and convenience,
which his change of life rendered superfluous and unsuitable. He
directed his course northwards, travelling principally by night—so painfully did he shrink from the gaze even of footfarers like himself; and
sleeping during the day in some hidden nook of wood or thicket, or
under the shadow of a great tree in a solitary field. So fine was the
season, that for three successive weeks he was able to travel thus
without inconvenience, lying down when the sun grew hot in the
forenoon, and generally waking when the first faint stars were hesi-
tating in the great darkening heavens that covered and shielded him.
For above every cloud, above every storm, rise up, calm, clear, divine,
the deep infinite skies; they embrace the tempest even as the sunshine;
by their permission it exists within their boundless peace: therefore it
cannot hurt, and must pass away, while there they stand as ever, domed
up eternally, lasting, strong, and pure.

Several times he attempted to get agricultural employment; but the
whiteness of his hands and the tone of his voice not merely suggested
unfitness for labour, but generated suspicion as to the character of one
who had evidently dropped from a rank so much higher, and was
seeking admittance within the natural masonic boundaries and secrets
and privileges of another. Disheartened somewhat, but hopeful, he
journeyed on. I say hopeful; for the blessed power of life in the
universe, in fresh air and sunshine absorbed by active exercise, in winds,
yea in rain, though it fell but seldom, had begun to work its natural
healing, soothing effect, upon his perturbed spirit. And there was room
for hope in his new endeavour. As his bodily strength increased, and his
health, considerably impaired by inward suffering, improved, the trouble of his soul became more endurable—and in some measure to endure
is to conquer and destroy. In proportion as the mind grows in the
strength of patience, the disturber of its peace sickens and fades away.
At length, one day, a widow lady in a village through which his road led
him, gave him a day's work in her garden. He laboured hard and well,
notwithstanding his soon-blistered hands, received his wages thankfully,
and found a resting-place for the night on the low part of a hay-stack
from which the upper portion had been cut away. Here he ate his
supper of bread and cheese, pleased to have found such comfortable
quarters, and soon fell fast asleep.

When he awoke, the whole heavens and earth seemed to give a full
denial to sin and sorrow. The sun was just mounting over the horizon,

looking up the clear cloud-mottled sky. From millions of water-drops hanging on the bending stalks of grass, sparkled his rays in varied refraction, transformed here to a gorgeous burning ruby, there to an emerald, green as the grass, and yonder to a flashing, sunny topaz. The chanting priest-lark had gone up from the low earth, as soon as the heavenly light had begun to enwrap and illumine the folds of its tabernacle; and had entered the high heavens with his offering, whence, unseen, he now dropped on the earth the sprinkled sounds of his overflowing blessedness. The poor youth rose but to kneel, and cry, from a bursting heart, "Hast Thou not, O Father, some care for me? Canst Thou not restore my lost honour? Can anything befall Thy children for which Thou hast no help? Surely, if the face of Thy world lie not, joy and not grief is at the heart of the universe. Is there none for me?"

The highest poetic feeling of which we are now conscious, springs not from the beholding of perfected beauty, but from the mute sympathy which the creation with all its children manifests with us in the groaning and travailing which look for the sonship. Because of our need and aspiration, the snowdrop gives birth in our hearts to a loftier spiritual and poetic feeling, than the rose most complete in form, colour, and odour. The rose is of Paradise—the snowdrop is of the striving, hoping, longing Earth. Perhaps our highest poetry is the expression of our aspirations in the sympathetic forms of visible nature. Nor is this merely a longing for a restored Paradise; for even in the ordinary history of men, no man or woman that has fallen, can be restored to the position formerly held. Such must rise to a yet higher place, whence they can behold their former standing far beneath their feet. They must be restored by the attainment of something better than they ever possessed before, or not at all. If the law be a weariness, we must escape it by taking refuge with the spirit, for not otherwise can we fulfil the law than by being above the law. To escape the overhanging rocks of Sinai, we must climb to its secret top.

> "Is thy strait horizon dreary?
> Is thy foolish fancy chill?
> Change the feet that have grown weary
> For the wings that never will."

Thus, like one of the wandering knights searching the wide earth for the Sangreal, did he wander on, searching for his lost honour, or rather (for that he counted gone for ever) seeking unconsciously for the peace of mind which had departed from him, and taken with it, not the joy merely, but almost the possibility, of existence.

At last, when his little store was all but exhausted, he was employed by a market gardener, in the neighbourhood of a large country town, to work in his garden, and sometimes take his vegetables to market. With him he continued for a few weeks, and wished for no change; until, one day driving his cart through the town, he saw approaching him an elderly gentleman, whom he knew at once, by his gait and carriage, to be a military man. Now he had never seen his uncle the retired officer, but it struck him that this might be he; and under the tyranny of his passion for concealment, he fancied that, if it were he, he might recognise him by some family likeness—not considering the improbability of his looking at him. This fancy, with the painful effect which the sight of an officer, even in plain clothes, had upon him, recalling the torture of that frightful day, so overcame him, that he found himself at the other end of an alley before he recollected that he had the horse and cart in charge. This increased his difficulty; for now he dared not return, lest his inquiries after the vehicle, if the horse had strayed from the direct line, should attract attention, and cause interrogations which he would be unable to answer. The fatal want of self-possession seemed again to ruin him. He forsook the town by the nearest way, struck across the country to another line of road, and before he was missed, was miles away, still in a northerly direction.

But although he thus shunned the face of man, especially of any one who reminded him of the past, the loss of his reputation in their eyes was not the cause of his inward grief. That would have been comparatively powerless to disturb him, had he not lost his own respect. He quailed before his own thoughts; he was dishonoured in his own eyes. His perplexity had not yet sufficiently cleared away to allow him to see the extenuating circumstances of the case; not to say the fact that the peculiar mental condition in which he was at the time, removed the case quite out of the class of ordinary instances of cowardice. He condemned himself more severely than any of his judges would have dared; remembering that portion of his mental sensations which had savoured of fear, and forgetting the causes which had produced it. He judged himself a man stained with the foulest blot that could cleave to a soldier's name, a blot which nothing but death, not even death, could efface. But, inwardly condemned and outwardly degraded, his dread of recognition was intense; and feeling that he was in more danger of being discovered where the population was sparser, he resolved to hide himself once more in the midst of poverty; and, with this view, found his way to one of the largest of the manufacturing towns.

He reached it during the strike of a great part of the workmen; so that, though he found some difficulty in procuring employment, as might be expected from his ignorance of machine-labour, he yet was sooner successful than he would otherwise have been. Possessed of a natural aptitude for mechanical operations, he soon became a tolerable workman; and he found that his previous education assisted to the fitting execution of those operations even which were most purely mechanical.

He found also, at first, that the unrelaxing attention requisite for the mastering of the many niceties of his work, of necessity drew his mind somewhat from its brooding over his misfortune, hitherto almost ceaseless. Every now and then, however, a pang would shoot suddenly to his heart, and turn his face pale, even before his consciousness had time to inquire what was the matter. So by degrees, as attention became less necessary, and the nervo-mechanical action of his system increased with use, his thoughts again returned to their old misery. He would wake at night in his poor room, with the feeling that a ghostly nightmare sat on his soul; that a want—a loss—miserable, fearful—was present; that something of his heart was gone from him; and through the darkness he would hear the snap of the breaking sword, and lie for a moment overwhelmed beneath the assurance of the incredible fact. Could it be true that *he* was a coward? that *his* honour was gone, and in its place a stain? that *he* was a thing for men—and worse, for women—to point the finger at, laughing bitter laughter? Never lover or husband could have mourned with the same desolation over the departure of the loved; the girl alone, weeping scorching tears over *her* degradation, could resemble him in his agony, as he lay on his bed, and wept and moaned.

His sufferings had returned with the greater weight, that he was no longer upheld by the "divine air" and the open heavens, whose sunlight now only reached him late in an afternoon, as he stood at his loom, through windows so coated with dust that they looked like frosted glass; showing, as it passed through the air to fall on the dirty floor, how the breath of life was thick with dust of iron and wood, and films

of cotton; amidst which his senses were now too much dulled by
custom to detect the exhalations from greasy wheels and overtasked
human-kind. Nor could he find comfort in the society of his fellow-
labourers. True, it was a kind of comfort to have those near him who
could not know of his grief; but there was so little in common between
them, that any interchange of thought was impossible. At least, so it
seemed to him. Yet sometimes his longing for human companionship
would drive him out of his dreary room at night, and send him
wandering through the lower part of the town, where he would gaze
wistfully on the miserable faces that passed him, as if looking for some
one—some angel, even there—to speak goodwill to his hungry heart.

Once he entered one of those gin-palaces, which, like the golden
gates of hell, entice the miserable to worse misery, and seated himself
close to a half-tipsy, good-natured wretch, who made room for him on
a bench by the wall. He was comforted even by this proximity to one
who would not repel him. But soon the paintings of warlike action—of
knights, and horses, and mighty deeds done with battle-axe, and broadsword, which adorned the panels all round, drove him forth even from
this heaven of the damned; yet not before the impious thought had
arisen in his heart, that the brilliantly painted and sculptural roof, with
the gilded vine-leaves and bunches of grapes trained up the windows, all
lighted with the great shining chandeliers, was only a microcosmic
repetition of the bright heavens and the glowing earth, that overhung
and surrounded the misery of man. But the memory of how kindly
they had comforted and elevated him, at one period of his painful
history, not only banished the wicked thought, but brought him more
quiet, in the resurrection of a past blessing, than he had known for
some time. The period, however, was now at hand when a new grief,
followed by a new and more elevated activity, was to do its part
towards the closing up of the fountain of bitterness.

Amongst his fellow-labourers, he had for a short time taken some
interest in observing a young woman, who had lately joined them.
There was nothing remarkable about her, except what at first sight
seemed a remarkable plainness. A slight scar over one of her rather
prominent eyebrows, increased this impression of plainness. But the
first day had not passed, before he began to see that there was
something not altogether common in those deep eyes; and the plain
look vanished before a closer observation, which also discovered, in the
forehead and the lines of the mouth, traces of sorrow or other suf-

fering. There was an expression, too, in the whole face, of fixedness of purpose, without any hardness of determination. Her countenance altogether seemed the index to an interesting mental history. Signs of mental trouble were always an attraction to him; in this case so great, that he overcame his shyness, and spoke to her one evening as they left the works. He often walked home with her after that; as, indeed, was natural, seeing that she occupied an attic in the same poor lodging-house in which he lived himself. The street did not bear the best character; nor, indeed, would the occupations of all the inmates of the house have stood investigation; but so retiring and quiet was this girl, and so seldom did she go abroad after work hours, that he had not discovered till then that she lived in the same street, not to say the same house, with himself.

He soon learned her history—a very common one as outward events, but not surely insignificant because common. Her father and mother were both dead, and hence she had to find her livelihood alone, and amidst associations which were always disagreeable, and sometimes painful. Her quick womanly instinct must have discovered that he too had a history; for though, his mental prostration favouring the operation of outward influences, he had greatly approximated in appearance to those amongst whom he laboured, there were yet signs, besides the educated accent of his speech, which would have distinguished him to an observer; but she put no questions to him, nor made any approach towards seeking a return of the confidence she reposed in him. It was a sensible alleviation to his sufferings to hear her kind voice, and look in her gentle face, as they walked home together; and at length the expectation of this pleasure began to present itself, in the midst of the busy, dreary work-hours, as the shadow of a heaven to close up the dismal, uninteresting day.

But one morning he missed her from her place, and a keener pain passed through him than he had felt of late; for he knew that the Plague was abroad, feeding in the low stagnant places of human abode; and he had but too much reason to dread that she might be now struggling in its grasp. He seized the first opportunity of slipping out and hurrying home. He sprang upstairs to her room. He found the door locked, but heard a faint moaning within. To avoid disturbing her, while determined to gain an entrance, he went down for the key of his own door, with which he succeeded in unlocking hers, and so crossed her threshold for the first time. There she lay on her bed, tossing in pain, and beginning to be delirious. Careless of his own life, and feeling that he could not die better than in helping the only friend he had; certain, likewise, of the difficulty of finding a nurse for one in this disease and of her station in life; and sure, likewise, that there could be no question of propriety, either in the circumstances with which they were surrounded, nor in this case of terrible fever almost as hopeless for her as dangerous to him, he instantly began the duties of a nurse, and returned no more to his employment. He had a little money in his possession, for he could not, in the way in which he lived, spend all his wages; so he proceeded to make her as comfortable as he could, with all the pent-up tenderness of a loving heart finding an outlet at length. When a boy at home, he had often taken the place of nurse, and he felt quite capable of performing its duties. Nor was his boyhood far behind yet, although the trials he had come through made it appear an age since he had lost his light heart. So he never left her bedside, except to procure what was necessary for her. She was too ill to oppose any of his measures, or to seek to prohibit his presence. Indeed, by the time he had returned with the first medicine, she was insensible; and she continued so through the whole of the following week, during which time he was constantly with her.

That action produces feeling is as often true as its converse; and it is not surprising that, while he smoothed the pillow for her head, he should have made a nest in his heart for the helpless girl. Slowly and unconsciously he learned to love her. The chasm between his early associations and the circumstances in which he found her, vanished as he drew near to the simple, essential womanhood. His heart saw hers and loved it; and he knew that, the centre once gained, he could, as from the fountain of life, as from the innermost secret of the holy place, the hidden germ of power and possibility, transform the outer intellect and outermost manners as he pleased. With what a thrill of joy, a feeling for a long time unknown to him, and till now never known in this form or with this intensity, the thought arose in his heart that here lay one who some day would love him; that he should have a place of refuge and rest; one to lie in his bosom and not despise him! "For," said he to himself, "I will call forth her soul from where it sleeps, like an unawakened echo, in an unknown cave; and like a child, of whom I once dreamed, that was mine, and to my delight turned in fear from all besides, and clung to me, this soul of hers will run with bewildered, half-sleeping eyes, and tottering steps, but with a cry of joy on its lips, to me as the life-giver. She will cling to me and worship me. Then will I tell her, for she must know all, that I am low and contemptible; that I am an outcast from the world, and that if she receive me, she will be to me as God. And I will fall down at her feet and pray her for comfort, for life, for restoration to myself; and she will throw herself beside me, and weep and love me, I know. And we will go through life together, working hard, but for each other; and when we die, she shall lead me into paradise as the prize her angel-hand found cast on a desert shore, from the storm of winds and waves which I was too weak to resist—and raised, and tended, and saved." Often did such thoughts as these pass through his mind while watching her bed; alternated, checked, and sometimes destroyed, by the fears which attended her precarious condition, but returning with every apparent betterment or hopeful symptom.

I will not stop to decide the nice question, how far the intention was right, of causing her to love him before she knew his story. If in the whole matter there was too much thought of self, my only apology is the sequel. One day, the ninth from the commencement of her illness, a letter arrived, addressed to her; which he, thinking he might prevent some inconvenience thereby, opened and read, in the confidence of that love which already made her and all belonging to her appear his own. It was from a soldier—*her lover*. It was plain that they had been betrothed before he left for the continent a year ago; but this was the first letter which he had written to her. It breathed changeless love, and hope, and confidence in her. He was so fascinated that he read it through without pause.

Laying it down, he sat pale, motionless, almost inanimate. From the hard-won sunny heights, he was once more cast down into the shadow of death. The second storm of his life began, howling and raging, with yet more awful lulls between. "Is she not *mine*?" he said, in agony. "Do I not feel that she is mine? Who will watch over her as I? Who will kiss her soul to life as I? Shall she be torn away from me, when my soul seems to have dwelt with hers for ever in an eternal house? But have I not a right to her? Have I not given my life for hers? Is he not a soldier, and are there not many chances that he may never return? And it may be that, although they were engaged in word, soul has never touched soul with them; their love has never reached that point where it passes from the mortal to the immortal, the indissoluble: and so, in a sense, she may be yet free. Will he do for her what I will do? Shall this precious heart of hers, in which I see the buds of so many beauties, be left to wither and die?"

But here the voice within him cried out, "Art thou the disposer of destinies? Wilt thou, in a universe where the visible God hath died for the Truth's sake, do evil that a good, which He might neglect or overlook, may be gained? Leave thou her to Him, and do thou right." And he said within himself, "Now is the real trial for my life! Shall I conquer or no?" And his heart awoke and cried, "I will. God forgive me for wronging the poor soldier! A brave man, brave at least, is better for her than I."

A great strength arose within him, and lifted him up to depart. "Surely I may kiss her once," he said. For the crisis was over, and she slept. He stooped towards her face, but before he had reached her lips he saw her eyelids tremble; and he who had longed for the opening of those eyes, as of the gates of heaven, that she might love him, stricken now with fear lest she should love him, fled from her, before the eyelids that hid such strife and such victory from the unconscious maiden had time to unclose. But it was agony—quietly to pack up his bundle of linen in the room below, when he knew she was lying awake above, with her dear, pale face, and living eyes! What remained of his money, except a few shillings, he put up in a scrap of paper, and went out with his bundle in his hand, first to seek a nurse for his friend, and then to go he knew not whither. He met the factory people with whom he had worked, going to dinner, and amongst them a girl who had herself but lately recovered from the fever, and was yet hardly able for work. She was the only friend the sick girl had seemed to have amongst the women at the factory, and she was easily persuaded to go and take charge of her. He put the money in her hand, begging her to use it for the invalid, and promising to send the equivalent of her wages for the time he thought she would have to wait on her. This he easily did by the sale of a ring, which, besides his mother's watch, was the only article of value he had retained. He begged her likewise not to mention his name in the matter; and was foolish enough to expect that she would entirely keep the promise she had made him.

Wandering along the street, purposeless now and bereft, he spied a recruiting party at the door of a public-house; and on coming nearer, found, by one of those strange coincidences which do occur in life, and which have possibly their root in a hidden and wondrous law, that it was a party, perhaps a remnant, of the very regiment in which he had himself served, and in which his misfortune had befallen him. Almost simultaneously with the shock which the sight of the well-known number on the soldiers' knapsacks gave him, arose in his mind the romantic, ideal thought, of enlisting in the ranks of this same regiment, and recovering, as a private soldier and unknown, that honour which as officer he had lost. To this determination, the new necessity in which he now stood for action and change of life, doubtless contributed, though unconsciously. He offered himself to the sergeant; and, notwith- standing that his dress indicated a mode of life unsuitable as the antecedent to a soldier's, his appearance, and the necessity for recruits combined, led to his easy acceptance.

The English armies were employed in expelling the enemy from an invaded and helpless country. Whatever might be the political motives which had induced the Government to this measure, the young man was now able to feel that he could go and fight, individually and for his part, in the cause of liberty. He was free to possess his own motives for joining in the execution of the schemes of those who commanded his commanders.

With a heavy heart, but with more of inward hope and strength than he had ever known before, he marched with his comrades to the seaport and embarked. It seemed to him that because he had done right in his last trial, here was a new glorious chance held out to his hand. True, it was a terrible change to pass from a woman in whom he had hoped to find healing, into the society of rough men, to march with them, *"mit gleichem Tritt und Schritt,"* up to the bristling bayonets or the horrid vacancy of the cannon mouth. But it was the only cure for the evil that consumed his life.

He reached the army in safety, and gave himself, with religious assiduity, to the smallest duties of his new position. No one had a brighter polish on his arms, or whiter belts than he. In the necessary movements, he soon became precise to a degree that attracted the attention of his officers; while his character was remarkable for all the virtues belonging to a perfect soldier.

One day, as he stood sentry, he saw the eyes of his colonel intently fixed on him. He felt his lip quiver, but he compressed and stilled it, and tried to look as unconscious as he could; which effort was assisted by the formal bearing required by his position. Now the colonel, such had been the losses of the regiment, had been promoted from a lieutenancy in the same, and had belonged to it at the time of the ensign's degradation. Indeed, had not the changes in the regiment been so great, he could hardly have escaped so long without discovery. But the poor fellow would have felt that his name was already free of reproach, if he had seen what followed on the close inspection which had awakened his apprehensions, and which, in fact, had convinced the colonel of his identity with the disgraced ensign. With a hasty and less soldierly step than usual, the colonel entered his tent, threw himself on his bed, and wept like a child. When he rose he was overheard to say these words— and these only escaped his lips: "He is nobler than I."

But this officer showed himself worthy of commanding such men as this private; for right nobly did he understand and meet his feelings. He uttered no word of the discovery he had made, till years afterwards; but it soon began to be remarked that whenever anything arduous, or in any manner distinguished, had to be done, this man was sure to be of the party appointed. In short, as often as he could, the colonel "set him in the forefront of the battle." Passing through all with wonderful escape, he was soon as much noticed for his reckless bravery, as hitherto for his precision in the discharge of duties, bringing only commendation and not honour. But his final lustration was at hand.

A great part of the army was hastening, by forced marches, to raise the siege of a town which was already on the point of falling into the hands of the enemy. Forming one of a reconnoitring party, which preceded the main body at some considerable distance, he and his companions came suddenly upon one of the enemy's outposts, occupying a high, and on one side precipitous rock, a short way from the town, which it commanded. Retreat was impossible, for they were already discovered, and the bullets were falling amongst them like the first of a hail-storm. The only possibility of escape remaining for them was a nearly hopeless improbability. It lay in forcing the post on this steep rock; which if they could do before assistance came to the enemy, they might, perhaps, be able to hold out, by means of its defences, till the arrival of the army. Their position was at once understood by all; and, by a sudden, simultaneous impulse, they found themselves half-way up the steep ascent, and in the struggle of a close conflict, without being aware of any order to that effect from their officer. But their courage was of no avail; the advantages of the place were too great; and in a few minutes the whole party was cut to pieces, or stretched helpless on the rock. Our youth had fallen amongst the foremost; for a musket ball had grazed his skull, and laid him insensible.

But consciousness slowly returned, and he succeeded at last in raising himself and looking around him. The place was deserted. A few of his friends, alive, but grievously wounded, lay near him. The rest were dead. It appeared that, learning the proximity of the English forces from this rencontre with part of their advanced guard, and dreading lest the town, which was on the point of surrendering, should after all be snatched from their grasp, the commander of the enemy's forces had ordered an immediate and general assault; and had for this purpose recalled from their outposts the whole of his troops thus stationed, that he might make the attempt with the utmost strength he could accumulate.

As the youth's power of vision returned, he perceived, from the height where he lay, that the town was already in the hands of the enemy. But looking down into the level space immediately below him, he started to his feet at once; for a girl, bare-headed, was fleeing towards the rock, pursued by several soldiers. "Aha!" said he, divining her purpose—the soldiers behind and the rock before her—"I will help you to die!" And he stooped and wrenched from the dead fingers of a sergeant the sword which they clenched by the bloody hilt. A new throb of life pulsed through him to his very finger-tips; and on the brink of the unseen world he stood, with the blood rushing through his veins in a wild dance of excitement. One who lay near him wounded, but recovered afterwards, said that he looked like one inspired. With a keen eye he watched the chase. The girl drew nigh; and rushed up the path near which he was standing. Close on her footsteps came the soldiers, the distance gradually lessening between them.

Not many paces higher up, was a narrower part of the ascent, where the path was confined by great stones, or pieces of rock. Here had been the chief defence in the preceding assault, and in it lay many bodies of his friends. Thither he went and took his stand.

On the girl came, over the dead, with rigid hands and flying feet, the bloodless skin drawn tight on her features, and her eyes awfully large and wild. She did not see him though she bounded past so near that her hair flew in his eyes. "Never mind!" said he, "we shall meet soon." And he stepped into the narrow path just in time to face her pursuers—between her and them. Like the red lightning the bloody sword fell, and a man beneath it. Cling! clang! went the echoes in the rocks—and another man was down; for, in his excitement, he was a destroying angel to the breathless pursuers. His stature rose, his chest dilated; and as the third foe fell dead, the girl was safe; for her body lay a broken, empty, but undesecrated temple, at the foot of the rock. That moment his sword flew in shivers from his grasp. The next instant he fell, pierced to the heart; and his spirit rose triumphant, free, strong, and calm, above the stormy world, which at length lay vanquished beneath him.

VII
The Wow O' Rivven
[The Bell]

Elsie Scott had let her work fall on her knees, and her hands on her work, and was looking out of the wide, low window of her room, which was on one of the ground floors of the village street. Through a gap in the household shrubbery of fuchsias and myrtles filling the window-sill, one passing on the foot-pavement might get a momentary glimpse of her pale face, lighted up with two blue eyes, over which some inward trouble had spread a faint, gauze-like haziness. But almost before her thoughts had had time to wander back to this trouble, a shout of children's voices, at the other end of the street, reached her ear. She listened a moment. A shadow of displeasure and pain crossed her countenance; and rising hastily, she betook herself to an inner apartment, and closed the door behind her.

Meantime the sounds drew nearer; and by and by, an old man, whose strange appearance and dress showed that he had little capacity either for good or evil, passed the window. His clothes were comfortable enough in quality and condition, for they were the annual gift of a benevolent lady in the neighbourhood; but, being made to accommodate his taste, both known and traditional, they were somewhat peculiar in cut and adornment. Both coat and trousers were of a dark grey cloth; but the former, which, in its shape, partook of the military, had a straight collar of yellow, and narrow cuffs of the same; while upon both sleeves, about the place where a corporal wears his stripes, was expressed, in the same yellow cloth, a somewhat singular device. It was as close an imitation of a bell, with its tongue hanging out of its mouth, as the tailor's skill could produce from a single piece of cloth. The origin of the military cut of his coat was well known. His preference for it arose in the time of the wars of the first Napoleon, when the threatened invasion of the country caused the organization of many volunteer regiments. The martial show and exercises captivated the poor man's fancy; and from that time forward nothing pleased his vanity, and consequently conciliated his good-will more, than to style

First appeared as "The Bell" in *Good Words* (1864); reprinted in *Adela Cathcart* (1864).

him by his favourite title—the *Colonel.* But the badge on his arm had a
deeper origin, which will be partially manifest in the course of the
story—if story it can be called. It was, indeed, the baptism of the fool,
the outward and visible sign of his relation to the infinite and unseen.
His countenance, however, although the features were not of any
peculiarly low or animal type, showed no corresponding sign of the
consciousness of such a relation, being as vacant as human countenance
could well be.

The cause of Elsie's annoyance was that the fool was annoyed; he
was followed by a troop of boys, who turned his rank into scorn, and
assailed him with epithets hateful to him. Although the most harmless
of creatures when let alone, he was dangerous when roused; and now he
stooped repeatedly to pick up stones and hurl them at his tormentors,
who took care, while abusing him, to keep at a considerable distance,
lest he should get hold of them. Amidst the sounds of derision that
followed him, might be heard the words frequently repeated—*"Come
hame, come hame."* But in a few minutes the noise ceased, either from
the interference of some friendly inhabitant, or that the boys grew
weary, and departed in search of other amusement. By and by, Elsie
might be seen again at her work in the window; but the cloud over her
eyes was deeper, and her whole face more sad.

Indeed, so much did the persecution of this poor man affect her,
that an onlooker would have been compelled to seek the cause in some
yet deeper sympathy than that commonly felt for the oppressed, even
by women. And such a sympathy existed, strange as it may seem,
between the beautiful girl (for many called her *a bonnie lassie*) and this
"tatter of humanity." Nothing would have been further from the
thoughts of those that knew them, than the supposition of any correspondence or connexion between them; yet this sympathy sprang in
part from a real similarity in their history and present condition.

All the facts that were known about *Feel Jock's* origin were these:
that seventy years ago, a man who had gone with his horse and cart
some miles from the village, to fetch home a load of peat from a
desolate *moss,* had heard, while toiling along as rough a road on as
lonely a hill-side as any in Scotland, the cry of a child; and, searching
about, had found the infant, hardly wrapt in rags, and untended, as if
the earth herself had just given him birth,—that desert moor, wide and
dismal, broken and watery, the only bosom for him to lie upon, and the

cold, clear night-heaven his only covering. The man had brought him
home, and the parish had taken parish-care of him. He had grown up,
and proved what he now was—almost an idiot. Many of the towns-
people were kind to him, and employed him in fetching water for them
from the river or wells in the neighbourhood, paying him for his trouble
in victuals, or whisky, of which he was very fond. He seldom spoke; and
the sentences he could utter were few; yet the tone, and even the words
of his limited vocabulary, were sufficient to express gratitude and some
measure of love towards those who were kind to him, and hatred of
those who teased and insulted him. He lived a life without aim, and
apparently to no purpose; in this resembling most of his more gifted
fellow-men, who, with all the tools and materials necessary for building
a noble mansion, are yet content with a clay hut.

Elsie, on the contrary, had been born in a comfortable farm-house,
amidst homeliness and abundance. But at a very early age, she had lost
both father and mother; not so early, however, but that she had faint
memories of warm soft times on her mother's bosom, and of refuge in
her mother's arms from the attacks of geese, and the pursuit of pigs.
Therefore, in after-times, when she looked forward to heaven, it was as
much a reverting to the old heavenly times of childhood and mother's
love, as an anticipation of something yet to be revealed. Indeed,
without some such memory, how should we ever picture to ourselves a
perfect rest? But sometimes it would seem as if the more a heart was
made capable of loving, the less it had to love; and poor Elsie, in passing
from a mother's to a brother's guardianship, felt a change of spiritual
temperature too keen. He was not a bad man, or incapable of benevo-
lence when touched by the sight of want in anything of which he would
himself have felt the privation; but he was so coarsely made, that only
the purest animal necessities affected him; and a hard word, or un-
feeling speech, could never have reached the quick of his nature
through the hide that enclosed it. Elsie, on the contrary, was exces-
sively and painfully sensitive, as if her nature constantly portended an
invisible multitude of half-spiritual, half-nervous antennae, which
shrank and trembled in every current of air at all below their own
temperature. The effect of this upon her behaviour was such, that she
was called odd; and the poor girl felt she was not like other people, yet
could not help it. Her brother, too, laughed at her without the slightest
idea of the pain he occasioned, or the remotest feeling of curiosity as to

what the inward and consistent causes of the outward abnormal condition might be. Tenderness was the divine comforting she needed; and it was altogether absent from her brother's character and behaviour.

Her neighbours looked on her with some interest, but they rather shunned than courted her acquaintance; especially after the return of certain nervous attacks, to which she had been subject in childhood, and which were again brought on by the events I must relate. It is curious how certain diseases repel, by a kind of awe, the sympathies of the neighbours: as if, by the fact of being subject to them, the patient were removed into another realm of existence, from which, like the dead with the living, she can hold communion with those around her only partially, and with a mixture of dread pervading the intercourse. Thus some of the deepest, purest wells of spiritual life, are, like those in old castles, choked up by the decay of the outer walls. But what tended more than anything, perhaps, to keep up the painful unrest of her soul (for the beauty of her character was evident in the fact, that the irritation seldom reached her *mind*), was a circumstance at which, in its present connexion, some of my readers will smile, and others feel a shudder corresponding in kind to that of Elsie.

Her brother was very fond of a rather small, but ferocious-looking bull-dog, which followed close at his heels, wherever he went, with hanging head and slouching gait, never leaping or racing about like other dogs. When in the house, he always lay under his master's chair. He seemed to dislike Elsie, and she felt an unspeakable repugnance to him. Though she never mentioned her aversion, her brother easily saw it by the way in which she avoided the animal; and attributing it entirely to fear—which indeed had a great share in the matter—he would cruelly aggravate it, by telling her stories of the fierce hardihood and relentless persistency of this kind of animal. He dared not yet further increase her terror by offering to set the creature upon her, because it was doubtful whether he might be able to restrain him; but the mental suffering which he occasioned by this heartless conduct, and for which he had no sympathy, was as severe as many bodily sufferings to which he would have been sorry to subject her. Whenever the poor girl happened inadvertently to pass near the dog, which was seldom, a low growl made her aware of his proximity, and drove her to a quick retreat. He was, in fact, the animal impersonation of the animal opposition which she had continually to endure. Like chooses like; and the bull-dog *in* her brother made choice of the bull-dog *out of* him for his companion. So her day was one of shrinking fear and multiform discomfort.

But a nature capable of so much distress, must of necessity be *capable* of a corresponding amount of pleasure; and in her case this was manifest in the fact, that sleep and the quiet of her own room restored her wonderfully. If she was only let alone, a calm mood, filled with images of pleasure, soon took possession of her mind.

Her acquaintance with the fool had commenced some ten years previous to the time I write of, when she was quite a little girl, and had come from the country with her brother, who, having taken a small farm close to the town, preferred residing in the town to occupying the farm-house, which was not comfortable. She looked at first with some terror on his uncouth appearance, and with much wonderment on his strange dress. This wonder was heightened by a conversation she over-heard one day in the street, between the fool and a little pale-faced boy, who, approaching him respectfully, said, "Weel, cornel!" "Weel, laddie!" was the reply. "Fat dis the wow say, cornel?" "Come hame, come hame!" answered the *colonel*, with both accent and quantity heaped on the word *hame*. What the *wow* could be, she had no idea; only, as the years passed on, the strange word became in her mind indescribably associated with the strange shape in yellow cloth on his sleeves. Had she been a native of the town, she could not have failed to know its import, so familiar was every one with it, although it did not belong to the local vocabulary; but, as it was, years passed away before she discovered its meaning. And when, again and again, the fool, attempting to convey his gratitude for some kindness she had shown him, mumbled over the words—*"The wow o' Rivven—the wow o' Rivven,"* the wonder would return as to what could be the idea associated with them in his mind, but she made no advance towards their explanation.

That, however, which most attracted her to the old man, was his persecution by the children. They were to him what the bull-dog was to her—the constant source of irritation and annoyance. They could hard-ly hurt him, nor did he appear to dread other injury from them than insult, to which, fool though he was, he was keenly alive. Human gad-flies that they were! they sometimes stung him beyond endurance, and he would curse them in the impotence of his anger. Once or twice Elsie had been so far carried beyond her constitutional timidity, by sympathy for the distress of her friend, that she had gone out and talked to the boys,—even scolded them, so that they slunk away ashamed, and began to stand as much in dread of her as of the clutches of their prey. So she, gentle and timid to excess, acquired among them the reputation of a termagant.* Popular opinion among children, as among men, is often just, but as often very unjust; for the same manifestations may proceed from opposite principles; and, therefore, as indices to character, may mislead as often as enlighten.

Next door to the house in which Elsie resided, dwelt a tradesman and his wife, who kept an indefinite sort of shop, in which various kinds of goods were exposed for sale. Their youngest son was about the same age as Elsie; and while they were rather more than children, and less than young people, he spent many of his evenings with her, somewhat to the loss of position in his classes at the parish school. They were, indeed, much attached to each other; and, peculiarly constituted as Elsie was, one may imagine what kind of heavenly messenger a companion stronger than herself must have been to her. In fact, if she could have framed the undefinable need of her child-like nature into an articulate prayer, it would have been—"Give me some one to love me stronger than I." Any love was helpful, yes, in its degree, saving to her poor troubled soul; but the hope, as they grew older together, that the powerful, yet tender-hearted youth, really loved her, and would one day make her his wife, was like the opening of heavenly eyes of life and love in the hitherto blank and death-like face of her existence. But nothing had been said of love, although they met and parted like lovers.

Doubtless, if the circles of their thought and feeling had continued as now to intersect each other, there would have been no interruption to their affection; but the time at length arrived when the old couple, seeing the rest of their family comfortably settled in life, resolved to make a gentleman of the youngest; and so sent him from school to college. The facilities existing in Scotland for providing a professional training enabled them to educate him as a surgeon. He parted from Elsie with some regret; but, far less dependent on her than she was on him, and full of the prospects of the future, he felt none of that sinking at the heart which seemed to lay her whole nature open to a fresh inroad of all the terrors and sorrows of her peculiar existence. No correspondence took place between them. New pursuits and relations,

*A turbulent girl.

and the development of his tastes and judgments, entirely altered the position of poor Elsie in his memory. Having been, during their intercourse, far less of a man than she of a woman, he had no definite idea of the place he had occupied in her regard; and in his mind she receded into the background of the past, without his having any idea that she would suffer thereby, or that he was unjust towards her; while, in her thoughts, his image stood in the highest and clearest relief. It was the centre-point from which and towards which all lines radiated and converged; and although she could not but be doubtful about the future, yet there was much hope mingled with her doubts.

But when, at the close of two years, he visited his native village, and she saw before her, instead of the homely youth who had left her that winter evening, one who, to her inexperienced eyes, appeared a finished gentleman, her heart sank within her, as if she had found Nature herself false in her ripening processes, destroying the beautiful promise of a former year by changing instead of developing her creations. He spoke kindly to her, but not cordially. To her ear the voice seemed to come from a great distance out of the past; and while she looked upon him, that optical change passed over her vision, which all have experienced after gazing abstractedly on any object for a time: his form grew very small, and receded to an immeasurable distance; till, her imagination mingling with the twilight haze of her senses, she seemed to see him standing far off on a hill, with the bright horizon of sunset for a background to his clearly defined figure.

She knew no more till she found herself in bed in the dark; and the first message that reached her from the outer world, was the infernal growl of the bull-dog from the room below. Next day she saw her lover walking with two ladies, who would have thought it some degree of condescension to speak to her; and he passed the house without once looking towards it.

One who is sufficiently possessed by the demon of nervousness to be glad of the magnetic influences of a friend's company in a public promenade, or of a horse beneath him in passing through a churchyard, will have some faint idea of how utterly exposed and defenceless poor Elsie now felt on the crowded thoroughfare of life. And so the insensibility which had overtaken her, was not the ordinary swoon with which Nature relieves the overstrained nerves, but the return of the epileptic fits of her early childhood; and if the condition of the poor girl had been pitiable before, it was tenfold more so now. Yet she did not complain, but bore all in silence, though it was evident that her health was giving way. But now, help came to her from a strange quarter; though many might not be willing to accord the name of help to that which rather hastened than retarded the progress of her decline.

She had gone to spend a few of the summer days with a relative in the country, some miles from her home, if home it could be called. One evening, towards sunset, she went out for a solitary walk. Passing from the little garden-gate, she went along a bare country road for some distance, and then turning aside by a footpath through a thicket of low trees, she came out in a lonely little churchyard on the hill-side. Hardly knowing whether or not she had intended to go there, she seated herself on a mound covered with long grass, one of many. Before her stood the ruins of an old church which was taking centuries to crumble. Little remained but the gable-wall, immensely thick, and covered with ancient ivy. The rays of the setting sun fell on a mound at its foot, not green like the rest, but of a rich, red-brown in the rosy sunset, and evidently but newly heaped up. Her eyes, too, rested upon it. Slowly the sun sank below the near horizon.

As the last brilliant point disappeared, the ivy darkened, and a wind arose and shook all its leaves, making them look cold and troubled; and to Elsie's ear came a low faint sound, as from a far-off bell. But close beside her—and she started and shivered at the sound—rose a deep, monotonous, almost sepulchral voice, *"Come Hame, come Hame! The wow, the wow!"*

At once she understood the whole. She sat in the churchyard of the ancient parish church of Ruthven; and when she lifted up her eyes, there she saw, in the half-ruined belfry, the old bell, all but hidden with ivy, which the passing wind had roused to utter one sleepy tone; and there, beside her, stood the fool with the bell on his arm; and to him and to her the *wow o' Rivven* said, *"Come hame, come hame!"* Ah, what did she want in the whole universe of God but a home? And though the ground beneath was hard, and the sky overhead far and boundless, and the hill-side lonely and companionless, yet somewhere within the visible, and beyond these the outer surfaces of creation, there might be a home for her; as round the wintry house the snows lie heaped up cold and white and dreary all the long *forenight,* while within, beyond the closed shutters, and giving no glimmer through the thick stone walls, the fires are blazing joyously, and the voices and laughter of young unfrozen children are heard, and nothing belongs to winter but the grey hairs on the heads of the parents, within whose warm hearts child-like voices are heard, and child-like thoughts move to and fro. The kernel of winter itself is spring, or a sleeping summer.

It was no wonder that the fool, cast out of the earth on a far more desolate spot than this, should seek to return within her bosom at this place of open doors, and should call it *home*. For surely the surface of the earth had no home for him. The mound at the foot of the gable contained the body of one who had shown him kindness. He had followed the funeral that afternoon from the town, and had remained behind with the bell. Indeed, it was his custom, though Elsie had not known it, to follow every funeral going to this, his favourite churchyard of Ruthven; and, possibly in imitation of its booming, for it was still tolled at the funerals, he had given the old bell the name of *the wow*, and had translated its monotonous clangour into the articulate sounds—*come hame, come hame*. What precise meaning he attached to the words, it is impossible to say; but it was evident that the place possessed a strange attraction for him, drawing him towards it by the cords of some spiritual magnetism. It is possible that in the mind of the idiot there may have been some feeling about this churchyard and bell, which, in the mind of another, would have become a grand poetic thought; a feeling as if the ghostly old bell hung at the church-door of the invisible world, and ever and anon rang out joyous notes (though they sounded sad in the ears of the living), calling to the children of the unseen to *come home, come home*. She sat for some time in silence; for the bell did not ring again, and the fool spoke no more; till the dews began to fall, when she rose and went home, followed by her companion, who passed the night in the barn.

From that hour Elsie was furnished with a visual image of the rest she sought; an image which, mingling with deeper and holier thoughts, became, like the bow set in the cloud, the earthly pledge and sign of the fulfilment of heavenly hopes. Often when the wintry fog of cold discomfort and homelessness filled her soul, all at once the picture of the little churchyard—with the old gable and belfry, and the slanting sunlight steeping down to the very roots of the long grass on the graves—arose in the darkened chamber *(camera obscura)* of her soul; and again she heard the faint Aeolian sound of the bell, and the voice of the prophet-fool who interpreted the oracle; and the inward weariness was soothed by the promise of a long sleep. Who can tell how many have been counted fools simply because they were prophets; or

how much of the madness in the world may be the utterance of
thoughts true and just, but belonging to a region differing from ours in
its nature and scenery!

But to Elsie looking out of her window came the mocking tones of
the idle boys who had chosen as the vehicle of their scorn the very
words which showed the relation of the fool to the eternal, and
revealed in him an element higher far than any yet developed in them.
They turned his glory into shame, like the enemies of David when they
mocked the would-be king. And the best in a man is often that which is
most condemned by those who have not attained to his goodness. The
words, however, even as repeated by the boys, had not solely awakened
indignation at the persecution of the old man: they had likewise
comforted her with the thought of the refuge that awaited both him
and her.

But the same evening a worse trial was in store for her. Again she
sat near the window, oppressed by the consciousness that her brother
had come in. He had gone up-stairs, and his dog had remained at the
door, exchanging surly compliments with some of his own kind, when
the fool came strolling past, and, I do not know from what cause, the
dog flew at him. Elsie heard his cry and looked up. Her fear of the
brute vanished in a moment before her sympathy for her friend. She
darted from the house, and rushed towards the dog to drag him off the
defenceless idiot, calling him by his name in a tone of anger and dislike.
He left the fool, and, springing at Elsie, seized her by the arm above the
elbow with such a grip that, in the midst of her agony, she fancied she
heard the bone crack. But she uttered no cry, for the most apprehensive
are sometimes the most courageous. Just then, however, her former lover
was coming along the street, and, catching a glimpse of what had
happened, was on the spot in an instant, took the dog by the throat
with a grip not inferior to his own, and having thus compelled him to
relax his hold, dashed him on the ground with a force that almost
stunned him, and then with a superadded kick sent him away limping
and howling; whereupon the fool, attacking him furiously with a stick,
would certainly have finished him, had not his master descried his
plight and come to his rescue.

Meantime the young surgeon had carried Elsie into the house; for,
as soon as she was rescued from the dog, she had fallen down in one of
her fits, which were becoming more and more frequent of themselves,
and little needed such a shock as this to increase their violence. He was

dressing her arm when she began to recover; and when she opened her eyes, in a state of half-consciousness, the first object she beheld, was his face bending over her. Recalling nothing of what had occurred, it seemed to her, in the dreamy condition in which the fit had left her, the same face, unchanged, which had once shone in upon her tardy spring-time, and promised to ripen it into summer. She forgot it had departed and left her in the wintry cold. And so she uttered wild words of love and trust; and the youth, while stung with remorse at his own neglect, was astonished to perceive the poetic forms of beauty in which the soul of the uneducated maiden burst into flower. But as her senses recovered themselves, the face gradually changed to her, as if the slow alteration of two years had been phantasmagorically compressed into a few moments; and the glow departed from the maiden's thoughts and words, and her soul found itself at the narrow window of the present, from which she could behold but a dreary country.—From the street came the iambic cry of the fool, "Come hame, come hame."

Tycho Brahe, I think, is said to have kept a fool, who frequently sat at his feet in his study, and to whose mutterings he used to listen in the pauses of his own thought. The shining soul of the astronomer drew forth the rainbow of harmony from the misty spray of words ascending ever from the dark gulf into which the thoughts of the idiot were ever falling. He beheld curious concurrences of words therein, and could read strange meanings from them—sometimes even received wondrous hints for the direction of celestial inquiry, from what, to any other, and it may be to the fool himself, was but a ceaseless and aimless babble. Such power lieth in words. It is not then to be wondered at, that the sounds I have mentioned should fall on the ears of Elsie, at such a moment, as a message from God himself. This then—all this dreariness—was but a passing show like the rest, and there lay somewhere for her a reality—a home. The tears burst up from her oppressed heart. She received the message, and prepared to go home. From that time her strength gradually sank, but her spirits as steadily rose.

The strength of the fool, too, began to fail, for he was old. He bore all the signs of age, even to the grey hairs, which betokened no wisdom. But one cannot say what wisdom might be in him, or how far he had not fought his own battle, and been victorious. Whether any notion of a continuance of life and thought dwelt in his brain, it is impossible to tell; but he seemed to have the idea that this was not his home; and those who saw him gradually approaching his end, might well anticipate for him a higher life in the world to come. He had passed through this world without ever awaking to such a consciousness of being as is common to mankind. He had spent his years like a weary dream through a long night,—a strange, dismal, unkindly dream; and now the morning was at hand. Often in his dream had he listened with sleepy senses to the ringing of the bell, but that bell would awake him at last. He was like a seed buried too deep in the soil, to which the light has never penetrated, and which, therefore, has never forced its way upwards to the open air, never experienced the resurrection of the dead. But seeds will grow ages after they have fallen into the earth; and, indeed, with many kinds, and within some limits, the older the seed before it germinates, the more plentiful the fruit. And may it not be believed of many human beings, that, the great Husbandman having sown them like seeds in the soil of human affairs, there they lie buried a life long; and only after the upturning of the soil by death, reach a position in which the awakening of their aspiration and the consequent growth become possible. Surely he has made nothing in vain.

A violent cold and cough brought him at last near to his end, and hearing that he was ill, Elsie ventured one bright spring day to go to see him. When she entered the miserable room where he lay, he held out his hand to her with something like a smile, and muttered feebly and painfully, "I'm gaein' to the wow, nae to come back again." Elsie could not restrain her tears; while the old man, looking fixedly at her, though with meaningless eyes, muttered, for the last time, *"Come hame! come hame!"* and sank into a lethargy, from which nothing could rouse him, till, next morning, he was waked by friendly death from the long sleep of this world's night. They bore him to his favourite churchyard, and buried him within the site of the old church, below his loved bell, which had ever been to him as the cuckoo-note of a coming spring. Thus he at length obeyed its summons, and went home.

Elsie lingered till the first summer days lay warm on the land. Several kind hearts in the village, hearing of her illness, visited her and ministered to her. Wondering at her sweetness and patience, they regretted they had not known her before. How much consolation might not their kindness have imparted, and how much might not their sympathy have strengthened her on her painful road! But they could not long have delayed her going home. Nor, mentally constituted as she was, would this have been at all to be desired. Indeed it was chiefly the expectation of departure that quieted and soothed her tremulous nature. It is true that a deep spring of hope and faith kept singing on in her heart, but this alone, without the anticipation of speedy release, could only have kept her mind at peace. It could not have reached, at least for a long time, the border land between body and mind, in which her disease lay.

One still night of summer, the nurse who watched by her bed-side heard her murmur through her sleep, "I hear it: *come hame—come hame.* I'm comin', I'm comin'—I'm gaein' hame to the wow, nae to come back." She awoke at the sound of her own words, and begged the nurse to convey to her brother her last request, that she might be buried by the side of the fool, within the old church of Ruthven. Then she turned her face to the wall, and in the morning was found quiet and cold. She must have died within a few minutes after her last words. She was buried according to her request; and thus she too went home.

Side by side rest the aged fool and the young maiden; for the bell called them and they obeyed; and surely they found the fire burning bright, and heard friendly voices, and felt sweet lips on theirs, in the home to which they went. Surely both intellect and love were waiting them there.

Still the old bell hangs in the old gable; and whenever another is borne to the old churchyard, it keeps calling to those who are left behind, with the same sad, but friendly and unchanging voice—"*Come hame! come hame! come hame!*"

"Thy sun shall no more go down; neither shall thy moon withdraw itself: for the LORD shall be thine everlasting light, and the days of thy mourning shall be ended." —*Isaiah lx. 20.*

VIII
Uncle Cornelius, His Story

It was a dull evening in November. A drizzling mist had been falling all day about the old farm. Harry Heywood and his two sisters sat in the house-place, expecting a visit from their uncle, Cornelius Heywood. This uncle lived alone, occupying the first floor above a chemist's shop in the town, and had just enough of money over to buy books that nobody seemed ever to have heard of but himself; for he was a student in all those regions of speculation in which anything to be called knowledge is impossible.

"What a dreary night!" said Kate. "I wish uncle would come and tell us a story."

"A cheerful wish," said Harry. "Uncle Cornie is a lively companion,—isn't he? He can't even blunder through a Joe Miller without tacking a moral to it, and then trying to persuade you that the joke of it depends on the moral."

"Here he comes!" said Kate, as three distinct blows with the knob of his walking-stick announced the arrival of Uncle Cornelius. She ran to the door to open it.

The air had been very still all day, but as he entered he seemed to have brought the wind with him, for the first moan of it pressed against rather than shook the casement of the low-ceiled room.

Uncle Cornelius was very tall, and very thin, and very pale, with large gray eyes that looked greatly larger because he wore spectacles of the most delicate hair-steel, with the largest pebble-eyes that ever were seen. He gave them a kindly greeting, but too much in earnest even in shaking hands to smile over it. He sat down in the armchair by the chimney corner.

I have been particular in my description of him, in order that my reader may give due weight to his words. I am such a believer in words, that I believe everything depends on who says them. Uncle Cornelius Heywood's story, told word for word by Uncle Timothy Warren, would not have been the same story at all. Not one of the listeners would have believed a syllable of it from the lips of round-bodied, red-faced,

Reprinted from *Works of Fancy and Imagination* (1871).

small-eyed, little Uncle Tim; whereas from Uncle Cornie,—disbelieve
one of his stories if you could!

One word more concerning him. His interest in everything con-
jectured or believed relative to the awful borderland of this world and
the next, was only equalled by his disgust at the vulgar, unimaginative
forms which curiosity about such subjects has assumed in the present
day. With a yearning after the unseen like that of a child for the lifting
of the curtain of a theatre, he declared that, rather than accept such a
spirit-world as the would-be seers of the nineteenth century thought or
pretended to reveal,—the prophets of a pauperized, workhouse immortality, invented by a poverty-stricken soul, and a sense so greedy that it
would gorge on carrion,—he would rejoice to believe that a man had
just as much of a soul as the cabbage of Iamblichus, namely, an aerial
double of his body.

"I'm so glad you're come, uncle!" said Kate. "Why wouldn't you
come to dinner? We have been so gloomy!"

"Well, Katey, you know I don't admire eating. I never could bear to
see a cow tearing up the grass with her long tongue." As he spoke he
looked very much like a cow. He had a way of opening his jaws while
he kept his lips closely pressed together, that made his cheeks fall in,
and his face look awfully long and dismal. "I consider eating," he went
on, "such an animal exercise that it ought always to be performed in
private. You never saw me dine, Kate."

"Never, uncle; but I have seen you drink;—nothing but water, I
must confess."

"Yes, that is another affair. According to one eye-witness, that is no
more than the disembodied can do. I must confess, however, that,
although well attested, the story is to me scarcely credible. Fancy a
glass of Bavarian beer lifted into the air without a visible hand, turned
upside down, and set empty on the table!—and no splash on the floor
or anywhere else!"

A solitary gleam of humour shone through the great eyes of the
spectacles as he spoke.

"Oh, uncle! how can you believe such nonsense!" said Janet.

"I did not say I believed it,—did I? But why not? The story has at
least a touch of imagination in it."

"That is a strange reason for believing a thing, uncle," said Harry.

"You might have a worse, Harry. I grant it is not sufficient; but it is better than that commonplace aspect which is the ground of most faith. I believe I did say that the story puzzled me."

"But how can you give it any quarter at all, uncle?"

"It does me no harm. There it is,—between the boards of an old German book. There let it remain."

"Well, you will never persuade me to believe such things," said Janet.

"Wait till I ask you, Janet," returned her uncle, gravely. "I have not the slightest desire to convince you. How did we get into this unprofitable current of talk? We will change it at once. How are consols, Harry?"

"Oh, uncle!" said Kate, "we were longing for a story, and just as I thought you were coming to one, off you go to consols!"

"I thought a ghost story at least was coming," said Janet.

"You did your best to stop it, Janet," said Harry.

Janet began an angry retort, but Cornelius interrupted her. "You never heard me tell a ghost story, Janet."

"You have just told one about a drinking ghost, uncle," said Janet,—in such a tone that Cornelius replied:

"Well, take that for your story, and let us talk of something else."

Janet apparently saw that she had been rude, and said as sweetly as she might,—"Ah! but you didn't make that one, uncle. You got it out of a German book."

"Make it!—Make a ghost story!" repeated Cornelius. "No; that I never did."

"Such things are not to be trifled with, are they?" said Janet.

"I at least have no inclination to trifle with them."

"But, really and truly, uncle," persisted Janet, "you don't believe in such things?"

"Why should I either believe or disbelieve in them? They are not essential to salvation, I presume."

"You must do the one or the other, I suppose."

"I beg your pardon. You suppose wrong. It would take twice the proof I have ever had to make me believe in them; and exactly your prejudice, and allow me to say ignorance, to make me disbelieve in them. Neither is within my reach. I postpone judgment. But you, young people, of course, are wiser, and know all about the question."

"Oh, uncle! I'm so sorry!" said Kate. "I am sure I did not mean to vex you."

"Not at all, not at all, my dear.—It wasn't you."

"Do you know," Kate went on, anxious to prevent anything unpleasant, for there was something very black perched on Janet's forehead,—"I have taken to reading about that kind of thing."

"I beg you will give it up at once. You will bewilder your brains till you are ready to believe anything, if only it be absurd enough. Nay, you may come to find the element of vulgarity essential to belief. I should be sorry to the heart to believe concerning a horse or dog what they tell you now-a-days about Shakspeare and Burns. What have you been reading, my girl?"

"Don't be alarmed, uncle. Only some Highland legends, which are too absurd either for my belief or for your theories."

"I don't know that, Kate."

"Why, what could you do with such shapeless creatures as haunt their fords and pools for instance? They are as featureless as the faces of the mountains."

"And so much the more terrible."

"But that does not make it easier to believe in them," said Harry.

"I only said," returned his uncle, "that their shapelessness adds to their horror."

"But you allowed,—almost, at least, uncle," said Kate, "that you could find a place in your theories even for those shapeless creatures."

Cornelius sat silent for a moment; then, having first doubled the length of his face, and restored it to its natural condition, said thoughtfully,—"I suspect, Katey, if you were to come upon an ichthyosaurus or a pterodactyl asleep in the shrubbery, you would hardly expect your report of it to be believed all at once either by Harry or Janet."

"I suppose not, uncle. But I can't see what——"

"Of course such a thing could not happen here and now. But there was a time when and a place where such a thing may have happened. Indeed, in my time, a traveller or two have got pretty soundly disbelieved for reporting what they saw,—the last of an expiring race, which had strayed over the natural verge of its history, coming to life in some neglected swamp, itself a remnant of the slime of Chaos."

"I never heard you talk like that before, uncle," said Harry. "If you go on like that, you'll land me in a swamp, I'm afraid."

"I wasn't talking to you at all, Harry. Kate challenged me to find a place for kelpies, and such like, in the theories she does me the honour of supposing I cultivate."

"Then you think, uncle, that all these stories are only legends which, if you could follow them up, would lead you back to some one of the awful monsters that have since quite disappeared from the earth."

"It is possible those stories may be such legends; but that was not what I intended to lead you to. I gave you that only as something like what I am going to say now. What if,—mind, I only suggest it,—what if the direful creatures, whose report lingers in these tales, should have an origin far older still? What if they were the remnants of a vanishing period of the earth's history long antecedent to the birth of mastodon and iguanodon; a stage, namely, when the world, as we call it, had not yet become quite visible, was not yet so far finished as to part from the invisible world that was its mother, and which, on its part, had not then become quite invisible,—was only almost such; and when, as a credible consequence, strange shapes of those now invisible regions, Gorgons and Chimaeras dire, might be expected to gloom out occasionally from the awful Fauna of an ever-generating world upon that one which was being born of it. Hence, the life-periods of a world being long and slow, some of these huge, unformed bulks of half-created matter might, somehow, like the megatherium of later times,—a baby creation to them,—roll at age-long intervals, clothed in a mighty terror of shapelessness, into the half-recognition of human beings, whose consternation at the uncertain vision were barrier enough to prevent all further knowledge of its substance."

"I begin to have some notion of your meaning, uncle," said Kate.

"But then," said Janet, "all that must be over by this time. That world has been invisible now for many years."

"Ever since you were born, I suppose, Janet. The changes of a world are not to be measured by the changes of its generations."

"Oh, but, uncle, there can't be any such things. You know that as well as I do."

"Yes, just as well, and no better."

"There can't be any ghosts now. Nobody believes such things."

"Oh, as to ghosts, that is quite another thing. I did not know you were talking with reference to them. It is no wonder if one can get nothing sensible out of you, Janet, when your discrimination is no greater than to lump everything marvellous, kelpies, ghosts, vampires, doubles, witches, fairies, nightmares, and I don't know what all, under the one head of ghosts; and we hadn't been saying a word about them. If one were to disprove to you the existence of the afreets of Eastern tales, you would consider the whole argument concerning the reappearance of the departed upset. I congratulate you on your powers of analysis and induction, Miss Janet. But it matters very little whether we believe in ghosts, as you say, or not, provided we believe that we are ghosts,—that within this body, which so many people are ready to consider their own very selves, there lies a ghostly embryo, at least, which has an inner side to it God only can see, which says I concerning itself, and which will soon have to know whether or not it can appear to those whom it has left behind, and thus solve the question of ghosts for itself, at least."

"Then you do believe in ghosts, uncle?" said Janet, in a tone that certainly was not respectful.

"Surely I said nothing of the sort, Janet. The man most convinced that he had himself had such an interview as you hint at, would find,—ought to find it impossible to convince any one else of it."

"You are quite out of my depth, uncle," said Harry. "Surely any honest man ought to be believed?"

"Honesty is not all, by any means, that is necessary to being believed. It is impossible to convey a conviction of anything. All you can do is to convey a conviction that you are convinced. Of course, what satisfied you might satisfy another; but, till you can present him with the sources of your conviction, you cannot present him with the conviction,—and perhaps not even then."

"You can tell him all about it, can't you?"

"Is telling a man about a ghost, affording him the source of your conviction? Is it the same as a ghost appearing to him? Really, Harry!—You cannot even convey the impression a dream has made upon you."

"But isn't that just because it is only a dream?"

"Not at all. The impression may be deeper and clearer on your mind than any fact of the next morning will make. You will forget the next day altogether, but the impression of the dream will remain through all the following whirl and storm of what you call facts. Now a conviction may be likened to a deep impression on the judgment or the reason, or both. No one can feel it but the person who is convinced. It cannot be conveyed."

"I fancy that is just what those who believe in spirit-rapping would say."

"There are the true and false of convictions, as of everything else. I mean that a man may take that for a conviction in his own mind which is not a conviction, but only resembles one. But those to whom you refer profess to appeal to facts. It is on the ground of those facts, and with the more earnestness the more reason they can give for receiving them as facts, that I refuse all their deductions with abhorrence. I mean that, if what they say is true, the thinker must reject with contempt the claim to anything like revelation therein."

"Then you do not believe in ghosts, after all?" said Kate, in a tone of surprise.

"I did not say so, my dear. Will you be reasonable, or will you not?"

"Dear uncle, do tell us what you really think."

"I have been telling you what I think ever since I came, Katey; and you won't take in a word I say."

"I have been taking in every word, uncle, and trying hard to understand it as well.—Did you ever see a ghost, uncle?"

Cornelius Heywood was silent. He shut his lips and opened his jaws till his cheeks almost met in the vacuum. A strange expression crossed the strange countenance, and the great eyes of his spectacles looked as if, at the very moment, they were seeing something no other spectacles could see. Then his jaws closed with a snap, his countenance brightened, a flash of humour came through the goggle eyes of pebble, and, at length, he actually smiled as he said—"Really, Katey, you must take me for a simpleton!"

"How, uncle?"

"To think, if I had ever seen a ghost, I would confess the fact before a set of creatures like you,—all spinning your webs like so many spiders to catch and devour old Daddy Longlegs."

By this time Harry had grown quite grave. "Indeed, I am very sorry, uncle," he said, "if I have deserved such a rebuke."

"No, no, my boy," said Cornelius; "I did not mean it more than half. If I had meant it, I would not have said it. If you really would like——" Here he paused.

"Indeed we should, uncle," said Kate, earnestly. "You should have heard what we were saying just before you came in."

"All you were saying, Katey?"

"Yes," answered Kate, thoughtfully. "The worst we said was that you could not tell a story without——well, we did say tacking a moral to it."

"Well, well! I mustn't push it. A man has no right to know what people say about him. It unfits him for occupying his real position amongst them. He, least of all, has anything to do with it. If his friends won't defend him, he can't defend himself. Besides, what people say is so often untrue!—I don't mean to others, but to themselves. Their hearts are more honest than their mouths. But Janet doesn't want a strange story, I am sure."

Janet certainly was not one to have chosen for a listener to such a tale. Her eyes were so small that no satisfaction could possibly come of it. "Oh! I don't mind, uncle," she said, with half-affected indifference, as she searched in her box for silk to mend her gloves.

"You are not very encouraging, I must say," returned her uncle, making another cow-face.

"I will go away, if you like," said Janet, pretending to rise.

"No, never mind," said her uncle hastily. "If you don't want me to tell it, I want you to hear it; and, before I have done, that may have come to the same thing perhaps."

"Then you really are going to tell us a ghost-story!" said Kate, drawing her chair nearer to her uncle's; and then, finding this did not satisfy her sense of propinquity to the source of the expected pleasure, drawing a stool from the corner, and seating herself almost on the hearth-rug at his knee.

"I did not say so," returned Cornelius, once more. "I said I would tell you a strange story. You may call it a ghost-story if you like; I do not pretend to determine what it is. I confess it will look like one though."

After so many delays, Uncle Cornelius now plunged almost hurriedly into his narration.

"In the year 1820," he said, "in the month of August, I fell in love." Here the girls glanced at each other. The idea of Uncle Cornie in love, and in the very same century in which they were now listening to the confession, was too astonishing to pass without ocular remark; but, if he observed it, he took no notice of it; he did not even pause. "In the month of September, I was refused. Consequently, in the month of October, I was ready to fall in love again. Take particular care of

yourself, Harry, for a whole month, at least, after your first disappointment; for you will never be more likely to do a foolish thing. Please
yourself after the second. If you are silly then, you may take what you
get, for you will deserve it,—except it be good fortune."

"Did you do a foolish thing then, uncle?" asked Harry, demurely.

"I did, as you will see; for I fell in love again."

"I don't see anything so very foolish in that."

"I have repented it since, though. Don't interrupt me again, please.
In the middle of October, then, in the year 1820, in the evening, I was
walking across Russell Square, on my way home from the British
Museum, where I had been reading all day. You see I have a full
intention of being precise, Janet."

"I'm sure I don't know why you make the remark to me, uncle,"
said Janet, with an involuntary toss of her head. Her uncle only went
on with his narrative.

"I begin at the very beginning of my story," he said; "for I want to
be particular as to everything that can appear to have had anything to
do with what came afterwards. I had been reading, I say, all the
morning in the British Museum; and, as I walked, I took off my
spectacles to ease my eyes. I need not tell you that I am short-sighted
now, for that you know well enough. But I must tell you that I was
short-sighted then, and helpless enough without my spectacles, although I was not quite so much so as I am now;—for I find it all
nonsense about short-sighted eyes improving with age. Well, I was
walking along the south side of Russell Square, with my spectacles in
my hand, and feeling a little bewildered in consequence,—for it was
quite the dusk of the evening, and short-sighted people require more
light than others. I was feeling, in fact, almost blind. I had got more
than half-way to the other side, when, from the crossing that cuts off
the corner in the direction of Montagu Place, just as I was about to turn
towards it, and old lady stepped upon the kerbstone of the pavement,
looked at me for a moment, and passed,—an occurrence not very
remarkable, certainly. But the lady was remarkable, and so was her
dress. I am not good at observing, and I am still worse at describing
dress, therefore, I can only say that hers reminded me of an old
picture,—that is, I had never seen anything like it, except in old
pictures. She had no bonnet, and looked as if she had walked straight
out of an ancient drawing-room in her evening attire. Of her face I shall
say nothing now. The next instant I met a man on the crossing, who

stopped and addressed me. So short-sighted was I that, although I recognized his voice as one I ought to know, I could not identify him until I had put on my spectacles, which I did instinctively in the act of returning his greeting. At the same moment I glanced over my shoulder after the old lady. She was nowhere to be seen.

" 'What are you looking at?' asked James Hetheridge.

" 'I was looking after that old lady,' I answered, 'but I can't see her.'

" 'What old lady?' said Hetheridge, with just a touch of impatience.

" 'You must have seen her,' I returned. 'You were not more than three yards behind her.'

" 'Where is she then?'

" 'She must have gone down one of the areas, I think. But she looked a lady, though an old-fashioned one.'

" 'Have you been dining?' asked James in a tone of doubtful inquiry.

" 'No,' I replied, not suspecting the insinuation; 'I have only just come from the Museum.'

" 'Then I advise you to call on your medical man before you go home.'

" 'Medical man!' I returned; 'I have no medical man. What do you mean? I never was better in my life.'

" 'I mean that there was no old lady. It was an illusion, and that indicates something wrong. Besides, you did not know me when I spoke to you.'

" 'That is nothing,' I returned. 'I had just taken off my spectacles, and without them I shouldn't know my own father.'

" 'How was it you saw the old lady, then?'

"The affair was growing serious under my friend's cross-questioning. I did not at all like the idea of his supposing me subject to hallucinations. So I answered, with a laugh, 'Ah! to be sure, that explains it. I am so blind without my spectacles, that I shouldn't know an old lady from a big dog.'

" 'There was no big dog,' said Hetheridge, shaking his head, as the fact for the first time dawned upon me that, although I had seen the old lady clearly enough to make a sketch of her, even to the features of her careworn, eager old face, I had not been able to recognise the well-known countenance of James Hetheridge.

" 'That's what comes of reading till the optic nerve is weakened,' he went on. 'You will cause yourself serious injury if you do not pull up in time. I'll tell you what; I'm going home next week,—will you go with me?'

" 'You are very kind,' I answered, not altogether rejecting the proposal, for I felt that a little change to the country would be pleasant, and I was quite my own master. For I had unfortunately means equal to my wants, and had no occasion to follow any profession,—not a very desirable thing for a young man, I can tell you, Master Harry. I need not keep you over the commonplaces of pressing and yielding. It is enough to say that he pressed and that I yielded. The day was fixed for our departure together; but something or other, I forget what, occurred, to make him advance the date, and it was resolved that I should follow later in the month.

"It was a drizzly afternoon in the beginning of the last week of October when I left the town of Bradford in a post-chaise to drive to Lewton Grange, the property of my friend's father. I had hardly left the town, and the twilight had only begun to deepen, when, glancing from one of the windows of the chaise, I fancied I saw, between me and the hedge, the dim figure of a horse keeping pace with us. I thought, in the first interval of unreason, that it was a shadow from my own horse, but reminded myself the next moment that there could be no shadow where there was no light. When I looked again, I was at the first glance convinced that my eyes had deceived me. At the second, I believed once more that a shadowy something, with the movements of a horse in harness, was keeping pace with us. I turned away again with some discomfort, and not till we had reached an open moorland road, whence a little watery light was visible on the horizon, could I summon up courage enough to look out once more. Certainly then there was nothing to be seen, and I persuaded myself that it had been all a fancy, and lighted a cigar. With my feet on the cushions before me, I had soon lifted myself on the clouds of tobacco far above all the terrors of the night, and believed them banished for ever. But, my cigar coming to an end just as we turned into the avenue that led up to the Grange, I found myself once more glancing nervously out of the window. The moment the trees were about me, there was, if not a shadowy horse out there by the side of the chaise, yet certainly more than half that conviction in here in my consciousness. When I saw my friend, however, standing on the doorstep, dark against the glow of the hall-fire, I forgot all about it; and I need not add that I did not make it a subject of conversation

when I entered, for I was well aware that it was essential to a man's
reputation that his senses should be accurate, though his heart might
without prejudice swarm with shadows, and his judgment be a very
stable of hobbies.

"I was kindly received. Mrs. Hetheridge had been dead for some
years, and Laetitia, the eldest of the family, was at the head of the
household. She had two sisters, little more than girls. The father was a
burly, yet gentlemanlike Yorkshire squire, who ate well, drank well,
looked radiant, and hunted twice a week. In this pastime his son joined
him when in the humour, which happened scarcely so often. I, who had
never crossed a horse in my life, took his apology for not being able to
mount me very coolly, assuring him that I would rather loiter about
with a book than be in at the death of the best-hunted fox in
Yorkshire.

"I very soon found myself at home with the Hetheridges; and very
soon again I began to find myself not so much at home; for Miss
Hetheridge,—Laetitia as I soon ventured to call her,—was fascinating. I
have told you, Katey, that there was an empty place in my heart. Look
to the door then, Katey. That was what made me so ready to fall in
love with Laetitia. Her figure was graceful, and I think, even now, her
face would have been beautiful but for a certain contraction of the skin
over the nostrils, suggesting an invisible thumb and forefinger pinching
them, which repelled me, although I did not then know what it
indicated. I had not been with her one evening before the impression it
made on me had vanished, and that so entirely that I could hardly recall
the perception of the peculiarity which had occasioned it. Her observation was remarkably keen, and her judgment generally correct. She had
great confidence in it herself; nor was she devoid of sympathy with
some of the forms of human imagination, only they never seemed to
possess for her any relation to practical life. That was to be ordered by
the judgment alone. I do not mean she ever said so. I am only giving the
conclusions I came to afterwards. It is not necessary that you should
have any more thorough acquaintance with her mental character. One
point in her moral nature, of especial consequence to my narrative, will
show itself by and by.

"I did all I could to make myself agreeable to her, and the more I
succeeded the more delightful she became in my eyes. We walked in the
garden and grounds together; we read, or rather I read and she
listened;—read poetry, Katey—sometimes till we could not read any

more for certain hazinesses and huskinesses which look now, I am afraid, considerably more absurd than they really were, or even ought to look. In short, I considered myself thoroughly in love with her."

"And wasn't she in love with you, uncle?"

"Don't interrupt me, child. I don't know. Honestly, I don't know. I hoped so then. I hope the contrary now. She liked me I am sure. That is not much to say. Liking is very pleasant and very cheap. Love is as rare as a star."

"I thought the stars were anything but rare, uncle."

"That's because you never went out to find one for yourself, Katey. They would prove a few miles apart then."

"But it would be big enough when I did find it."

"Right, my dear. That is the way with love.—Laetitia was a good housekeeper. Everything was punctual as clockwork. I use the word advisedly. If her father, who was punctual to one date,—the dinner-hour,—made any remark to the contrary as he took up the carving-knife, Laetitia would instantly send one of her sisters to question the old clock in the hall, and report the time to half a minute. It was sure to be found that, if there was a mistake, the mistake was in the clock. But although it was certainly a virtue to have her household in such perfect order, it was not a virtue to be impatient with every infringe-ment of its rules on the part of others. She was very severe, for instance, upon her two younger sisters if, the moment after the second bell had rung, they were not seated at the dinner-table, washed and aproned. Order was a very idol with her. Hence the house was too tidy for any sense of comfort. If you left an open book on the table, you would, on returning to the room a moment after, find it put aside. What the furniture of the drawing-room was like, I never saw; for not even on Christmas Day, which was the last day I spent there, was it uncovered. Everything in it was kept in bibs and pinafores. Even the carpet was covered with a cold and slippery sheet of brown holland. Mr. Hetheridge never entered that room, and therein was wise. James remonstrated once. She answered him quite kindly, even playfully, but no change followed. What was worse, she made very wretched tea. Her father never took tea; neither did James. I was rather fond of it, but I soon gave it up. Everything her father partook of was first-rate. Every-thing else was somewhat poverty-stricken. My pleasure in Laetitia's society prevented me from making practical deductions from such trifles."

"I shouldn't have thought you knew anything about eating, uncle," said Janet.

"The less a man eats, the more he likes to have it good, Janet. In short,—there can be no harm in saying it now,—Laetitia was so far from being like the name of her baptism,—and most names are so good that they are worth thinking about; no children are named after bad ideas,— Laetitia was so far unlike hers as to be stingy,—an abominable fault. But, I repeat, the notion of such a fact was far from me then. And now for my story.

"The first of November was a very lovely day, quite one of the 'halcyon days' of 'St. Martin's summer.' I was sitting in a little arbour I had just discovered, with a book in my hand,—not reading, however, but day-dreaming,—when, lifting my eyes from the ground, I was startled to see, through a thin shrub in front of the arbour, what seemed the form of an old lady seated, apparently reading from a book on her knee. The sight instantly recalled the old lady of Russell Square. I started to my feet, and then, clear of the intervening bush, saw only a great stone such as abounded on the moors in the neighbourhood, with a lump of quartz set on the top of it. Some childish taste had put it there for an ornament. Smiling at my own folly, I sat down again, and reopened my book. After reading for a while, I glanced up again, and once more started to my feet, overcome by the fancy that there verily sat the old lady reading. You will say it indicated an excited condition of the brain. Possibly; but I was, as far as I can recall, quite collected and reasonable. I was almost vexed this second time, and sat down once more to my book. Still, every time I looked up, I was startled afresh. I doubt, however, if the trifle is worth mentioning, or has any significance even in relation to what followed.

"After dinner I strolled out by myself, leaving father and son over their claret. I did not drink wine; and from the lawn I could see the windows of the library, whither Laetitia commonly retired from the dinner-table. It was a very lovely soft night. There was no moon, but the stars looked wider awake than usual. Dew was falling, but the grass was not yet wet, and I wandered about on it for half an hour. The stillness was somehow strange. It had a wonderful feeling in it as if something were expected,—as if the quietness were the mould in which some event or other was about to be cast.

"Even then I was a reader of certain sorts of recondite lore. Suddenly I remembered that this was the eve of All Souls. This was the night on which the dead came out of their graves to visit their old homes. 'Poor dead!' I thought with myself; 'have you any place to call a home now? If you have, surely you will not wander back here, where all that you called home has either vanished or given itself to others, to be their home now and yours no more! What an awful doom the old fancy has allotted you! To dwell in your graves all the year, and creep out, this one night, to enter at the midnight door, left open for welcome! A poor welcome truly!—just an open door, a clean-swept floor, and a fire to warm your rain-sodden limbs! The household asleep, and the house-place swarming with the ghosts of ancient times,—the miser, the spendthrift, the profligate, the coquette,—for the good ghosts sleep, and are troubled with no waking like yours! Not one man, sleepless like yourselves, to question you, and be answered after the fashion of the old nursery rhyme:—

> " 'What makes your eyes so holed?'
> 'I've lain so long among the mould.'
> 'What makes your feet so broad?'
> 'I've walked more than ever I rode!'

" 'Yet who can tell?' I went on to myself. 'It may be your hell to return thus. It may be that only on this one night of all the year you can show yourselves to him who can see you, but that the place where you were wicked is the Hades to which you are doomed for ages.' I thought and thought till I began to feel the air alive about me, and was enveloped in the vapours that dim the eyes of those who strain them for one peep through the dull mica windows that will not open on the world of ghosts. At length I cast my fancies away, and fled from them to the library, where the bodily presence of Laetitia made the world of ghosts appear shadowy indeed.

" 'What a reality there is about a bodily presence!' I said to myself, as I took my chamber-candle in my hand. 'But what is there more real in a body?' I said again, as I crossed the hall. 'Surely nothing,' I went on, as I ascended the broad staircase to my room. 'The body must vanish. If there be a spirit, that will remain. A body can but vanish. A ghost can appear.'

"I woke in the morning with a sense of such discomfort as made me spring out of bed at once. My foot lighted upon my spectacles. How they came to be on the floor I could not tell, for I never took them off when I went to bed. When I lifted them I found they were in two pieces; the bridge was broken. This was awkward. I was so utterly helpless without them! Indeed, before I could lay my hand on my hair-brush I had to peer through one eye of the parted pair. When I looked at my watch after I was dressed, I found I had risen an hour earlier than usual. I groped my way down-stairs to spend the hour before breakfast in the library.

"No sooner was I seated with a book than I heard the voice of Laetitia scolding the butler, in no very gentle tones, for leaving the garden-door open all night. The moment I heard this, the strange occurrences I am about to relate began to dawn upon my memory. The door had been open the night long between All Saints and All Souls. In the middle of that night I awoke suddenly. I knew it was not the morning by the sensations I had, for the night feels altogether different from the morning. It was quite dark. My heart was beating violently, and I either hardly could or hardly dared breathe. A nameless terror was upon me, and my sense of hearing was, apparently by the force of its expectation, unnaturally roused and keen. There it was,—a slight noise in the room!—slight, but clear, and with an unknown significance about it! It was awful to think it would come again. I do believe it was only one of those creaks in the timbers which announce the torpid, age-long, sinking flow of every house back to the dust,—a motion to which the flow of the glacier is as a torrent, but which is no less inevitable and sure. Day and night it ceases not; but only in the night, when house and heart are still, do we hear it. No wonder it should sound fearful! for are we not the immortal dwellers in ever-crumbling clay? The clay is so near us, and yet not of us, that its every movement starts a fresh dismay. For what will its final ruin disclose? When it falls from about us, where shall we find that we have existed all the time?

"My skin tingled with the bursting of the moisture from its pores. Something was in the room beside me. A confused, indescribable sense of utter loneliness, and yet awful presence, was upon me, mingled with a dreary, hopeless desolation, as of burnt-out love and aimless life. All at once I found myself sitting up. The terror that a cold hand might be laid upon me, or a cold breath blow on me, or a corpse-like face bend down through the darkness over me, had broken my bonds!—I would meet half way whatever might be approaching. The moment that my will burst into action the terror began to ebb.

"The room in which I slept was a large one, perfectly dreary with tidiness. I did not know till afterwards that it was Laetitia's room, which she had given up to me rather than prepare another. The furniture, all but one article, was modern and commonplace. I could not help remarking to myself afterwards how utterly void the room was of the nameless charm of feminine occupancy. I had seen nothing to wake a suspicion of its being a lady's room. The article I have excepted was an ancient bureau, elaborate and ornate, which stood on one side of the large bow window. The very morning before, I had seen a bunch of keys hanging from the upper part of it, and had peeped in. Finding, however, that the pigeon-holes were full of papers, I closed it at once. I should have been glad to use it, but clearly it was not for me. At that bureau the figure of a woman was now seated in the posture of one writing. A strange dim light was around her, but whence it proceeded I never thought of inquiring. As if I, too, had stepped over the bourne, and was a ghost myself, all fear was now gone. I got out of bed, and softly crossed the room to where she was seated. 'If she should be beautiful!' I thought,—for I had often dreamed of a beautiful ghost that made love to me. The figure did not move. She was looking at a faded brown paper. 'Some old love-letter,' I thought, and stepped nearer. So cool was I now, that I actually peeped over her shoulder. With mingled surprise and dismay I found that the dim page over which she bent was that of an old account-book. Ancient household records, in rusty ink, held up to the glimpses of the waning moon, which shone through the parting in the curtains, their entries of shillings and pence!—Of pounds there was not one. No doubt pounds and farthings are much the same in the world of thought—the true spirit-world; but in the ghost-world this eagerness over shillings and pence must mean something awful! To think that coins which had since been worn smooth in other pockets and purses, which had gone back to the Mint, and been melted down, to come out again and yet again with the heads of new kings and queens,—that dinners, eaten by men and women and children whose bodies had since been eaten by the worms,—that polish for the floors, inches of whose thickness had since been worn away,—that the hundred nameless trifles of a life utterly vanished, should be perplexing, annoying, and worst of all, interesting the soul of a ghost who had been in Hades for centuries! The writing was very old-fashioned, and the words were contracted. I could read nothing but the moneys and one single entry,—'Corinths, Vs.'

"Currants for a Christmas pudding, most likely!—Ah, poor lady! the pudding and not the Christmas was her care; not the delight of the children over it, but the beggarly pence which it cost. And she cannot get it out of her head, although her brain was 'powdered all as thin as flour' ages ago in the mortar of Death. 'Alas, poor ghost!' It needs no treasured hoard left behind, no floor stained with the blood of the murdered child, no wickedly hidden parchment of landed rights!—An old account-book is enough for the hell of the house-keeping gentle-woman!

"She never lifted her face, or seemed to know that I stood behind her. I left her, and went into the bow window, where I could see her face. I was right. It was the same old lady I had met in Russell Square, walking in front of James Hetheridge. Her withered lips went moving as if they would have uttered words had the breath been commissioned thither; her brow was contracted over her thin nose; and once and again her shining forefinger went up to her temple as if she were pondering some deep problem of humanity. How long I stood gazing at her I do not know, but at last I withdrew to my bed, and left her struggling to solve that which she could never solve thus. It was the symbolic problem of her own life, and she had failed to read it. I remember nothing more. She may be sitting there still, solving at the insolvable.

"I should have felt no inclination, with the broad sun of the squire's face, the keen eyes of James, and the beauty of Laetitia before me at the breakfast-table, to say a word about what I had seen, even if I had not been afraid of the doubt concerning my sanity which the story would certainly awaken. What with the memories of the night and the want of my spectacles, I passed a very dreary day, dreading the return of the night, for, cool as I had been in her presence, I could not regard the possible reappearance of the ghost with equanimity. But when the night did come, I slept soundly till the morning.

"The next day, not being able to read with comfort, I went wandering about the place, and at length began to fit the outside and inside of the house together. It was a large and rambling edifice, parts of it very old, parts comparatively modern. I first found my own window, which looked out of the back. Below this window, on one side, there was a door. I wondered whither it led, but found it locked. At the moment James approached from the stables. 'Where does this door lead?' I asked him. 'I will get the key,' he answered. 'It is rather a queer old place. We used to like it when we were children.' 'There's a stair, you see,' he said, as he threw the door open. 'It leads up over the kitchen.' I followed him up the stair. 'There's a door into your room,' he said, 'but it's always locked now.—And here's Grannie's room, as they call it, though why, I have not the least idea,' he added, as he pushed open the door of an old-fashioned parlour, smelling very musty. A few old books lay on a side-table. A china bowl stood beside them, with some shrivelled, scentless rose-leaves in the bottom of it. The cloth that covered the table was riddled by moths, and the spider-legged chairs were covered with dust.

"A conviction seized me that the old bureau must have belonged to this room, and I soon found the place where I judged it must have stood. But the same moment I caught sight of a portrait on the wall above the spot I had fixed upon. 'By Jove!' I cried, involuntarily, 'that's the very old lady I met in Russell Square!''

" 'Nonsense!' said James. 'Old-fashioned ladies are like babies,— they all look the same. That's a very old portrait.'

" 'So I see,' I answered. 'It is like a Zucchero.

" 'I don't know whose it is,' he answered hurriedly, and I thought he looked a little queer.

" 'Is she one of the family?' I asked.

" 'They say so; but who or what she was, I don't know. You must ask Letty,' he answered.

" 'The more I look at it,' I said, 'the more I am convinced it is the same old lady.'

" 'Well,' he returned with a laugh, 'my old nurse used to say she was rather restless. But it's all nonsense.'

" 'That bureau in my room looks about the same date as this furniture,' I remarked.

" 'It used to stand just there,' he answered, pointing to the space under the picture. 'Well I remember with what awe we used to regard it; for they said the old lady kept her accounts at it still. We never dared touch the bundles of yellow papers in the pigeon-holes. I remember thinking Letty a very heroine once when she touched one of them with the tip of her forefinger. She had got yet more courageous by the time she had it moved into her own room.'

" 'Then that is your sister's room I am occupying?' I said.

" 'Yes.'

" 'I am ashamed of keeping her out of it.'

" 'Oh! she'll do well enough.'

" 'If I were she though,' I added, 'I would send that bureau back to its own place.'

" 'What do you mean, Heywood? Do you believe every old wife's tale that ever was told?'

" 'She may get a fright some day,—that's all!' I replied.

"He smiled with such an evident mixture of pity and contempt that for the moment I almost disliked him; and feeling certain that Laetitia would receive any such hint in a somewhat similar manner, I did not feel inclined to offer her any advice with regard to the bureau.

"Little occurred during the rest of my visit worthy of remark. Somehow or other I did not make much progress with Laetitia. I believe I had begun to see into her character a little, and therefore did not get deeper in love as the days went on. I know I became less absorbed in her society, although I was still anxious to make myself agreeable to her,—or perhaps, more properly, to give her a favourable impression of me. I do not know whether she perceived any difference in my behaviour, but I remember that I began again to remark the pinched look of her nose, and to be a little annoyed with her for always putting aside my book. At the same time, I daresay I was provoking, for I never was given to tidiness myself.

"At length Christmas Day arrived. After breakfast, the squire, James, and the two girls arranged to walk to church. Laetitia was not in the room at the moment. I excused myself on the ground of a headache, for I had had a bad night. When they left, I went up to my room, threw myself on the bed, and was soon fast asleep.

"How long I slept I do not know, but I woke again with that indescribable yet well-known sense of not being alone. The feeling was scarcely less terrible in the daylight than it had been in the darkness. With the same sudden effort as before, I sat up in the bed. There was the figure at the open bureau, in precisely the same position as on the former occasion. But I could not see it so distinctly. I rose as gently as I could, and approached it, after the first physical terror. I am not a coward. Just as I got near enough to see the account book open on the folding cover of the bureau, she started up, and, turning, revealed the face of Laetitia. She blushed crimson.

" 'I beg your pardon, Mr. Heywood,' she said, in great confusion; 'I thought you had gone to church with the rest.'

" 'I had lain down with a headache, and gone to sleep,' I replied.

'But,—forgive me, Miss Hetheridge,' I added, for my mind was full of the dreadful coincidence,—'don't you think you would have been better at church than balancing your accounts on Christmas Day?'

" 'The better day the better deed,' she said, with a somewhat offended air, and turned to walk from the room.

" 'Excuse me, Laetitia,' I resumed, very seriously, 'but I want to tell you something.'

"She looked conscious. It never crossed me, that perhaps she fancied I was going to make a confession. Far other things were then in my mind. For I thought how awful it was, if she too, like the ancestral ghost, should have to do an age-long penance of haunting that bureau and those horrid figures, and I had suddenly resolved to tell her the whole story. She listened with varying complexion and face half turned aside. When I had ended, which I fear I did with something of a personal appeal, she lifted her head and looked me in the face, with just a slight curl on her thin lip, and answered me. 'If I had wanted a sermon, Mr. Heywood, I should have gone to church for it. As for the ghost, I am sorry for you.' So saying she walked out of the room.

"The rest of the day I did not find very merry. I pleaded my headache as an excuse for going to bed early. How I hated the room now! Next morning, immediately after breakfast, I took my leave of Lewton Grange."

"And lost a good wife, perhaps, for the sake of a ghost, uncle!" said Janet.

"If I lost a wife at all, it was a stingy one. I should have been ashamed of her all my life long."

"Better than a spendthrift," said Janet.

"How do you know that?" returned her uncle. "All the difference I see is, that the extravagant ruins the rich, and the stingy robs the poor."

"But perhaps she repented, uncle," said Kate.

"I don't think she did, Katey. Look here."

Uncle Cornelius drew from the breast-pocket of his coat a black-edged letter.

"I have kept up my friendship with her brother," he said. "All he knows about the matter is, that either we had a quarrel, or she refused me;—he is not sure which. I must say for Laetitia, that she was no tattler. Well, here's a letter I had from James this very morning. I will read it to you.

" 'My dear Heywood,—We have had a terrible shock this morning.

Letty did not come down to breakfast, and Lizzie went to see if she was ill. We heard her scream, and, rushing up, there was poor Letty, sitting at the old bureau, quite dead. She had fallen forward on the desk, and her housekeeping-book was crumpled up under her. She had been so all night long, we suppose, for she was not undressed, and was quite cold. The doctors say it was disease of the heart.'

"There!" said Uncle Cornie, folding up the letter.

"Do you think the ghost had anything to do with it, uncle?" asked Kate, almost under her breath.

"How should I know, my dear? Possibly."

"It's very sad," said Janet; "but I don't see the good of it all. If the ghost had come to tell that she had hidden away money in some secret place in the old bureau, one would see why she had been permitted to come back. But what was the good of those accounts after they were over and done with? I don't believe in the ghost."

"Ah, Janet, Janet! but those wretched accounts were not over and done with, you see. That is the misery of it."

Uncle Cornelius rose without another word, bade them good-night, and walked out into the wind.

IX
The Butcher's Bills

I

Husband and Wife

I am going to tell a story of married life. My title will prepare the reader for something hardly heroic; but I trust it will not be found lacking in the one genuine and worthy interest a tale ought to have—namely, that it presents a door through which we may walk into one region or another of the human heart, and there find ourselves not altogether unacquainted or from home.

There was a law among the Jews which forbade the yoking together of certain animals, either because, being unequal in size or strength, one of them must be oppressed, or for the sake of some lesson thus embodied to the Eastern mind—possibly for both reasons. Half the tragedy would be taken out of social life if this law could be applied to human beings in their various relations. I do not say that this would be well, or that we could afford to lose the result of the tragedy thus occasioned. Neither do I believe that there are so many instances of unequal yoking as the misprising judgments of men by men and women by women might lead us to imagine. Not every one declared by the wisdom of acquaintance to have thrown himself or herself away must therefore be set down as unequally yoked. Or it may even be that the inequality is there, but the loss on the other side. How some people could ever have come together must always be a puzzle until one knows the history of the affair; but not a few whom most of us would judge quite unsuited to each other do yet get on pretty well from the first, and better and better the longer they are together, and that with mutual advantage, improvement, and development. Essential humanity is deeper than the accidents of individuality; the common is more powerful than the peculiar; and the honest heart will always be learning to act more and more in accordance with the laws of its being. It must

Reprinted from *The Gifts of the Child Christ, and Other Tales* (1882).

be of much more consequence to any lady that her husband should be a man on whose word she can depend than that he should be of a gracious presence. But if instead of coming nearer to a true understanding of each other, the two should from the first keep falling asunder, then something tragic may almost be looked for.

Duncan and Lucy Dempster were a couple the very mention of whose Christian names together would have seemed amusing to the friends who had long ceased to talk of their unfitness. Indeed, I doubt if in their innermost privacy they ever addressed each other except as Mr. and Mrs. Dempster. For the first time to see them together, no one could help wondering how the conjunction could have been effected. Dempster was of Scotch descent, but the hereditary high cheek-bone seemed to have got into his nose, which was too heavy a pendant for the low forehead from which it hung. About an inch from the end it took a swift and unexpected curve downwards, and was a curious and abnormal nose, which could not properly be assorted with any known class of noses. A long upper lip, a large, firm, and not quite ugly mouth, with a chin both long and square, completed a face which, with its low forehead, being yet longer than usual, had a particularly equine look. He was rather under the middle height, slender, and well enough made—altogether an ordinary mortal, known on 'Change as an able, keen, and laborious man of business. What his special business was I do not know. He went to the city by the eight o'clock omnibus every morning, dived into a court, entered a little square, rushed up two flights of stairs to a couple of rooms, and sat down in the back one before an office table on a hair-seated chair. It was a dingy place—not so dirty as it looked, I daresay. Even the windows, being of bad glass, did, I believe, look dirtier than they were. It was a place where, so far as the eye of an outsider could tell, much or nothing might be doing. Its occupant always wore his hat in it, and his hat always looked shabby. Some people said he was rich, others that he would be one day. Some said he was a responsible man, whatever the epithet may have been intended to mean. I believe he was quite as honest as the recognized laws of his trade demanded—and for how many could I say more? Nobody said he was avaricious—but then he moved amongst men whose very notion was first to make money, after that to be religious, or to enjoy themselves, as the case might be. And no one either ever said of him that he was a good man, or a generous. He was about forty years of age, looking somehow as if he had never been younger. He had had a

fair education—better than is generally considered necessary for mer-
cantile purposes—but it would have been hard to discover any signs of it
in the spending of his leisure. On Sunday mornings he went with his
wife to church, and when he came home had a good dinner, of which
now and then a friend took his share. If no stranger was present he took
his wine by himself, and went to sleep in his easy chair of marone-
coloured leather, while his wife sat on the other side of the fire if it was
winter, or a little way off by the open window if it was summer, gently
yawned now and then, and looked at him with eyes a little troubled.
Then he went off again by the eight o'clock omnibus on Monday
morning, and not an idea more or less had he in his head, not a
hair's-breadth of difference was there in his conduct or pursuits, that he
had been to church and had spent the day out of business. That may,
however, for anything I know, have been as much the clergyman's fault
as his. He was the sort of man you might call machine-made, one in
whom humanity, if in no wise caricatured, was yet in no wise ennobled.

His wife was ten years younger than he—hardly less than beautiful—
only that over her countenance seemed to have gathered a kind of haze
of commonness. At first sight, notwithstanding, one could not help
perceiving that she was china and he was delft. She was graceful as she
sat, long-necked, slope-shouldered, and quite as tall as her husband,
with a marked daintiness about her in the absence of the extremes of
the fashion, in the quality of the lace she wore on her black silk dress,
and in the wide white sleeves of fine cambric that covered her arms
from the shoulder to the wrist. She had a morally delicate air, a look of
scrupulous nicety and lavender-stored linen. She had long dark lashes;
and when they rose, the eyelids revealed eyes of uncommon beauty.
She had good features, good teeth, and a good complexion. The main
feeling she produced and left was of ladyhood—little more.

Sunday afternoon came fifty-two times in the year. I mention this
because then always, and nearly then only, could one calculate on
seeing them together. It came to them in a surburb of London, and the
look of it was dull. Doubtless Mr. Dempster's dinner and his repose
after it were interesting to him, but I cannot help thinking his wife
found it dreary. She had, however, got used to it. The house was a good
old one, of red brick, much larger than they required, but not expensive, and had a general look of the refinement of its mistress. In the
summer the windows of the dining-room would generally be open, for
they looked into a really lovely garden behind the house, and the scent

of the jasmine that crept all around them would come in plentifully. I
wonder what the scent of jasmine did in Duncan Dempster's world.
Perhaps it never got farther than the general ante-chamber of the
sensorium. It often made his wife sad—she could not tell why. To him I
daresay it smelt agreeable, but I can hardly believe it ever woke in him
that dreamy sensation it gave her—of something she had not had
enough of, she could not say what. When the heat was gone off a little
he would walk out on the lawn, which was well kept and well watered,
with many flowering shrubs about it. Why he did so, I cannot tell. He
looked at nothing in particular, only walked about for a few minutes,
no doubt derived some pleasure of a mild nature from something, and
walked in again to tea. One might have expected he would have
cultivated the acquaintance of his garden a little, if it were only for the
pleasure the contrast would give him when he got back to his loved
office, for a greater contrast could not well have been found than
between his dingy dreary haunt on weekdays—a place which nothing
but duty could have made other than repugnant to any free soul—and
this nest of greenery and light and odour. Sweet scents floated in clouds
invisible about the place; flower eyes and stars and bells and bunches
shone and glowed and lurked all around; his very feet might have
learned a lesson of that which is beyond the sense from the turf he
trod; but all the time, if he were not exactly seeing in his mind's eye the
walls and tables of his office in the City square, his thoughts were not
the less brooding over such business as he there transacted. For Mr.
Dempster's was not a free soul. How could it be when all his energies
were given to making money? This he counted his *calling*—and I believe
actually contrived to associate some feeling of duty with the notion of
leaving behind him a plump round sum of money, as if money in
accumulation and following flood, instead of money in peaceful current, were the good thing for the world! Hence the whole realm of real
life, the universe of thought and growth, was a high-hedged park to
him, within which he never even tried to look—not even knowing that
he was shut out from it, for the hedge was of his own growing. What
shall ever wake such a man to a sense of indwelling poverty, or make
him begin to hunger after any lowliest expansion? Does a reader retort,
"The man was comfortable, and why should he be troubled?" If the
end of being, I answer, is only comfort in self, I yield. But what if there
should be at the heart of the universe a Thought to which the being of
such men is distasteful? What if to that Thought they look blots in

light, ugly things? May there not lie in that direction some possible reason why they should bethink themselves? Dempster, however, was not yet a clinker out of which all the life was burned, however much he looked like one. There was in him that which might yet burn—and give light and heat.

On the Sunday evenings Mrs. Dempster would have gladly gone to church again, if only—though to herself she never allowed this for one of her reasons—to slip from under the weight of her husband's presence. He seldom spoke to her more than a sentence at a time, but he did like to have her near him, and I suppose held, through the bare presence, some kind of dull one-sided communication with her; what did a woman know about business? and what did he know about except business? It is true he had a rudimentary pleasure in music—and would sometimes ask her to play to him, when he would listen, and after his fashion enjoy. But although here was a gift that might be developed until his soul could echo the music of the spheres, the embodied souls of Handel or Mendelssohn were to him but clouds of sound wrapped about kernels—let me say of stock or bonds.

For a year or so after their marriage it had been the custom that, the first thing after breakfast on Monday morning, she should bring him her account-book, that they might together go over her week's expenses. She must cultivate the business habits in which, he said, he found her more than deficient. How could he endure in a wife what would have been preposterous in a clerk, and would have led to his immediate dismissal? It was in his eyes necessary that the same strict record of receipt and expenditure should be kept in the household as in the office; how else was one to know in what direction things were going? he said. He required of his wife, therefore, that every individual thing that cost money, even to what she spent upon her own person, should be entered in her book. She had no money of her own, neither did he allow her any special sum for her private needs; but he made her a tolerably liberal weekly allowance, from which she had to pay everything except house-rent and taxes, an arrangement which I cannot believe a good one, as it will inevitably lead some conscientious wives to self-denial severer than necessary, and on the other hand will tempt the vulgar nature to make a purse for herself by mean savings off everybody else. It was especially distasteful to Mrs. Dempster to have to set down every little article of personal requirement that she bought. It would probably have seemed to her but a trifle had they both been young

when they married, and had there been that tenderness of love between
them which so soon sets everything more than right; but as it was, she
could never get over the feeling that the man was strange to her. As it
was she would have got over this. But there was in her a certain
constitutional lack of precision, combined with a want of energy and a
weakness of will, that rendered her more than careless where her liking
was not interested. Hence, while she would have been horrified at
playing a wrong note or singing out of tune, she not only had no
anxiety, for the thing's own sake, to have her accounts correct, but
shrunk from every effort in that direction. Now I can perfectly understand her recoil from the whole affair, with her added dislike to the
smallness of the thing required of her; but seeing she did begin with
doing it after a fashion, it is not so easy to understand why, doing it,
she should not make a consolation of doing it with absolute exactness.
Not even her dread of her husband's dissatisfaction—which was by no
means small—could prevail to make her, instead of still trusting a
memory that constantly played her false, put down a thing at once, nor
postpone it to a far less convenient season. Hence it came that her
accounts, though never much out, never balanced; and the weekly
audit, while it grew more and more irksome to the one, grew more and
more unsatisfactory to the other. For to Mr. Dempster's dusty eyes
exactitude wore the robe of rectitude, and before long, precisely and
merely from the continued unsatisfactory condition of her accounts, he
began, in a hidden corner of his righteous soul, to reflect on the moral
condition of his wife herself as unsatisfactory. Now such it certainly
was, but he was not the man to judge it correctly, or to perceive the
true significance of her failing. In business, while scrupulous as to the
requirements of custom and recognized right, he nevertheless did things
from which her soul would have recoiled like "the tender horns of
cockled snails"; yet it was to him not merely a strange and inexplicable
fact that she should *never* be able to show to a penny, nay, often not to
a shilling or eighteenpence, how the week's allowance went, but a
painful one as indicating something beyond perversity. And truly it was
no very hard task he required of her, for, seeing they had no children,
only three servants, and saw little company, her housekeeping could
not be a very heavy or involved affair. Perhaps if it had been more
difficult she would have done it better, but anyhow she hated the
whole thing, procrastinated, and setting down several things together,
was *sure* to forget some article or mistake some price; yet not one atom

more would she distrust her memory the next time she was tempted. But it was a small fault at worst, and if her husband had loved her enough to understand the bearings of it in relation to her mental and moral condition he would have tried to content himself that at least she did not exceed her allowance; and would of all things have avoided making such a matter a burden upon the consciousness of one so differently educated, if not constituted, from himself. It is but fair to add on the other side that, if she had loved him after anything like a wifely ideal, which I confess was not yet possible to her, it would not have been many weeks before she had a first correct account to show him. Convinced, at length, that accuracy was not to be had from her, and satisfying himself with dissatisfaction, he one morning threw from him the little ruled book, and declared, in a wrath which he sought to smother into dignified but hopeless rebuke, that he would trouble himself with her no further. She burst into tears, took up the book, left the room, cried a little, resolved to astonish him the next Monday, and never set down another item. When it came, and breakfast was over, he gave her the usual cheque, and left at once for town. Nor had the accounts ever again been alluded to between them.

Now this might have been very well, or at least not very ill, if both had done tolerably well thereafter—that is, if the one had continued to attend to her expenditure as well as before, and the other, when he threw away the account-book, had dismissed from his mind the whole matter. But Dempster was one of those dangerous men—more dangerous, however, to themselves than to others—who never forget, that is, get over, an offence or disappointment. They respect themselves so much, and, out of their respect for themselves, build so much upon success, set so much by never being defeated but always gaining their point, that when they are driven to confess themselves foiled, the confession is made from the "poor dumb mouth" of a wound that cannot be healed. It is there for ever—will be there at least until they find another God to worship than their own paltry selves. Hence it came that the bourn between the two spiritual estates yawned a little wider at one point, and a mist of dissatisfaction would not unfrequently rise from a certain stagnant pool in its hollow. The cause was paltry in one sense, but nothing to which belongs the name of *Cause* can fail to mingle the element of awfulness even with its paltriness. Its worst effect was that it hindered approximation in other parts of their marching natures.

And as to Mrs. Dempster, I am sorry for the apparent justification which what I have to confess concerning her must give to the severe whims of such husbands as hers: from that very Monday morning she began to grow a little careless about her expenditure—which she had never been before. By degrees bill after bill was allowed to filch from the provision of the following week, and when that was devoured, then from that of the week after. It was not that she was in the least more expensive upon herself, or that she consciously wasted anything; but, altogether averse to housekeeping, she ceased to exercise the same outlook upon the expenditure of the house, did not keep her horses together, left the management more and more to her cook; while the consciousness that she was not doing her duty made her more and more uncomfortable, and the knowledge that things were going farther and farther wrong, made her hate the idea of accounts worse and worse, until she came at length to regard them with such a loathing as might have fitted some extreme of moral evil. The bills which were supposed by her husband to be regularly settled every week were at last months behind, and the week's money spent in meeting the most pressing of its demands, while what it could no longer cover was cast upon the growing heap of evil for the time to come.

I must say this for her, however, that there was a small sum of money she expected on the death of a crazy aunt, which, if she could but lay hold of it without her husband's knowledge, she meant to devote to the clearing off of everything, when she vowed to herself to do better in the time to come.

The worst thing in it all was that her fear of her husband kept increasing, and that she felt more and more uncomfortable in his presence. Hence that troubled look in her eye, always more marked when her husband sat dozing in his chair of a Sunday afternoon.

It was natural, too, that, although they never quarrelled, their intercourse should not grow of a more tender character. Seldom was there a salient point in their few scattered sentences of conversation, except, indeed, it were some piece of news either had to communicate. Occasionally the wife read something from the newspaper, but never except at her husband's request. In general he enjoyed his newspaper over a chop at his office. Two or three times since their marriage—now eight years—he had made a transient resolve pointing at the improvement of her mind, and to that end had taken from his great glass-armoured bookcase some *standard* work—invariably, I believe, upon party-politics—from which he had made her read him a chapter. But, unhappily, she had always got to the end of it without gaining the slightest glimmer of a true notion of what the author was driving at.

It almost moves me to pity to think of the vagueness of that rudimentary humanity in Mr. Dempster which made him dream of doing something to improve his wife's mind. What did he ever do to improve his own? It is hard to understand how horses find themselves so comfortable in their stables that, be the day ever so fine, the country ever so lovely, the air ever so exhilarating, they are always rejoiced to get back into their dull twilight: it is harder to me to understand how Mr. Dempster could be so comfortable in his own mind that he never wanted to get out of it, even at the risk of being beside himself; but no doubt the dimness of its twilight had a good deal to do with his content. And then there is that in every human mind which no man's neighbour, nay, no man himself, can understand. My neighbour may in his turn be regarding my mind as a gloomy place to live in, while I find it no undesirable residence—though chiefly because of the number of windows it affords me for looking out of it. Still, if Dempster's dingy office in the City was not altogether a sufficing type of the mind that used it, I consider it a very fairly good one.

But wherein was Mrs. Dempster so very different from her husband as I rudely fancy some of my readers imagining her? Whatever may have been her reasons for marrying him—one would suppose they must have been weighty—to do so she must have been in a very undeveloped condition, and in that condition she still remained. I do not mean that she was less developed than ninty-nine out of the hundred: most women affect me only as valuable crude material out of which precious things are making. How much they might be, must be, shall be! For now they stand like so many Lot's-wives—so many rough-hewn marble blocks, rather, of which a Divinity is shaping the ends. Mrs. Dempster had all the making of a lovely woman, but notwithstanding her grace, her beauty, her sweetness, her lark-like ballading too, she was a very ordinary woman in that region of her which knew what she meant when she said "I." Of this fact she had hardly a suspicion, however; for until aspiration brings humility, people are generally pretty well satisfied with themselves, having no idea what poor creatures they are. She saw in her mirror a superior woman, regarded herself as one of the finer works of creation. The worst was that from the first she had counted herself superior to her husband, and in marrying him had felt not merely that she was conferring a favour, which every husband would allow, but that she was lowering herself without elevating him. Now it is true that she was pleasanter to look at, that her manners were sweeter, and her notions of the becoming far less easily satisfied than his; also that she was a little less deficient in vague reverence for certain forms of the higher than he. But I know of nothing in her to determine her classification as of greater value than he, except indeed that she was on the whole rather more honest. She read novels and he did not; she passed shallow judgment, where he scorned to judge; she read all the middling poetry that came in her way, and copied books full of it; but she could no more have appreciated one of Milton's or Shakspere's smallest poems than she could have laughed over a page of Chinese. She liked to hear this and that popular preacher, and when her husband called his sermons humbug, she heard it with a shocked countenance; but was she better or worse than her husband when, admiring them as she did, she permitted them to have no more influence upon her conduct than if they had been the merest humbug ever uttered by ambitious demagogue? In truth, I cannot see that in the matter of worth there was much as yet to choose between them.

It is hardly necessary, then, to say that there was little appreciable approximation of any kind going on between them. If only they would have read Dickens together! Who knows what might have come of it! But this dull close animal proximity, without the smallest conscious nearness of heart or mind or soul—and so little chance, from very lack of wants, for showing each other kindnesses—surely it is a killing sort of thing! And yet, and yet, there is always a something—call it habit, or any poorest name you please—grows up between two who are much together, at least when they neither quarrel nor thwart each other's designs, which, tending with its roots towards the deeper human, blossoms into—a wretched little flower indeed, yet afar off partaking of the nature of love. The Something seldom reveals its existence until they are parted. I suspect that with not a few, Death is the love-messenger at the stroke of whose dart the stream of love first begins to flow in the selfish bosom.

It is now necessary to mention a little break in the monotony of Mrs. Dempster's life, which, but for what came afterwards, could claim no record. One morning her page announced Major Strong, and possibly she received the gentleman who entered with a brighter face than she had ever shown her husband. The major had just arrived from India. He had been much at her father's house while she was yet a mere girl, being then engaged to one of her sisters, who died after he went abroad, and before he could return to marry her. He was now a widower, a fine-looking, frank, manly fellow. The expression of his countenance was little altered, and the sight of him revived in the memory of Mrs. Dempster many recollections of a happy girlhood, when the prospect of such a life as she now led with tolerable content would have seemed simply unendurable. When her husband came home she told him as much as he cared to hear of the visitor she had had, and he made no objection to her asking him to dine the next Sunday. When he arrived Mr. Dempster saw a man of his own age, bronzed and big, with not much waist left, but a good carriage and pleasant face. He made himself agreeable at dinner, appreciated his host's wine, and told good stories that pleased the business man as showing that he knew "what was what." He accorded him his more particular approval, speaking to his wife, on the ground that he was a man of the world, with none of the army slang about him. Mr. Dempster was not aware that he had himself more business peculiarities than any officer in her majesty's service had military ones.

After this Major Strong frequently called upon Mrs. Dempster. They were good friends, and did each other no harm whatever, and the husband neither showed nor felt the least jealousy. They sang together, occasionally went out shopping, and three or four times went together to the play. Mr. Dempster, so long as he had his usual comforts, did not pine in his wife's absence, but did show a little more pleasure when she came home to him than usually when he came home to her. This lasted for a few months. Then the major went back to India, and for a time the lady missed him a good deal, which, considering the dulness of her life, was not very surprising or reprehensible.

II

An Astonishment

Now comes the strange part of my story.

One evening the housemaid opened the door to Mr. Dempster on his return from the city; and perhaps the fact that it was the maid, and not the page as usual, roused his observation, which, except in business matters, was not remarkably operative. He glanced at the young woman, when an eye far less keen than his could not have failed to remark a strangely excited expression on her countenance.

"Where is the boy?" he asked.

"Just run to the doctor's, sir," she answered.

Then first he remembered that when he left in the morning his wife had not been feeling altogether well, but he had never thought of her since.

"How is your mistress?" he said.

"She's rather poorly, sir, but—but—she's as well as could be expected."

"What does the fool mean?" said Dempster to himself, and very nearly said it aloud, for he was not over polite to any in his service. But he did not say it aloud. He advanced into the hall with deliberation, and made for the stair.

"Oh, please, sir," the maid cried in a tone of perturbation, when, turning from shutting the door, she saw his intention, "you can't go up to mis'ess's room just at this minute, sir. Please go in the dining-room, sir."

"What do you mean?" he asked, turning angrily upon the girl, for of all things he hated mystery.

Like every one else in the house, and office both, she stood in awe of him, and his look frightened her.

"Please go in the dining-room," she gasped entreatingly.

"What!" he said and did turn towards the dining-room, "is your mistress so ill she can't see me?"

"Oh, no, sir!—at least I don't know exactly. Cook's with her, sir. She's over the worst, anyhow."

"What on earth do you mean, girl? Speak out, will you? What is the matter with your mistress?"

As he spoke he stepped into the room, the maid following him. The same moment he spied a whitish bundle of something on the rug in front of the fire.

"What do you mean by leaving things like that in the dining-room?" he went on more angrily still.

"Please, sir," answered the girl, going and lifting the bundle carefully, "it's the baby!"

"The baby!" shouted Mr. Dempster, and looked at her from head to foot. "What baby?" Then bethinking himself that it must belong to some visitor in the drawing-room with his wife, he moderated his tone. "Make haste; take it away!" he said. "I don't want babies here! There's a time and a place for everything!—What *are* you about?"

For, instead of obeying her master and taking it away, the maid was carefully looking in the blanket for the baby. Having found it and turned aside the covering from its face, she came nearer, and holding up the little vision, about the size and colour of a roll of red wax taper, said:—

"Look at it, sir! It's your own, and worth looking at."

Never before had she dared speak to him so!

I will not venture to assert that Mr. Dempster turned white, but his countenance changed, and he dropped into the chair behind him, feeling less of a business man than had been his consciousness for the last twenty years. He was hit hard. The absolutely Incredible had hit him. Babies might be born in a day, but surely not without previous preparation on the part of nature at least, if not on that of the mother; and in this case if the mother had prepared herself, certainly she had not prepared him for the event. It was as if the treasure of Nature's germens were tumbling all together. His head swam. He could not speak a word.

"Yes, sir," the maid went on, relieved of her trepidation in perceiving that her master too was mortal, and that her word had such power over him—proud also of knowing more of his concerns than he did himself, "she was took about an hour and a half ago. We've kep' sendin' an' sendin' after the doctor, but he ain't never been yet; only cook, she knows a deal an' she says she's been very bad, sir. But the young gentleman come at last, bless him! and now she's doin' as well as could be expected, sir—cook says."

"God bless me!" said the astonished father, and relapsed into the silence of bewilderment.

Eight years married with never a glimmer of offspring—and now, all at once, and without a whisper of warning, the father of a "young gentleman!" How could it be other than perplexing—discomposing, indeed!—yet it was right pleasant too. Only it would have been more pleasant if experience could have justified the affair! Nature—no, not Nature—or, if Nature, then Nature sure in some unnatural mood, had stolen a march upon him, had gone contrary to all that had ever been revealed of her doings before! and why had she pitched on him—just him, Duncan Dempster, to exercise one of her more grotesque and wayward moods upon?—to play at hide-and-seek with after this fashion? She had not treated him with exactly proper respect, he thought, or, rather vaguely felt.

"Business is business," he remarked, under his breath, "and this cannot be called proper business behaviour. What is there about me to make game of? Really, my wife ought——"

What his wife ought or ought not to have done, however, had not yet made itself clear to him, and his endeavour to excogitate being in that direction broken off, gave way to the pleasure of knowing himself a father, or perhaps more truly of having an heir. In the strength of it he rose, went to the cellaret, and poured himself out a glass of his favourite port, which he sat down to drink in silence and meditation. He was rather a picture just then and there, though not a very lovely one, seated, with his hat still on his head, in the middle of the room, upon a chair half-way between the dining-table and the sideboard, with his glass of wine in his hand. He was pondering partly the pleasure, but still mainly the peculiarity of his position. A bishop once told me that, shortly after he had been raised to the episcopal dignity, a friend's horses, whose driver had tumbled off the box drunk, ran away with him, and upset the carriage. He crept out of the window over his head, and the first thought that came to him as he sat perched on the side of the carriage, while it was jumbled along by the maddened horses, was, "What do bishops do in such circumstances?" Equally perplexing was the question Dempster had to ask himself: how husbands who, after being married eight years, suddenly and unexpectedly received the gift of a first-born, were in the habit of comporting themselves! He poured himself out another glass, and with it came the reflection, both amusing and consoling, that his brother, who was confidently expecting his tidy five figures to crown the earthly bliss of one or more of his large family some day, would be equally but less agreeably surprised. "Serve him right!" he said to himself. "What business have they to be looking out for my death?" And for a moment the heavens appeared a little more just than he was ordinarily in the habit of regarding them. He said to himself he would work harder than ever now. There would now be some good in making money! He had never given his mind to it yet, he said: now the world should see what he could do when he did give his mind to it!

Hitherto gathering had been his main pleasure, but with the thought of his money would now not seldom be mingled the thought of the little thing in the blanket! He began to find himself strangely happy. I use the wrong phrase—for the fact is, he had never yet found himself at all; he knew nothing of the person except a self-painted and immensely flattered portrait that hung in the innermost chamber of his heart—I mean the innermost chamber he knew anything of: there were many chambers there of which he did not even know the doors. Yet a few minutes as he sat there, and he was actually cherishing a little pride in the wife who had done so much better for him than he had at length come to expect. If not a good accountant, she was at least a good wife, and a very fair housekeeper: he had no doubt she would prove a good mother. He would gladly have gone to her at once, to let her know how much he was pleased with her behaviour. As for that little bit of red clay—"terra cotta," he called it to himself, as he looked round with a smile at the blanket, which the housemaid had replaced on the rug before the fire—who could imagine him a potentate upon 'Change— perhaps in time a director of European affairs! He was not in the way of joking—of all things about money; the very thought of business filled him from top to toe with seriousness; but he did make that small joke, and accompany it with a grim smile.

He was startled from his musing by the entrance of the doctor, who had in the meantime arrived and seen the lady, and now came to look at the baby. He congratulated Mr. Dempster on having at length a son and heir, but warned him that his wife was far from being beyond danger yet. The whole thing was entirely out of the common, he said, and she must be taken the greatest possible care of. The words woke a gentle pity in the heart of the man, for by nature all men have some tenderness for women in such circumstances, but they did not trouble him greatly—for such dangers belonged to their calling, their *business* in life, and, doubtless, if she had attended to that business earlier she would have found it easier.

"Did you ever know such a thing before, doctor?" he asked, with the importance of one honoured by a personal visit from the Marvellous.

"Never in my own practice," answered the doctor, whom the cook had instructed in the wonders of the case, "but I have read of such a thing." And Mr. Dempster swelled like a turkey-cock.

It was several days before he was allowed to see the mother. Perhaps had she expressed a strong desire to see him, it might have been risked sooner, but she had neither expressed nor manifested any. He kissed her, spoke a few stupid words in a kind tone, asking her how she did, but paying no heed to her answer, and turned aside to look at the baby.

Mrs. Dempster recovered but slowly, and not very satisfactorily. She did not seem to care much about the child. She tried to nurse him, but was not very successful. She took him when the nurse brought him, and yielded him again with the same indifference, showing neither pleasure to receive nor unwillingness to part with him. The nurse did not fail to observe it and remark upon it: *she* had never seen a mother care so little for her child! there was little of the mother in *her* any way! it was no wonder she was so long about it. It troubled the father a little that she should not care for his child: some slight fermentation had commenced in the seemingly dead mass of human affection that had lain so long neglected in his being, and it seemed strange to him that, while he was living for the child in the City, she should be so indifferent to him at home. For already he had begun to keep his vow, already his greater keenness in business was remarked in the City. But it boded little good for either that the gift of God should stir up in him the worship of Mammon. More sons are damned by their fathers' money than by anything else whatever outside of themselves.

There was the excuse to be made for Mrs. Dempster that she continued far from strong—and her husband made it: he would have made it more heartily if he had himself ever in his life known what it was to be ill. By degrees she grew stronger, however, until, to persons who had not known her before, she would have seemed in tolerable health. For a week or two after she was again going about the house, she continued to nurse the baby, but after that she became unable to do so, and therewith began to neglect him entirely. She never asked to see him, and when the nurse brought him would turn her head aside, and tell her to take it away. So far from his being a pleasure to her, the very sight of the child brought the hot dew upon her forehead. Her husband frowned and wondered, but, unaccustomed to open his mind either to her or to any one else, not unwisely sought to understand the thing before speaking of it, and in the meantime commenced a genuine attempt to make up to the baby for his mother's neglect. Almost without a notion how even to take him in his arms, he would now send for him the moment he had had his tea, and after a fashion, ludicrous in the eyes of the nurse, would dandle and caress him, and strut about with him before his wife, glancing up at her every now and then, to point the lesson that such was the manner in which a parent ought to behave to a child. In his presence she never made any active show of her dislike, but her look seemed all the time fixed on something far away, as if she had nothing to do with the affair.

III

Another Astonishment

But a second and very different astonishment awaited Mr. Dempster. Again one evening, on his return from the City, he saw a strange look on the face of the girl who opened the door—but this time it was a look of fear.

"Well?" he said, in a tone at once alarmed and peremptory.

She made no answer, but turned whiter than before.

"Where is your mistress?" he demanded.

"Nobody knows, sir," she answered.

"Nobody knows! What would you have me understand by such an answer?"

"It's the bare truth, sir. Nobody knows where she is."

"God bless me!" cried the husband. "What does it all mean?"

And again he sunk down upon a chair—this time in the hall, and stared at the girl as if waiting further enlightenment.

But there was little enough to be had. Only one point was clear: his wife was nowhere to be found. He sent for every one in the house, and cross-questioned each to discover the last occasion on which she had

been seen. It was some time since she had been missed; how long before
that she had been seen there was no certainty to be had. He ran to the
doctor, then from one to another of her acquaintance, then to her
mother, who lived on the opposite side of London. She, like the rest,
could tell him nothing. In her anxiety she would have gone back with
him, but he was surly, and would not allow her. It was getting towards
morning before he reached home, but no relieving news awaited him.
What to think was as much a perplexity to him as what to do. He was
not in the agony in which a man would have been who thoroughly
loved his wife, but he cared enough about her to feel uncomfortable;
and the cries of the child, who was suffering from some ailment, made
him miserable: in his perplexity and dull sense of helplessness he
wondered whether she might not have given the baby poison before she
went. Then the thing would make such a talk! and, of all things,
Duncan Dempster hated being talked about. How busy people's brains
would be with all his affairs! How many explanations of the mystery
would be suggested on 'Change! Some would say, "What business had a
man like him with a fine lady for a wife? one so much younger than
himself too!" He could remember making some remark of another,
before he was married. "Served him right!" they would say. And with
that the first movement of suspicion awoke in him—purely and solely
from his own mind's reflection of the imagined minds of others. While
in his mind's ear he heard them talking, almost before he knew what
they meant the words came to him: "There was that Major Strong, you
know!"

"She's gone to him!" he cried aloud, and, springing from the bed on
which he had thrown himself, he paced the chamber in a fury. He had
no word for it but hers that he was now in India! They had only been
waiting till—By heaven, that child was none of his! And therewith
rushed into his mind the conviction that everything was thus explained.
No man ever yet entertained an unhappy suspicion, but straightway an
army of proofs positive came crowding to the service of the lie. It is
astounding with what manifest probability everything will fall in to
prove that a fact which has no foundation whatever! There is no end to
the perfection with which a man may fool himself while taking absolute
precautions against being fooled by others. Every fact, being a living
fact, has endless sides and relations; but of all these, the man whose
being hangs upon one thought, will see only those sides and relations
which fall in with that thought. Dempster even recalled the words of

the maid, "It's mis'ess's," as embodying the girl's belief that it was not master's. Where a man, whether by nature jealous or not, is in a jealous condition, there is no need of an Iago to parade before him the proofs of his wrong. It was because Shakespere would neither have Desdemona less than perfect, nor Othello other than the most trusting and least suspicious of men, that he had to invent an all but incredible villain to effect the needful catastrophe.

But why should a man, who has cared so little for his wife, become instantly, upon the bare suspicion, so utter a prey to consuming misery? There was a character in his suffering which could not be attributed to any degree of anger, shame, or dread of ridicule. The truth was, there lay in his being a possibility of love to his wife far beyond anything his miserably stunted consciousness had an idea of; and the conviction of her faithlessness now wrought upon him in the office of Death, to let him know what he had lost. It magnified her beauty in his eyes, her gentleness, her grace; and he thought with a pang how little he had made of her or it.

But the next moment wrath at the idea of another man's child being imposed upon him as his, with the consequent loss of his precious money, swept every other feeling before it. For by law the child was his, whoever might be the father of it. During a whole minute he felt on the point of tying a stone about its neck, carrying it out, and throwing it into the river Lea. Then, with the laugh of a hyena, he set about arranging in his mind the proofs of her guilt. First came eight childless years with himself; next the concealment of her condition, and the absurd pretence that she had known nothing of it; then the trouble of mind into which she had fallen; then her strange unnatural aversion to her own child; and now, last of all, conclusive of a guilty conscience, her flight from his house. He would give himself no trouble to find her; why should he search after his own shame! He would neither attempt to conceal nor to explain the fact that she had left him—people might say what they pleased—try him for murder if they liked! As to the child she had so kindly left to console him for her absence, he would not drown him, neither would he bring him up in his house; he would give him an ordinary education, and apprentice him to a trade. For his money, he would leave it to a hospital—a rich one, able to defend his will if disputed. For what was the child? A monster—a creature that had no right to existence!

Not one of those who knew him best would have believed him

capable of being so moved, nor did one of them now know it, for he hid his suffering with the success of a man not unaccustomed to make a mask of his face. There are not a few men who, except something of the nature of a catastrophe befall them, will pass through life without having or affording a suspicion of what is in them. Everything hitherto had tended to suppress the live elements of Duncan Dempster; but now, like the fire of a volcano in a land of ice, the vitality in him had begun to show itself.

Sheer weariness drove him, as the morning began to break, to lie down again; but he neither undressed nor slept, and rose at his usual hour. When he entered the dining-room, where breakfast was laid as usual—only for one instead of two—he found by his plate, among letters addressed to his wife, a packet directed to himself. It had not been through the post, and the address was in his wife's hand. He opened it. A sheet of paper was wrapped around a roll of unpaid butcher's bills, amounting to something like eighty pounds, and a note from the butcher craving immediate settlement. On the sheet of paper was written, also in his wife's hand, these words: "I am quite unworthy of being your wife any longer"; that was all.

Now here, to a man who had loved her enough to understand her, was a clue to the whole—to Dempster it was the strongest possible confirmation of what he had already concluded. To him it appeared as certain as anything he called truth, that for years, while keeping a fair face to her husband—a man who had never refused her anything—he did not recall the fact that almost never had she asked or he offered anything—she had been deceiving him, spending money she would not account for, pretending to pay everything when she had been ruining his credit with the neighbourhood, making him, a far richer man than any but himself knew, appear to be living beyond his means, when he was every month investing far more than he spent. It was injury upon injury! Then, as a last mark of her contempt, she had taken pains that these beggarly butcher's bills should reach him from her own hand! He would trouble himself about such a woman not a moment longer!

He went from breakfast to his omnibus as usual, walked straight to his office, and spent the day according to custom. I need hardly say that the first thing he did was to write a cheque for the butcher. He made no further inquiry after her whatever, nor was any made of him there, for scarcely one of the people with whom he did business had been to his house, or had even seen his wife.

In the suburb where he lived it was different; but he paid no heed to any inquiry, beyond saying he knew nothing about her. To her relatives he said that if they wanted her they might find her for themselves. She had gone to please herself, and he was not going to ruin himself by running about the world after her.

Night after night he came home to his desolate house; took no comfort from his child; made no confession that he stood in need of comfort. But he had a dull sensation as if the sun had forsaken the world, and an endless night had begun. The simile, of course, is mine—the sensation only was his; *he* could never have expressed anything that went on in the region wherein men suffer.

A few days made a marked difference in his appearance. He was a hard man; but not so hard as people had thought him; and besides, *no* man can rule his own spirit except he has the spirit of right on his side; neither is any man proof against the inroads of good. Even Lady Macbeth was defeated by the imagination she had braved. Add to this, that no man can, even by those who understand him best, be labelled as a box containing such and such elements, for the humanity in him is deeper than any individuality, and may manifest itself at some crisis in a way altogether beside expectation.

His feeling was not at first of an elevated kind. After the grinding wrath had abated, self-pity came largely to the surface—not by any means a grand emotion, though very dear to boys and girls in their first consciousness of self, and in them pardonable enough. On the same ground it must be pardoned in a man who, with all his experience of the world, was more ignorant of the region of emotion, and more undeveloped morally, than multitudes of children: in him it was an indication that the shell was beginning to break. He said to himself that he was old beside her, and that she had begun to weary of him, and despise him. Gradually upon this, however, supervened at intervals a faint shadow of pity for her who could not have been happy or she would not have left him.

Days and weeks passed, and there was no sign of Mrs. Dempster. The child was not sent out to nurse, and throve well enough. His father never took the least notice of him.

IV

What It Meant

Some of my readers, perhaps all of them, will have concluded that Mrs. Dempster was a little out of her mind. Such, indeed, was the fact, and one not greatly to be wondered at, after such a peculiar experience as she had had. Some small degree of congestion, and the consequent pressure on some portion of the brain, had sent certain faculties to sleep, and, perhaps, roused others into morbid activity. That it is impossible to tell where sanity ends and insanity begins, is a trite remark indeed; but like many things which it is useless to say, it has the more need to be thought of. If I yield to an impulse of which I know I shall be ashamed, is it not the act of a madman? And may not the act lead to a habit, and at length to a despised, perhaps feared and hated, old age, twisting at the ragged ends of a miserable life?

However certain it is that mental disorder had to do with Mrs. Dempster's departure from her home, it is almost as certain she would never have gone had it not been for the unpaid bills haunting her consciousness, a combination of demon and ghost. The misery had all the time been growing upon her, and must have had no small share in the subversion of her microcosm. When that was effected, the evil thing that lay at the root of it all rose and pounced upon her. Wrong is its own avenger. She had been doing wrong, and knowingly for years, and now the plant of evil was blossoming towards its fruit. If one say the evil was but a trifle, I take her judgment, not his, upon that. She had been lazy towards duty, had persistently turned aside from what she knew to be her business, until she dared not even look at it. And now that the crisis was at hand, as omened by that letter from the butcher, with the sense of her wrong-doing was mingled the terror of her husband. What would he think, say, and do? Not yet had she, after all these years, any deep insight into his character; else perhaps she might have read there that, much as he loved money, the pleasure of seeing signal failure follow the neglect of his instructions would quite compensate him for the loss. What the bills amounted to, she had not an idea. Not until she had made up her mind to leave her home could she muster the courage to get them together. Then she even counted up the total and set down the sum in her memory—which sum thereafter haunted her like the name of her devil.

As to the making up of her mind—she could remember very little of that process—or indeed of the turning of her resolve into action. She left the house in the plainest dress her wardrobe could afford her, and with just one half-crown in her pocket. Her design was to seek a situation, as a refuge from her husband and his wrath. It was a curious thing, that, while it gave her no trouble to leave her baby, whom indeed she had not that day seen, and to whom for some time she had ceased to be necessary, her only notion was to get a place as nurse.

At that time, I presume, there were few or no such offices for engaging servants as are now common; at all events, the plan Mrs. Dempster took, when she had reached a part of London she judged sufficiently distant for her purpose, was to go from shop to shop inquiring after a situation. But she met with no prospect of success, and at last, greatly in need of rest and refreshment, went into a small coffee shop. The woman who kept it was taken by her appearance, her manners, and her evident trouble, and, happening to have heard of a lady who wanted a nurse, gave her the address. She went at once, and applied for the place. The lady was much pleased with her, and agreed to take her, provided she received a satisfactory character of her. For such a demand Mrs. Dempster was unprepared; she had never thought what reference she could give, and, her resources for deception easily exhausted, gave, driven to extremity, the name and address of her mother. So met the extremes of loss and salvation! She returned to the coffee shop, and the lady wrote at once to the address of the young woman's late mistress, as she supposed.

The kindness of her new friend was not exhausted; she gave her a share of her own bed that night. Mrs. Dempster had now but two shillings, which she offered her, promising to pay her the rest out of the first wages she received. But the good woman would take no more than one of them, and that in full payment of what she owed her, and Mrs. Dempster left the shop in tears, to linger about the neighbourhood until the hour should arrive at which the lady had told her to call again. Apparently she must have cherished the hope that her mother, divining her extremity, would give her the character she could honestly claim. But as she drew near the door which she hoped would prove a refuge, her mother was approaching it also, and at the turning of a corner they ran into each other's arms. The elderly lady had a hackney coach waiting for her in the next street, and Mrs. Dempster, too tired to resist, got into it at once at her mother's desire. Ere they reached the mother's house, which, as I have said, was a long way from Mr. Dempster's, the daughter told everything, and the mother had perceived more than the daughter could tell: her eyes had revealed that all was not right behind them. She soothed her as none but a mother can, easily persuading her she would make everything right, and undertaking herself to pay the money owing to the butcher. But it was soon evident that for the present there must be no suggestion of her going back to her husband; for, imagining from something, that her mother was taking her to him, she jumped up and had all but opened the door of the cab when her mother succeeded in mastering her. As soon as she was persuaded that such had never been the intention, she was quiet. When they reached the house she was easily induced to go to bed at once.

Her mother lived in a very humble way, with one servant, a trustworthy woman. To her she confided the whole story, and with her consulted as to what had better be done. Between them they resolved to keep her, for a while at least, in retirement and silence. To this conclusion they came on the following grounds: First, the daughter's terror and the mother's own fear of Mr. Dempster; next, it must be confessed, the resentment of both mistress and servant because of his rudeness when he came to inquire after her; third, the evident condition of the poor creature's mind; and last, the longing of the two women to have her to themselves, that they might nurse and cosset her to their hearts' content.

They were to have more of this indulgence, however, than, for her sake, they would have desired, for before morning she was very ill. She had brain fever, in fact, and they had their hands full, especially as they desired to take every precaution to prevent the neighbourhood from knowing there was any one but themselves in the house.

It was a severe attack, but she passed the crisis favourably, and began to recover. One morning, after a quieter night than usual, she called her mother, and told her she had had a strange dream—that she had a baby somewhere, but could not find him, and was wandering about looking for him.

"Wasn't it a curious dream, mamma?" she said. "I wish it were a true one. I knew exactly what my baby was like, and went into house after house full of children, sure that I could pick him out of thousands. I was just going up to the door of the Foundling Hospital to look for him there when I woke."

As she ceased, a strange trouble passed like a cloud over her forehead and eyes, and her hand, worn almost transparent by the fever, followed it over forehead and eyes. She seemed trying to recall something forgotten. But her mother thought it better to say nothing.

Each of the two nights following she had the same dream.

"Three times, mother," she said. "I am not superstitious, as you know, but I can't help feeling as if it must mean something. I don't know what to make of it else—except it be that I haven't got over the fever yet. And, indeed, I am afraid my head is not quite right, for I can't be sure sometimes, such a hold has my dream of me, that I haven't got a baby somewhere about the world. Give me your hand, mother, and sing to me."

Still her mother thought it more prudent to say nothing, and do what she could to divert her thoughts; for she judged it must be better to let her brain come right, as it were, of itself.

In the middle of the next night she woke her with a cry.

"O, mother, mother! I know it all now. I am not out of my mind any more. How I came here I cannot tell—but I know I have a husband and a baby at Hackney—and—oh, such a horrible roll of butcher's bills!"

"Yes, yes, my dear! I know all about it," answered her mother. "But never mind; you can pay them all yourself now, for I heard only yesterday that your aunt Lucy is dead, and has left you the hundred pounds she promised you twenty years ago."

"Oh, bless her!" cried Mrs. Dempster, springing out of bed, much to the dismay of her mother, who boded a return of the fever. "I must go home to my baby at once. But tell me about it, mamma. How did I come here? I seem to remember being in a carriage with you, and that is the last I know."

Then, upon condition that she got into bed at once, and promised not to move until she gave her leave, her mother consented to tell her all she knew. She listened in silence, with face flushed and eyes glowing, but drank a cooling draught, lay down again, and at daybreak was fast asleep. When she awoke she was herself again.

V

What Came of It

Meantime, things were going, as they should, in rather a dull fashion with Duncan Dempster. His chariot wheels were gone, and he drove heavily. The weather was good; he seldom failed of the box-seat on the omnibus; a ray of light, the first he had ever seen there, visited his table, reflected from a new window on the opposite side of a court into the heart of his dismal back office; and best of all, business was better than usual. Yet was Dempster not cheerful. He was not, indeed, a man an acquaintance would ever have thought of calling cheerful; but in grays there are gradations; and however differently a man's barometer may be set from those of other people, it has its ups and downs, its fair weather and foul. But not yet had he an idea how much his mental equilibrium had been dependent upon the dim consciousness of having that quiet uninterested wife in the comfortable house at Hackney. It had been stronger than it seemed, the spidery, invisible line connecting that office and that house, along which had run twice a day the hard dumpling that dwelt in Mr. Dempster's bosom. Vaguely connected with that home after all must have been that endless careful gathering of treasure in the city; for now, though he could no more stop making money than he could stop breathing, it had not the same interest as formerly. Indeed, he had less interest than before in keeping his lungs themselves going. But he kept on doing everything as usual.

Not one of the men he met ever said a word to him about his wife. The general impression was that she had left him for preferable society, and no one wondered at her throwing aside such "a dry old stick," whom even the devoted slaves of business contemned as having nothing in him but business.

A further change was, however, in progress within him. The first sign of it was that he began to doubt whether his wife had indeed been false to him—had forsaken him in any other company than that of Death. But there was one great difficulty in the way of the conclusion. It was impossible for him to imagine suicide as proceeding from any cause but insanity, and what could have produced the disorder in one who had no cares or anxieties, everything she wanted, and nothing to

trouble her, a devoted husband, and a happy home? Yet the mere idea
made him think more pitifully, and so more tenderly of her than
before. It had not yet occurred to him to consider whether he might
not have had something to do with her conduct or condition. Blame
was a thing he had never made acquaintance with—least of all in the
form of self-blame. To himself he was simply all right—the poised
centre of things capable of righteous judgment on everyone else. But it
must not be forgotten how little he knew about his own affairs at all;
his was a very different condition from that of one who had closed his
eyes and hardened his heart to suspicions concerning himself. His eyes
had never yet been opened to anything but the order of things in the
money world—its laws, its penalties, its rewards—those he did understand. But apparently he was worth troubling. A slow dissatisfaction
was now preying upon him—a sense of want—of not having something
he once had, a vague discomfort, growing restless. The feeling was no
doubt the worse that the birth of the child had brought such a sudden
rush of fresh interest into his occupation, which doubt concerning that
birth had again so suddenly checked; but even if the child should prove
after all his own, a supposition he was now willing to admit as possibly
a true one, he could never without his mother feel any enthusiasm
about him, even such enthusiasm as might be allowed to a man who
knew money from moonshine, and common sense from hysterics. Yet
once and again, about this time, the nurse coming into the room after a
few minutes' absence, found him bending over the sleeping infant, and,
as she described him, "looking as if he would have cried if he had only
known how."

One frosty evening in late autumn the forsaken husband came from
London—I doubt if he would now have said "home"—as usual, on the
top of the omnibus. His was a tough nature physically, as well as
morally, and if he had found himself inside an omnibus he would have
thought he was going to die. The sun was down. A green hue rose from
the horizon half-way to the zenith, but a pale yellow lingered over the
vanished sun, like the gold at the bottom of a chrysolite. The stars were
twinkling small and sharp in the azure overhead. A cold wind blew in
little gusts, now from this side, now from that, as they went steadily
along. The horses' hoofs rang loud on the hard road. The night got hold
of him: it was at this season, and on nights like these, that he had
haunted the house of Lucy's father, doing his best to persuade her to
make him, as he said, a happy man. It now seemed as if then, and then

only, he had been a happy man. Certainly, of all his life, it was the time when he came nearest to having a peep out of the upper windows of the house of life. He had been a dweller in the lower regions, a hewer of wood to the god of the cellar; and after his marriage, he had gone straight down again to the temple of the earthy god—to a worship whose god and temple and treasure caves will one day drop suddenly from under the votary's feet, and leave him dangling in the air without even a pocket about him—without even his banker's book to show for his respectability.

The night, I say, recalled the lovely season of his courtship, and again, in the mirror of loss, he caught a glimpse of things beyond him. Ah, if only that time and its hopes had remained with him! How different things would have been now! If Lucy had proved what he thought her!—remained what she seemed—the gentle, complaisant, yielding lady he imagined her, promising him a life of bliss! Alas, she would not even keep account of five pounds a week to please him! He never thought whether he, on his part, might not have, in some measure, come short of her expectations in a husband; whether she, the more lovely in inward design and outward fashion, might not have indulged yet more exquisite dreams of bliss which, by devotion to his ideal of life, he had done his part in disappointing. He only thought what a foolishness it all was; that thus it would go on to the end of the book; that youth after youth would have his turn of such a wooing, and such a disappointment. Sunsets, indeed! The suns of man's happiness never did anything but set! Out of money even—and who could say there was any poetry in that?—there was not half the satisfaction to be got that one expected. It was all a mess of expectations and disappointments mashed up together—nothing more. That was the world—on a fair judgment.

Such were his reflections till the driver pulled up for him to get down at his own gate. As he got down the said driver glanced up curiously at the row of windows on the first floor, and as soon as Mr. Dempster's back was turned, pointed to them with the butt-end of his whip, and nodded queerly to the gentleman who sat on his other side.

"That's more'n I've seen this six weeks," he said. "There's something more'n common up this evenin', sir."

There was light in the drawing-room—that was all the wonder; but at those windows Mr. Dempster himself looked so fixedly that he had nearly stumbled up his own door-steps.

He carried a latch-key now, for he did not care to stand at the door till the boy answered the bell; people's eyes, as they passed, seemed to burn holes in the back of his coat.

He opened the street door quietly, and went straight up the stair to the drawing-room. Perhaps he thought to detect some liberty taken by his servants. He was a little earlier than usual. He opened that door, took two steps into the room, and stood arrested, motionless. With his shabby hat on his head, his shabby greatcoat on his back—for he grudged every penny spent on his clothes—his arms hanging down by his sides, and his knees bent, ready to tremble, he looked not a little out of keeping in the soft-lighted, dainty, delicate-hued drawing-room. Could he believe his eyes? The light of a large lamp was centred upon a gracious figure in white—his wife, just as he used to see her before he married her! That was the way her hair would break loose as she ran down the stair to meet him!—only then there was no baby in her lap for it to fall over like a torrent of unlighted water over a white stone! It was a lovely sight.

He had stood but a moment when she looked up and saw him. She started, but gave no cry louder than a little moan. Instantly she rose. Turning, she laid the baby on the sofa, and flitted to him like a wraith. Arrived where he stood yet motionless, she fell upon her knees and clasped his. He was far too bewildered now to ask himself what husbands did in such circumstances, and stood like a block.

"Husband! husband!" she cried, "forgive me." With one hand she hid her face, although it was bent to the ground, and with the other held up to him a bit of paper. He took it from the thin white fingers; it might explain something—help him out of this bewilderment, half nightmare, half heavenly vision. He opened it. Nothing but a hundred-pound note! The familiar sight of bank paper, however, seemed to restore his speech.

"What does this mean, Lucy? Upon my word! Permit me to say——"

He was growing angry.

"It is to pay the butcher," she said, with a faltering voice.

"Damn the butcher!" he cried. "I hope you've got something else to say to me! Where have you been all this time?"

"At my mother's. I've had a brain fever, and been out of my mind. It was all about the butcher's bill."

Dempster stared. Perhaps he could not understand how a woman who would not keep accounts should be to such a degree troubled at the result of her neglect.

"Look at me, if you don't believe me," she cried, and as she spoke she rose and lifted her face to his.

He gazed at it for a moment—pale, thin, and worn; and out of it shone the beautiful eyes, larger than before, but shimmering uncertain like the stars of a humid night, although they looked straight into his.

Something queer was suddenly the matter with his throat—something he had never felt before—a constriction such as, had he been superstitious, he might have taken for the prologue to a rope. Then the thought came—what a brute he must be that his wife should have been afraid to tell him her trouble! Thereupon he tried to speak, but his throat was irresponsive to his will. Eve's apple kept sliding up and down in it, and would not let the words out. He had never been so served by members of his own body in his life before! It was positive rebellion, and would get him into trouble with his wife. There it was! Didn't he say so?

"Can't you forgive me, Mr. Dempster?" she said, and the voice was so sweet and so sad! "It is my own money. Aunt Lucy is dead, and left it me. I think it will be enough to pay all my debts; and I promise you—I do promise you that I will set down every halfpenny after this. Do try me once again—for baby's sake."

This last was a sudden thought. She turned and ran to the sofa. Dempster stood where he was, fighting the strange uncomfortable feeling in his throat. It would not yield a jot. Was he going to die suddenly of choking? Was it a judgment upon him? Diphtheria, perhaps! It was much about in the City!

She was back, and holding up to him their sleeping child.

The poor fellow was not half the brute he looked—only he could *not* tell what to do with that confounded lump in his throat! He dared not try to speak, for it only choked him the more. He put his arms round them both, and pressed them to his bosom. Then the lump in his throat melted and ran out at his eyes, and all doubt vanished like a mist before the sun. But he never knew that he had wept. His wife did, and that was enough.

The next morning, for the first time in his life, he lost the eight o'clock omnibus.

The following Monday morning she brought her week's account to him. He turned from it testily, but she insisted on his going over it.

There was not the mistake of a halfpenny. He went to town with a smile in his heart, and that night brought her home a cheque for ten pounds instead of five.

One day, in the middle of the same week, he came upon her sitting over the little blue-and-red-ruled book with a troubled countenance. She took no notice of his entrance.

"Do leave those accounts," he said, "and attend to me."

She shook her head impatiently, and made him no other answer. One moment more, however, and she started up, threw her arms about his neck, and cried triumphantly,

"It's buttons!—fourpence-halfpenny I paid for buttons!"'

X

Birth, Dreaming, Death
[The Schoolmaster's Story]

"In a little room, scantily furnished, lighted, not from the window, for it was dark without, and the shutters were closed, but from the peaked flame of a small, clear-burning lamp, sat a young man, with his back to the lamp and his face to the fire. No book or paper on the table indicated labour just forsaken; nor could one tell from his eyes, in which the light had all retreated inwards, whether his consciousness was absorbed in thought, or reverie only. The window curtains, which scarcely concealed the shutters, were of coarse texture, but of brilliant scarlet,—for he loved bright colours; and the faint reflection they threw on his pale, thin face, made it look more delicate than it would have seemed in pure daylight. Two or three bookshelves, suspended by cords from a nail in the wall, contained a collection of books, poverty-stricken as to numbers, with but few to fill up the chronological gap between the Greek New Testament and stray volumes of the poets of the present century. But his love for the souls of his individual books was the stronger that there was no possibility of its degenerating into avarice for the bodies or outsides whose aggregate constitutes the piece of house-furniture called a library.

"Some years before, the young man (my story is so short, and calls in so few personages, that I need not give him a name) had aspired, under the influence of religious and sympathetic feeling, to be a clergyman; but Providence, either in the form of poverty, or of theological difficulty, had prevented his prosecuting his studies to that end. And now he was only a village schoolmaster, nor likely to advance further. I have said *only* a village schoolmaster; but is it not better to be a teacher *of* babes than a preacher *to* men, at any time; not to speak of those troublous times of transition, wherein a difference of degree must so often assume the appearance of a difference of kind? That man is more happy—I will not say more blessed—who, loving boys and girls, is loved and revered by them, than he who, ministering unto men and women, is compelled to pour his words into the filter of religious

Reprinted from *Adela Cathcart* (1864).

suspicion, whence the water is allowed to pass away unheeded, and only the residuum is retained for the analysis of ignorant party-spirit.

"He had married a simple village girl, in whose eyes he was nobler than the noblest—to whom he was the mirror, in which the real forms of all things around were reflected. Who dares pity my poor village schoolmaster? I fling his pity away. Had he not found in her love the verdict of God, that he was worth loving? Did he not in her possess the eternal and the unchangeable? Were not her eyes openings through which he looked into the great depths that could not be measured or represented? She was his public, his society, his critic. He found in her the heaven of his rest. God gave unto him immortality, and he was glad. For his ambition, it had died of its own mortality. He read the words of Jesus, and the words of great prophets whom he has sent; and learned that the wind-tossed anemone is a word of God as real and true as the unbending oak beneath which it grows—that reality is an absolute existence precluding degrees. If his mind was, as his room, scantily furnished, it was yet lofty; if his light was small, it was brilliant. God lived, and he lived. Perhaps the highest moral height which a man can reach, and at the same time the most difficult of attainment, is the willingness to be *nothing* relatively, so that he attain that positive excellence which the original conditions of his being render not merely possible, but imperative. It is nothing to a man to be greater or less than another; to be esteemed or otherwise by the public or private world in which he moves. Does he, or does he not, behold and love and live the unchangeable, the essential, the divine? This he can only do according as God has made him. He can behold and understand God in the least degree, as well as in the greatest, only by the godlike within him; and he that loves thus the good and great has no room, no thought, no necessity for comparison and difference. The truth satisfies him. He lives in its absoluteness. God makes the glow-worm as well as the star; the light in both is divine. If mine be an earth-star to gladden the wayside, I must cultivate humbly and rejoicingly its green earth-glow, and not seek to blanch it to the whiteness of the stars that lie in the fields of blue. For to deny God in my own being is to cease to behold him in any. God and man can meet only by the man's becoming that which God meant him to be. Then he enters into the house of life, which is greater than the house of fame. It is better to be a child in a green field than a knight of many orders in a state ceremonial.

"All night long he had sat there, and morning was drawing nigh. He has not heard the busy wind all night, heaping up snow against the house, which will make him start at the ghostly face of the world when at length he opens the shutters, and it stares upon him so white. For up in a little room above, white-curtained, like the great earth without, there has been a storm, too, half the night—moanings and prayers—and some forbidden tears; but now, at length, it is over; and through the portals of two mouths instead of one, flows and ebbs the tide of the great air-sea which feeds the life of man. With the sorrow of the mother, the new life is purchased for the child; our very being is redeemed from nothingness with the pains of a death of which we know nothing.

"An hour has gone by since the watcher below has been delivered from the fear and doubt that held him. He has seen the mother and the child—the first she has given to life and him, and has returned to his lonely room, quiet and glad.

"But not long did he sit thus before thoughts of doubt awoke in his mind. He remembered his scanty income, and the somewhat feeble health of his wife. One or two small debts he had contracted seemed absolutely to press on his bosom; and the newborn child—'oh! how doubly welcome,' he thought, 'if I were but half as rich again as I am!'—brought with it, as its own love, so its own care. The dogs of need, that so often hunt us up to heaven, seemed hard upon his heels; and he prayed to God with fervour; and as he prayed he fell asleep in his chair, and as he slept he dreamed. The fire and the lamp burned on as before, but threw no rays into his soul; yet now, for the first time, he seemed to become aware of the storm without; for his dream was as follows:—

"He lay in his bed, and listened to the howling of the wintry wind. He trembled at the thought of the pitiless cold, and turned to sleep again, when he thought he heard a feeble knocking at the door. He rose in haste, and went down with a light. As he opened the door, the wind, entering with a gust of frosty particles, blew out his candle; but he found it unnecessary, for the grey dawn had come. Looking out, he saw nothing at first; but a second look, turned downwards, showed him a little half-frozen child, who looked quietly, but beseechingly, in his face. His hair was filled with drifted snow, and his little hands and cheeks were blue with cold. The heart of the schoolmaster swelled to bursting with the spring-flood of love and pity that rose up within it. He lifted the child to his bosom, and carried him into the house, where,

in the dream's incongruity, he found a fire blazing in the room in which
he now slept. The child said never a word. He set him by the fire, and
made haste to get hot water, and put him in a warm bath. He never
doubted that this was a stray orphan who had wandered to him for
protection, and he felt that he could not part with him again; even
though the train of his previous troubles and doubts once more passed
through the mind of the dreamer, and there seemed no answer to his
perplexities for the lack of that cheap thing, gold—yea, silver. But when
he had undressed and bathed the little orphan, and having dried him on
his knees, set him down to reach something warm to wrap him in, the
boy suddenly looked up in his face, as if revived, and said with a
heavenly smile, 'I am the child Jesus.' 'The child Jesus!' said the
dreamer, astonished. 'Thou art like any other child.' 'No, do not say
so,' returned the boy; 'but say, *Any other child is like me.'* And the
child and the dream slowly faded away; and he awoke with these words
sounding in his heart—'Whosoever shall receive one of such children in
my name, receiveth me; and whosoever shall receive me, receiveth not
me, but him that sent me.' It was the voice of God saying to him:
'Thou wouldst receive the child whom I sent thee out of the cold,
stormy night; receive the new child out of the cold waste into the warm
human house, as the door by which it can enter God's house, its home.
If better could be done for it, or for thee, would I have sent it hither?
Through thy love, my little one must learn my love and be blessed. And
thou shalt not keep it without thy reward. For thy necessities—in thy
little house, is there not yet room? in thy barrel, is there not yet meal?
and thy purse is not empty quite. Thou canst not eat more than a
mouthful at once. I have made thee so. Is it any trouble to me to take
care of thee? Only I prefer to feed thee from my own hand, and not
from thy store.' And the schoolmaster sprang up in joy, ran up stairs,
kissed his wife, and clasped the baby in his arms in the name of the
child Jesus. And in that embrace, he knew that he received God to his
heart. Soon, with a tender, beaming face, he was wading through the
snow to the school-house, where he spent a happy day amidst the rosy
faces and bright eyes of his boys and girls. These, likewise, he loved the
more dearly and joyfully for that dream, and those words in his heart;
so that, amidst their true child-faces, (all going well with them, as not
unfrequently happened in his schoolroom), he felt as if all the elements
of Paradise were gathered around him, and knew that he was God's
child, doing God's work.

"But while that dream was passing through the soul of the husband, another visited the wife, as she lay in the faintness and trembling joy of the new motherhood. For although she that has been mother before, is not the less a new mother to the new child, her former relation not covering with its wings the fresh bird in the nest of her bosom, yet there must be a peculiar delight in the thoughts and feelings that come with the first-born.—As she lay half in a sleep, half in a faint, with the vapours of a gentle delirium floating through her brain, without losing the sense of existence she lost the consciousness of its form, and thought she lay, not a young mother in her bed, but a nosegay of wild flowers in a basket, crushed, flattened and half-withered. With her in the basket lay other bunches of flowers, whose odours, some rare as well as rich, revealed to her the sad contrast in which she was placed. Beside her lay a cluster of delicately curved, faintly tinged, tea-scented roses; while she was only blue hyacinth bells, pale primroses, amethyst anemones, closed blood-coloured daisies, purple violets, and one sweet-scented, pure white orchis. The basket lay on the counter of a well-known little shop in the village, waiting for purchasers. By and by her own husband entered the shop, and approached the basket to choose a nosegay. 'Ah!' thought she, 'will he choose me? How dreadful if he should not, and I should be left lying here, while he takes another! But how should he choose me? They are all so beautiful; and even my scent is nearly gone. And he cannot know that it is I lying here. Alas! alas!' But as she thought thus, she felt his hand clasp her, heard the ransom-money fall, and felt that she was pressed to his face and lips, as he passed from the shop. He *had* chosen her; he *had* known her. She opened her eyes: her husband's kiss had awakened her. She did not speak, but looked up thankfully in his eyes, as if he had, in fact, like one of the old knights, delivered her from the transformation of some evil magic, by the counter-enchantment of a kiss, and restored her from a half-withered nosegay to be a woman, a wife, a mother. The dream comforted her much, for she had often feared that she, the simple, so-called uneducated girl, could not be enough for the great school-master. But soon her thoughts flowed into another channel; the tears rose in her dark eyes, shining clear from beneath a stream that was not of sorrow; and it was only weakness that kept her from uttering audible words like these:—'Father in heaven, shall I trust my husband's love, and doubt thine? Wilt thou meet less richly the fearing hope of thy child's heart, than he in my dream met the longing of his wife's? He was perfected in my eyes by the love he bore me—shall I find thee less complete? Here I lie on thy world, faint, and crushed, and withered; and my soul often seems as if it had lost all the odours that should float up in the sweet-smelling savour of thankfulness and love to thee. But thou hast only to take me, only to choose me, only to clasp me to thy bosom, and I shall be a beautiful singing angel, singing to God, and comforting my husband while I sing. Father, take me, possess me, fill me!"

"So she lay patiently waiting for the summer-time of restored strength that drew slowly nigh. With her husband and her child near her, in her soul, and God everywhere, there was for her no death, and no hurt. When she said to herself, 'How rich I am!' it was with the riches that pass not away—the riches of the Son of man; for in her treasures, the human and the divine were blended—were one.

"But there was a hard trial in store for them. They had learned to receive what the Father sent: they had now to learn that what he gave he gave eternally, after his own being—his own glory. For ere the mother awoke from her first sleep, the baby, like a frolicsome child-angel, that but tapped at his mother's window and fled,—the baby died; died while the mother slept away the pangs of its birth; died while the father was teaching other babes out of the joy of his new fatherhood.

"When the mother woke, she lay still in her joy—the joy of a doubled life; and knew not that death had been there, and had left behind only the little human coffin.

" 'Nurse, bring me the baby,' she said at last. 'I want to see it.'

"But the nurse pretended not to hear.

" 'I want to nurse it. Bring it.'

"She had not yet learned to say *him;* for it was her first baby.

"But the nurse went out of the room, and remained some minutes away. When she returned, the mother spoke more absolutely, and the nurse was compelled to reply—at last.

" 'Nurse, do bring me the baby; I am quite able to nurse it now.'

" 'Not yet, if you please, ma'am. Really you must rest a while first. Do try to go to sleep.'

"The nurse spoke steadily, and looked her, too, straight in the face; and there was a constraint in her voice, a determination to be calm, that at once roused the suspicion of the mother; for though her first-born was dead, and she had given birth to what was now, as far as the eye could reach, the waxen image of a son, a child had come from God, and had departed to him again; and she *was* his mother.

"And the fear fell upon her heart that it might be as it was; and, looking at her attendant with a face blanched yet more with fear than with suffering, she said,

" 'Nurse, is the baby——?'

"She could not say *dead;* for to utter the word would be at once to make it possible that the only fruit of her labour had been pain and sorrow.

"But the nurse saw that further concealment was impossible; and, without another word, went and fetched the husband, who, with face pale as the mother's, brought the baby, dressed in its white clothes, and laid it by its mother's side, where it lay too still.

" 'Oh, ma'am, do not take on so,' said the nurse, as she saw the face of the mother grow like the face of the child, as if she were about to rush after him into the dark.

"But she was not 'taking on' at all. She only felt that pain at her heart, which is the farewell kiss of a long-cherished joy. Though cast out of paradise into a world that looked very dull and weary, yet, used to suffering, and always claiming from God the consolation it needed, and satisfied with that, she was able, presently, to look up in her husband's face, and try to reassure him of her well-being by a dreary smile.

" 'Leave the baby,' she said; and they left it where it was. Long and earnestly she gazed on the perfect tiny features of the little alabaster countenance, and tried to feel that this was the child she had been so long waiting for. As she looked, she fancied she heard it breathe, and she thought–'What if it should be only asleep!' but, alas! the eyes would not open, and when she drew it close to her, she shivered to feel it so cold. At length, as her eyes wandered over and over the little face, a look of her husband dawned unexpectedly upon it; and, as if the wife's heart awoke the mother's, she cried out, 'Baby! baby!' and burst into tears, during which weeping she fell asleep.

"When she awoke, she found the babe had been removed while she slept. But the unsatisfied heart of the mother longed to look again on the form of the child; and again, though with remonstrance from the nurse, it was laid beside her. All day and all night long, it remained by her side, like a little frozen thing that had wandered from its home, and now lay dead by the door.

"Next morning the nurse protested that she must part with it, for it made her fret; but she knew it quieted her, and she would rather keep her little lifeless babe. At length the nurse appealed to the father; and the mother feared he would think it necessary to remove it; but to her joy and gratitude he said, 'No, no; let her keep it as long as she likes.' And she loved her husband the more for that; for he understood her.

"Then she had the cradle brought near the bed, all ready as it was for a live child that had open eyes, and therefore needed sleep—needed the lids of the brain to close, when it was filled full of the strange colours and forms of the new world. But this one needed no cradle, for it slept on. It needed, instead of the little curtains to darken it to sleep, a great sunlight to wake it up from the darkness, and the ever-satisfied rest. Yet she laid it in the cradle, which she had set near her, where she could see it, with the little hand and arm laid out on the white coverlet. If she could only keep it so! Could not something be done, if not to awake it, yet to turn it to stone, and let it remain so for ever? No; the body must go back to its mother, the earth, and the *form* which is immortal, being the thought of God, must go back to its Father—the Maker. And as it lay in the white cradle, a white coffin was being made for it. And the mother thought: 'I wonder which trees are growing coffins for my husband and me.'

"But ere the child, that had the prayer of Job in his grief, and had died from its mother's womb, was carried away to be buried, the mother prayed over it this prayer:—'O God, if thou wilt not let me be a mother, I have one refuge: I will go back and be a child: I will be thy child more than ever. My mother-heart will find relief in childhood towards its Father. For is it not the same nature that makes the true mother and the true child? Is it not the same thought blossoming upward and blossoming downward? So there is God the Father and God the Son. Thou wilt keep my little son for me. He has gone home to be nursed for me. And when I grow well, I will be more simple, and truthful, and joyful in thy sight. And now thou art taking away my child, my plaything, from me. But I think how pleased I should be, if I had a daughter, and she loved me so well that she only smiled when I took her plaything from her. Oh! I will not disappoint thee—thou shalt have thy joy. Here I am, do with me what thou wilt; I will only smile.'

"And how fared the heart of the father? At first, in the bitterness of his grief, he called the loss of his child a punishment for his doubt and unbelief; and the feeling of punishment made the stroke more

keen, and the heart less willing to endure it. But better thoughts woke
within him ere long.

"The old woman who swept out his schoolroom, came in the
evening to inquire after the mistress, and to offer her condolences on
the loss of the baby. She came likewise to tell the news, that a certain
old man of little respectability had departed at last, unregretted by a
single soul in the village but herself, who had been his nurse through the
last tedious illness.

"The schoolmaster thought with himself:

" 'Can that soiled and withered leaf of a man, and my little
snow-flake of a baby, have gone the same road? Will they meet by the
way? Can they talk about the same thing—anything? They must part on
the borders of the shining land, and they could hardly speak by the
way.'

" 'He will live four-and-twenty hours, nurse,' the doctor had said.

" 'No, doctor; he will die to-night,' the nurse had replied; during
which whispered dialogue, the patient had lain breathing quietly, for
the last of suffering was nearly over.

He was at the close of an ill-spent life, not so much selfishly
towards others as indulgently towards himself. He had failed of true joy
by trying often and perseveringly to create a false one; and now, about
to knock at the gate of the other world, he bore with him no burden of
the good things of this; and one might be tempted to say of him, that it
were better he had not been born. The great majestic mystery lay
before him—but when would he see its majesty?

"He was dying thus, because he had tried to live as Nature said he
should not live; and he had taken his own wages—for the law of the
Maker is the necessity of his creature. His own children had forsaken
him, for they were not perfect as their Father in heaven, who maketh
his sun to shine on the evil and on the good. Instead of doubling their
care as his need doubled, they had thought of the disgrace he brought
on them, and not of the duty they owed him; and now, left to die alone
for them, he was waited on by this hired nurse, who, familiar with
death-beds, knew better than the doctor, knew that he could live only a
few hours.

"Stooping to his ear, she had told him, as gently as she could,—for
she thought she ought not to conceal it—that he must die that night. He
had lain silent for a few moments; then had called her, and, with
broken and failing voice, had said, 'Nurse, you are the only friend I

have; give me one kiss before I die.' And the woman-heart had answered the prayer.

" 'And,' said the old woman, 'he put his arms round my neck, and gave me a long kiss, such a long kiss! and then he turned his face away, and never spoke again.'

"So, with the last unction of a woman's kiss, with this baptism for the dead, he had departed.

" 'Poor old man! he had not quite destroyed his heart yet,' thought the schoolmaster. 'Surely it was the child-nature that woke in him at the last, when the only thing left for his soul to desire, the only thing he could think of as a preparation for the dread something, was a kiss. Strange conjunction, yet simple and natural! Eternity—a kiss. Kiss me; for I am going to the Unknown!—Poor old man!' the schoolmaster went on in his thoughts, 'I hope my baby has met him, and put his tiny hand in the poor old shaking hand, and so led him across the borders into the shining land, and up to where Jesus sits, and said to the Lord: "Lord, forgive this old man, for he knew not what he did." And I trust the Lord has forgiven him.'

"And then the bereaved father fell on his knees, and cried out:

" 'Lord, thou hast not punished me. Thou wouldst not punish for a passing thought of troubled unbelief, with which I strove. Lord, take my child and his mother and me, and do what thou wilt with us. I know thou givest not, to take again.'

"And ere the schoolmaster could call his protestantism to his aid, he had ended his prayer with the cry:

" 'And O God! have mercy upon the poor old man, and lay not his sins to his charge.'

"For, though a woman's kiss may comfort a man to eternity, it is not all he needs. And the thought of his lost child had made the soul of the father compassionate."

He ceased, and we sat silent.

"That Holy Thing"

Written for My Friends, Christmas, 1877, Nervi (Italy)

They all were looking for a king
   To slay their foes and lift them high:
Thou cam'st a little baby thing
   That made a woman cry.

O son of man, to right my lot
   Nought but thy presence can avail;
Yet on the road thy wheels are not,
   Nor on the sea thy sail!

My fancied ways why shouldst thou heed?
   Thou com'st down thine own secret stair;
Com'st down to answer all my need,
   Yea, every bygone prayer!
                        —*George MacDonald*